Art and Understanding

DEREK CLIFFORD

Art and Understanding

TOWARDS A HUMANIST AESTHETIC

LONDON: EVELYN, ADAMS & MACKAY

TO KENDAL DIXON

© 1968 Derek Clifford
First published in 1968 by Evelyn, Adams & Mackay Ltd
9 Fitzroy Square, London W.1, and in the U.S.A. by
New York Graphic Society, Greenwich, Connecticut.
S.B.N. 238 78810 5. All rights reserved.
The text is set in 'Monotype' Ehrhardt. Printed and
bound in England by W & J Mackay & Co Ltd, Chatham.

Contents

ACKNOWLEDGEMENTS

A book of this sort depends in the long run upon all that its writer has ever read, seen, heard, or overheard, a great heap of indebtedness which can only be acknowledged in a general way. Specifically I am grateful to the owners and guardians of the objects which I have illustrated for their permission to do so. In the few cases where I have been unable for one reason or another to discover who, if anybody, might be supposed to have rights of reproduction I hope I may be forgiven the trespass. I must also mention by name Messrs Chatto and Windus for authorizing the quotations from Aldous Huxley's *Doors of Perception*.

Of an altogether different order is my gratitude to Mr Maurice Ash and to Mr George Rylands. The most important item in a writer's equipment is the belief that what he is doing may be of some interest to somebody at some time; it is not always easy to be sure of this and words that help one to believe it are particularly welcome. At a critical moment in the making of this book Mr Ash and Mr Rylands not only made helpful suggestions of a general kind, of which I have tried to take advantage, but encouraged me to suppose that I was, perhaps, not merely adding two inches to the annual mileage of books on the shelves of the copyright libraries. For this kind of help no thanks are enough.

List of Illustrations

Introduction

The object of life, after all, is not to understand things, but to maintain one's defences and equilibrium and live as well as one can . . . But it is widely and reasonably felt that those people are better able to deal with our present difficulties whose defences are strong enough for them to be able to afford to understand things.
    WILLIAM EMPSON, *Seven Types of Ambiguity* (1930)

THERE lingers in the innocent amongst us a conviction that somewhere, somehow, there are things indisputably good, or beautiful. It comes as a shock, therefore, when we hear that those who ought best to be able to distinguish their absolute and unchanging quality disagree amongst themselves where it is to be found. We cannot fail to be aware that differences of opinion do exist, but unless we have abandoned ourselves to cynicism we hug the certainty that some things ought to be immune from disparagement.

Of universally applauded artists who is more aloofly certain in his greatness than Michelangelo? Sir Joshua Reynolds in his last Discourse said of him: 'If I were now to begin the world again, I would tread in the steps of that great master: to kiss the hem of his garment, to catch the slightest of his perfections, would be glory and distinction enough for an ambitious man.' Yet of his fresco on the wall of the Sistine Chapel which many today would regard as his finest achievement the late Bernard Berenson wrote contemptuously: 'As for Michelangelo, he lived to paint the dyspeptic over-trained athletes who fill his Wagnerian *Last Judgement*.' (Plate 2.) What has happened between Reynolds's time and Berenson's that two sensitive men with trained minds should reach dissimilar conclusions? And what of Michelangelo himself? Was the judgement of this superman so astray that he was deceived in thinking his work of 1540 an advance on that of 1520? Or was it simply that he could not achieve the earlier height and knew it? Strike Vulcan, would that thou couldst! Or, as we are now inclined to think, was Berenson himself wrong and did the superman go from strength to strength? Is the *Last Judgement* finer than the *Creation of Man*? And are we to look for his greatest work of all in his last, in the poor hacked marble of the last *Pieta*? Or are better and worse, good and bad, nothing at all to do with the matter?

When Goethe climbed into the galleries of the Sistine Chapel and saw Michelangelo's frescoes face to face, he said: 'I am so taken with Michelangelo, that after him I have no taste even for nature herself. . . . Oh, that there were only some means of fixing such paintings in my soul. . . . Then we went to the *Loggie*, painted by Raphaelle, and scarcely dare I say that we could not endure to look at them. The eye had been so dilated and spoiled by those great forms, and the glorious finish of every part, that it was not able to follow these ingenious windings of the Arabesques; and the Scripture histories, however beautiful they were, did not stand examination after the former. And yet to see these works frequently one after another, and to compare them together at leisure, and without prejudice, must be a source of great pleasure,—for at first all sympathy is more or less exclusive.' (Plate 3.) Is even greatness of this order so unstable, so subject to mood, so at the mercy of what comes before and what comes after?

Michelangelo himself said of such artists as Van der Weyden, Van der Goes, and Memlinc: 'they paint with a view to extreme exactness . . . without reason or art, without symmetry or proportion, without skilful choice or boldness'. If this is true, and if the implication is true that painters should not lack these qualities, what is it that has kept the work of these men sweet for all these years? Or are they sweet only for some of us and not for others? (Plate 4.)

John Ruskin, we know, was commonly carried away by the charm of overforceful expression, but when he called 'the mannerism of Canaletto the most degraded I know in the whole range of art' he presumably meant something of what he said. Henry James was a much more sober and considered writer, but his criticism in 1872 of Canaletto's associate Francesco Guardi sounds oddly to our ears today: 'A Tiepolo of landscape we may call this gentleman. A comparison of his cold, colourless, sceptical reflections of Venetian splendour with the glowing fidelity and sincerity of such a picture as Van der Heyden's *Quay in Leyden* is really a theme for the philosopher. It vividly suggests that painfully frequent phenomenon in mental history, the demoralizing influence of lavish opportunity. The Italian, born amid lovely circumstances, and debauched, as it were, by the very grace of his daily visions, dispenses with effort and insights and trusts to mere artifice and manner— and a very light manner at that. He has some shallow faith that the charm of his subject will save him. The Dutchman, familiar with a meaner and dustier range of effect, feels that, unless he is faithful, he is nothing. He must confer a charm as well as borrow one; he must bring his grist to the mill and grind it with his own strength; and his little picture, therefore, lives and speaks and tells of perfection; while those of Guardi are as torpid and silent as decay.' (Plates 5, 6.) A *Tiepolo of Landscape* would not generally be regarded as a term of denigration in the middle of the twentieth century.

After this who is safe? Certainly not the masters nearer to our own day. Nor do we altogether expect it, for we have been brought up on the strange romantic notion that a great artist is unguessed at in his own time and that a man to become a god must necessarily have died first.

Henry James, who was not an insensitive critic, wrote of the 1876 exhibition of the

Impressionists at Durand-Ruel's: 'This little band is on all grounds less interesting than the group out of which Millais and Holman Hunt rose to fame. None of its members show signs of possessing first-rate talent.' Unlike many art critics James did not mind committing himself even if it meant withdrawal later. Of Whistler he wrote that his 'productions are pleasant things to have about, so long as one regards them as simple objects—as incidents of furniture and decoration. The spectator's quarrel with them begins when he feels it to be expected of him to regard them as pictures'; but as the years passed Henry James's opinion of Whistler's work became more favourable. (Plate 7.)

Sickert, Whistler's disciple, was even more decisive about Manet's famous *Dejeuner sur l'Herbe*, which he described as 'just as purely a studio confection as any of the swashbucklers of Meissonier. It was larger and not so efficient. There is very little doubt that the seated Meissonier model with the carved ham and the glass of Tokay that I saw within a year at Mr Sampson's gallery . . . is the better and more able painting, and that the *Dejeuner sur l'Herbe* would not hold its own at the Hôtel Drouot or the Christies of a hundred years hence, if it were not already safely embalmed in the mausoleum of a public gallery.' (Plate 9.) And again, commenting on Clive Bell's description of Cézanne 'as the type of the perfect artist', Sickert responded: 'he is the *arch* type of the imperfect artist. . . . He is perhaps the worst draughtsman that ever was. . . . The often quoted saying of Cézanne's that he wished to make of Impressionism something durable like the art of the Museums has been quoted too often. I know he wanted to, and tried to, while countless others before him and after him not only wanted to do so, but did it, and will do it when Cézanne is only remembered as a curious and pathetic by-product of the Impressionist group, and when Cubism has gone as lightly as it has come.'

These are all cases in which intelligent people have been discussing the relative merits of works of art; when unintelligent people enter, as they not infrequently do, this same field, the consequences are even more confusing through their application of inappropriate scales of value. In 1965 the Trustees of the Tate Gallery in London spent £60,000 on Picasso's *The Three Dancers*. (Plate 10.) The days when such a purchase might have been expected to shock the public were over, but Baroness Summerskill, a political appointee to the British House of Lords, treated her fellow legislators to the following: 'I think it is a pity, because that money could have been spent on a new hospital or providing a new operating theatre. I was Member of Parliament for Fulham, where many artists live. They agreed with me that art should be judged by the amount of satisfaction it gave to the viewer. I fail to see what satisfaction this particular fabrication could give.' The questioner is unknown to the world at large, but the question she asked could readily be paralleled from the records of the legislature of every land which has ever spent public money upon the acquisition of works of art.

The question is a typically muddled one, for it holds within it several different problems and the germs of many more. When unravelled they are these. First, was this picture of more value to the community than a new hospital or operating theatre? And implicitly the general question—How are we to assess the value to our society of art in relation to hospitals, and operating theatres . . . and to main drainage, telephones, road upkeep, propaganda for anti-vivisection, colour television, national defence, and all the remainder of those desirable things which might be thought to enter into competition for £60,000? But at the same time the question implied that whereas there *might be* pictures which were worth an operating theatre this was not one of them. This forces one to infer that the questioner considered herself a better judge of what a picture was worth (in terms of operating theatres) than the Trustees of the Tate Gallery.

But what does qualify a person to be a judge of pictures? Having raised these considerations, the questioner went some way to suggesting an answer antagonistic to her point of view when she sought strength from the fact that the 'artists of Fulham' agreed with her as to the function of art: though she did not say whether the Fulham artists agreed with her that *The Three Dancers* did not fulfil that function.

When we fancy we are on firm ground in believing that this politician considered 'a work of art should be judged by the amount of satisfaction it gives to the viewer' we find from a supplementary question which she later put in Parliament that we are not, for she asked: 'Would not some pseudo-intellectual snob pay a large sum for a doodle to which Picasso put his name?' Thus implying that some people get satisfaction from pictures for reasons which she clearly thought were wrong ones.

For what reasons do people like works of art? Are there good reasons for liking pictures and are there bad reasons?

It is not enough to dismiss this ill-considered protest as yet another shot fired by a Philistine against Enlightenment, and then to give it no further attention. According to a percipient philosopher, the Abbé Dubos, who wrote in 1719, when these matters were the subject of careful thought and intelligent debate, the best judge of a picture was the public and not the specialist in artistic technique. According to Dubos art satisfies the basic human need for our feelings to be active, 'a swift shifting of our emotional life comes from the first need of man'—which is to escape boredom. If, then, art satisfies a need that is basic to all men, then all men who experience this fulfilment are the appropriate judges of what does or does not do the trick—the customer is always right. The spokesman of the British Government said that they had entrusted the responsibility for buying *The Three Dancers* to 'eminent and distinguished artists'. But the Abbé would have held that anybody, even Baroness Summerskill, was as good a judge of a Picasso as they were. The Abbé may not have been right, but we cannot lightly assume that he was wrong. The Philistine may have as much right to be heard as the rest of us.

If, however, we do not accept that a person who knows nothing of pictures is a proper judge of them, we may take the opposite view that a painter is a right person. If we do this we shall find ourselves in a difficulty. One of the more amusing books that a million monkeys tapping a million typewriters for a million years might compose would be an anthology of what painters said about the work of other painters.

It would be reasonable to object that artists are, in fact, bad judges of art because they are already committed to a point of view, to an aesthetic or technical creed, and are therefore likely to be biased in their judgements; they are partisans before they start. In fact, those who wish to establish a bench of judges in this affair generally agree to place on it not artists themselves but connoisseurs, art historians, and 'art experts' (whatever they may be), whose credentials are either that they have spent the greater part of their time and energy assessing and enjoying works of art, or else that they have studied deeply the relevant documents, and have established themselves as accurate scholars of the subject, or, at the lowest level, that they have profitably bought and sold a great many pictures. If the monkeys in their creative task should compose a more interesting anthology than the sayings of artists about the work of artists, it would surely be a collection of the writings and sayings of art specialists running wild in their chosen field.

It is not unnatural that many people should seek a Court of the Absolute to which they can appeal. They recognize that the Philistines are unlikely to be sound guides; indeed, the Enlightenment clearly tells them so. Nor on the other hand do they feel that the artist, busily grinding his own axe, is a safe judge of the temper of another's chisel; not illogically they are inclined to entrust themselves to the men and women who have set up as experts. For, so the argument runs, is it not reasonable, if you have no experience of motor cars, to consult someone who has seen, studied, and perhaps owned many, before you buy one? If you are ill you go to a physician, don't you, rather than to a postman or a stockbroker? The doctor may diagnose your complaint incorrectly, advise the wrong treatment, and indeed kill you, but he is less likely to do this than any of the other technicians proposed and you will have the satisfaction of dying with the best advice. It is as satisfactory as being bombed in an air-raid shelter; there is nothing to attribute to your own negligence.

In the matter of the mystery of the human body most of us recognize our own incompetence because of the complexity and seriousness of the problem. But art is different—we suppose it is neither complex nor serious. The pronouncements of the art experts seem to us no more than the incantations of would-be wizards who, if they are honest, which is to say the least doubtful, have, by refining too much upon their feelings, puffed out a dense cloud or fog of words which may do things to Danae, but not to us. So we, many of us, share the view of the Abbé Dubos that in matters of art we may both diagnose and prescribe at the same time, secretly believing that what is good for us would certainly be good for others.

But the experts I have quoted have a standard of judgement. We know that, however fallible a doctor may be, he designs to restore us to health. The motor-car expert knows that we require it to transport us from here to there, and even if we do not brief him as to our specific requirements he will probably balance safety, reliability, comfort, capacity and economy when pronouncing judgement, and will also ensure that the vehicle he recommends will, in fact, move. But the art expert? What are his standards? When he says a picture is good can he say good for what? And our own standards, if we claim the right to judge for ourselves, what are they?

The sixteenth-century Italian philologist, Castelvetro, held that the justification of a work of art was solely in the delight it caused; and his fellow countryman, Bruni, carried the view further: 'We are not shocked', he said, 'when a poem contains wickedness, we are concerned solely in the artist's success or failure, it is the artist we are concerned with not the moralist.' But if art is merely a matter of giving pleasure there is no other good or bad about it and it becomes a question of what pleases most people most and longest. In which case we are either each one of us the only possible judge and our judgement is good for no one but ourselves (when indeed there would be an end of disputing about tastes), or else, given our contemporary democratic faith as a sort of moral overrider, are not the majority to be the judges? Those who throw up their sweaty night-caps and cry 'Ho!'? Better the experts than this.

The Trustees of the Tate Gallery are presumably thought by some to be such experts. They placed beside *The Three Dancers*, in letters of unusual size, an Apologia. If Baroness Summerskill's approach to the problem was muddleheaded and dishonest, the Trustees in their inflated document did quite as well. Its existence implied that those who saw the picture could not be left to find in it their own satisfaction, but that they must be conditioned to approve it. In paragraph after paragraph was blatantly built up the whole apparatus of conditioning until the viewer was reduced to an unresisting frame of mind. Assertions of doubtful critical validity were introduced in the reasonable certainty that no one would dare to question them; but at the same time, lest there should be signs of doubt, the viewer was carefully placed so that not only the Tate Gallery Trustees in London but *cognoscenti* in New York and in Paris were shown to be against him if he demurred. And, as if this were not enough, the viewer was finally invited to feel sympathy with the artist because the picture was associated in his mind with the death of a friend, and gratitude to him for having friendly feelings towards Great Britain. After this who could dare to dislike his picture?

If the Philistine's criticisms could incline one to like a bad picture, the method of the Tate Gallery Trustees might go far towards creating dislike for a moderately good one. But . . . can conditioning of this sort, even when it works antithetically, create an authentic response? And is 'liking' what we want from a picture? And can we rightly speak of the visual appearance of anything as good or bad?

The sort of disagreement provoked by the purchase of *The Three Dancers* occurs often;

so often that it scarcely warrants publicity. What matters is that the state of affairs revealed by it is one of confusion of mind rather than a difference of taste.

Our disagreement is interesting; our stupidity and prejudice are not. We frequently disagree. But are we all, in fact, disagreeing about the same thing? And what is this thing?

It is clear that we are at the beginning of a long inquiry, but one that is worth making unless we are content to range ourselves under the banner of the Enlightenment on the one hand or of the Philistines on the other without knowing for what we fight or why. Perhaps art is too serious for this sort of competitive one-upmanship. Then again, perhaps it matters no more than the contests of the Red and Green Stables in the chariot races of the Romans. At least let us try to find out.

In a world where all things appear to obey the law of cause and effect we must believe that some cause produces criticism and praise of the same picture, and that where there are divergencies of taste there are always causes for them.

What are these causes? Can we discover any general laws that govern these divergencies? If we do succeed in finding traces of general laws that control individual taste we shall be on the way to uncovering the hidden laws that govern those changes of fashion which have seemed to some observers merely capricious. And lastly, if we find that we have achieved some understanding of the springs of taste and the operations of fashion we shall certainly want to consider whether we have been given any pointers to the fundamental problem: what is the nature of the good?

There are many ways in which such an inquiry might be conducted. One might, for example, start by assuming the existence of an absolute and then set out to prove it by working backwards. It would be possible and more in line with modern practice to conduct a sort of prolonged skittle game with all previous theories on the subject. But it will be better to start at the beginning, or at least as near the beginning as we can, rather than at the end; for if there is in this matter an absolute good it will wait for us to approach it by orderly steps, but may resist an attempt to pluck it from the heart of the dark. This will, perhaps, involve us in making some very simple comments on the obvious, yet it is well known that it is the obvious which is most often overlooked and there should be no harm in that. And, after all, if we follow the course of inspiration and hunch, unaided by reason, how are we to be sure that we have not become possessed of a chimera?

I Bronze figure from Urartu (*c.* 800 BC)

PART ONE

The Object and the Image

1. The Function of Sensation

But it seems to me that those sciences are vain and full of error . . . of which neither the beginning, the middle nor the end is dependent on one of the five senses. And if we doubt the certainty of everything which comes to us through the senses, how much more should we doubt those things which cannot be tested by the senses, such as the nature of God and the soul and such things.

LEONARDO DA VINCI

VISION is a sensation, the product of a mechanical process which links the object outside with the 'us' which is inside. It is not the only link, but it is an important one without which we should have to live and think very differently.

If we say we see something, we intend it to be understood that we are experiencing in a particular way a certain sensation. We are able to associate this sensation with others so that it has meaning. The other sensations are not necessarily visual; indeed, it would mean very little if they were only visual, for a visual experience supported only by other visual experiences is like trying to explain a thing in terms of itself: we advance, but we get no further. To understand we need to establish cross-references so that every meaningful thing in our lives is the point at which a multitude of lines cross. The more relationships there are and the more lines that cross at that point, the more certainly is identity established and the more meaningful the place of intersection becomes. Our visual experience of an object is one line only, our other senses draw other lines to it, and at the heart of the intersection grows up our idea, what the object is to us.

It is a common notion that all the tables we have ever seen contribute to our idea of the table we are now looking at; but it is not so common a notion that behind every vision and idea of the table is the sensation of touching the table, and that we would not be able to interpret our vision of the table at all if we did not have the idea of solidity, weight, smoothness and roughness, heat and cold, to attribute to it.

If we had no experience of touch we might still have visual sensations; but until we were able to discern, or to invent, a relationship of behaviour amongst these sensations, what we saw would be as meaningless as the fuzz a newly born child sees. If we see what we do not understand we stretch out our hands as children do to touch it, to feel its shape and weight and consistency. We are able to do this because of the way our hands are constructed. A dog which can only grasp with its mouth lives less in a world of touch than his master who has

3

an opposed thumb; consequently it sees in a different way and cannot recognize a picture or a mirror image. The edge and weight of things which is so material a consideration to us, and which we can assess so accurately by passing our hands around, is to our dog a minor feature of a world of smells. Those experiences which enable a dog to recognize things, to some degree sounds, to a greater degree odours, the sensations which replace for him the sense of touch, are missing from a picture. The image which we carry within our minds is more clearly visual than that which he carries within his.

The human mind is an organizing machine, and it gives to sensations a meaning if it can, but without the experience of touch to aid it the meaning that resulted from vision would be unlike anything we are accustomed to call meaning. And this, in fact, is precisely the situation of those who, being blind almost from birth, are restored to sight after a cataract operation. Their sightless environment is not without meaning to such people, but its meaning has been established by patterns of touch and smell and sound and taste. The sensation of sight has played no part hitherto in the construction of their perceived world and what they see is as meaningless at first as a language unlearned. Quickly, much more quickly than with infants, the adult relates this new sensation to the old ones, but his attitude will be slightly different from those whose world has always included vision. For example, to most people a table is an object visually conceived which has certain characteristics, but to the man with new sight it is an object, solid, with a horizontal surface which can be used in a certain way *and which has a certain appearance*. Some objects do indeed occasionally appear to the rest of us in this sort of blind-man's order. For example, a violet may be conceived primarily as a smell which looks like *that*, rather than as a flower which smells like *this*.

When we say a sensation has meaning we are saying that it is recognizable because it relates to other sensations which are already an accepted part of the pattern of our consciousness. That in which we can see no meaning is rejected by our minds and remains either part of the great moat of oblivion with which we surround ourselves, or else hovers like a question-mark on the fringe of our awareness. The man with newly recovered sight experiences for a short while something that rarely comes the way of the rest of us, visual perception without recognition, a sensation without meaning.

Our five senses have a purpose in common. They each contribute to the survival of the organism which we are, though each contributes in a different way.

We live in a changing universe. Were it not so we should have no need of senses. In a changeless creation matter would need to take no measures to survive, its eternity would be its being; existence would be like a conjuring trick that cannot fail. Once any change is admitted, if it is only the slow crumbling of granitic hills, all change is admitted. Changelessness is a property of a universe either totally without forces or of one in which the forces are in eternal static balance . . . which comes to much the same thing. But a world in which great forces are in marginal unbalance is a world of change, and in order to survive in it living matter has acquired means of adjustment.

The first function of our senses is to enable us to adjust ourselves to changing circumstances, to enable us to act appropriately in any situation.

Whatever we believe about the existence or non-existence of matter it is a fact within the experience of all of us that a human organism can be destroyed by the impact of other material bodies. If you drive a piece of sharpened steel into a man's body in the right place he ceases to be a man. It is the displacement within his system caused by two solids trying to occupy the same space which kills him. It is his sense of touch which tells him of the impending danger as the point pierces his skin, and it is the sense of touch that continues to protest that something is amiss until sensation ceases. The Byzantine philosophers, St John of Damascus and Nemesius of Emesa, were right to hold that touch was the most fundamental of the five senses and coterminous with life itself.

Taste and smell are extensions of the sense of touch. In both cases there is physical contact between specialized nerve-ends and the matter about which the sensation informs us. Taste has the same function as the other senses inasmuch as we depend upon it for advanced information about what is poised to pass into our stomachs; but it also has the added function of encouraging appetite. Without the pleasure of the palate eating would be a tedious orgy, a merely negative avoidance of pain and discomfort rather than a positive encouragement to excess. It is in taste that the element of apparently unmotivated discrimination is greatest; so evidently so that we transfer the word for it to the other senses whenever irrational choice is in question. We speak of taste in music, taste in colours, taste in clothes, taste in behaviour, when what we wish to convey is the idea of a discriminating level of sensibility. Taste, over a relatively small field, gives direct instructions to accept or reject without reference to reason.

Smell, over a narrower field, does a similar thing. To my English Setter bitch, the sense of smell is finer than any other; to her each odour appears to have an exhilarating message, whereas with us, who are not often concerned to make smells meaningful, the sense of smell is transient and relatively undeveloped. Smells, good and bad alike, are rarely distinguishable for long, their message has to be taken, as with violets, almost at the first whiff or not at all. It is this quality of transience which, because of its direct relationship to a moment of time, explains the power of perfume to evoke old memories. Neither in self-defence nor in the hunt for food does man rely much on his sense of smell. He can hear over greater distances and in more varying conditions than he can smell; and he can gather a far greater range of useful information through his eyes than his nose. Men and women who have no sense of smell have no difficulty in surviving and do not usually appear to be impoverished personalities.

Sight and hearing are known as our finer senses because man has organized them in a more meaningful way than he has the others, nor are they directly related to matter in the way that taste and smell are.

Vision gives man advance information about the objects that are his fellow inhabitants of space. He sees them while they are still beyond touch, recognizes their nature from their visual attributes, and is given time to adjust himself to their presence. Vision acts as an extension of touch, so much so that it is almost possible to feel the pain before the blow falls. Vision not only gives warning that danger threatens, it identifies the danger, its timing, its route of approach, and at the same time provides information for countering or evading it.

Sound, on the other hand, does very much less than this. Its chief function is to alert the organism and no more. There is a knock on the door; is it a friend bearing gifts or a bailiff with a writ? We must look in order to decide. We have learned to organize sound so that it shall give us specific information; but essentially there need be no distinction between our friend's knock at the door and the bailiff's until we evolve a code which enables us to distinguish them so that we can act appropriately. There are certainly some sounds which do more than alert us. There are some, like the roar of a lion, which have no ambiguity; they signify danger and even tell us what sort of danger it is. They indicate with greater or lesser accuracy from which direction the danger threatens, but they tell us little else. Our eyes tell us of the tree that we may climb to safety, but we cannot hear it. Our eyes tell us if the lion is caged, but we cannot hear that it is so. The lion's image in our minds is identified with the lion itself, but we do not identify the lion with its roar; when we hear the lion we are aware that behind the roar is a visible presence, but when we see the beast we do not necessarily think of its noise at all.

We cannot touch sound. It is a product of activity and activity is not in normal terms a thing we can touch, or taste, or smell, or even see. Consequently our organizing minds have arranged sounds into language which has one sort of meaning, and into music which has another; but these sounds have no meaning of themselves which is of much consequence to us. Sound plays a large part in our higher life, but it does so because we have cultivated it. If we are to survive in a world of perils our need to be alerted is so great that our hearing must be a sensitive instrument with a greater range, and a capacity susceptible to many more nuances, than its prime function requires. It is out of this exuberant excess of sensibility that we have fashioned language and music.

Unlike taste and smell, neither sight nor hearing are directly in contact with matter itself, but only with manifestations of matter. In the one case we are made aware of an activity by the way in which it creates vibrations which we are able to sense as sound: it is not the trumpet we hear, but the air passing through it as modified by the trumpet. In the other we depend upon the way light is modified by the object upon which it plays: it is not a table we see, but the image in our minds created by the light which reflects from the table. But we do not identify sounds with their source in the way that we do visual images.

We speak of the sound of the drum, but we do not speak of the visual image of the drum, because we tacitly accept that what we see *is* the drum, whereas what we hear is only its vibrations. This is because the visual image tells us a great deal more about the important properties of the object out there as a physical presence than any of its audible manifestations can do.

The first function of all four secondary senses is to enable us to act appropriately in any situation. Sometimes we refer what we see to the corroborating testimony of the other senses; the milk looks 'off' so we sniff it, the bulb may be fused so we shake it to hear the loose filament rattle, but these are exceptional cases; normally all other sensations, even that of the master sensation touch itself, we are accustomed to refer to vision for confirmation or elaboration. We hear the roar and look for the lion; we smell the gas and look for the tap that has been left on; we taste the bitter food and look to see what it is so that we may avoid it.

The senses are not merely parallel forms of sensation as we are sometimes inclined to consider them; each one not only has a different apparatus for conveying sensation to the brain, but each also stands in a different relationship both to the object sensed and to ourselves. The modern passion for equality must not trick us into supposing them to be of equal significance. The sense of touch is the master and sight is its principal assistant.

The Making of the Synthesis

Although we discuss these senses and their functions as though they were separate, we shall make a mistake if we do not remember that our final mental image is a synthesis. We live so much in a world that analyses and separates and breaks down that we are in danger of losing the ability to synthesize, to unite and to build up. But a thing is more than the sum of its parts, and our idea of an object is more than the sight, smell, touch, taste and sound of it. A child does not at first isolate what he sees in the way that he learns to do later. His perceptions are not separate activites; they are his process of 'being'. He tends to perceive situations as a whole and an object as inseparable from its background. If he is accustomed to see his toy on the bed he will look for it there even though he knows that he has only just seen it on the floor in the next room. My dogs behave in much the same way: if a rabbit breaks through the hedge and runs across the garden they pursue it as long as they can see it, but once it is out of sight they return to the gap in the hedge where it first appeared with every sign of expecting to find it there again. A child soon learns to make allowances for the spatial jumps that an object can make; my dogs do not. The child learns not only that his toy has a different aspect but that it is part of a different field of perception when seen from one side of the room from the other. Out of this grows his notion of a toy as a separate thing. When he learns that in the dark he can touch his toy but not see it he will learn to distinguish between the two sensations, and the process of analysis is well begun. But even at the end of it all, when the adult mind has isolated the perceptual factors of the toy, and even identified to the last atom its physical properties, what remains important is the totally perceived world of which the toy is a part. And this is a world of which we may not often be aware, but the hidden vestiges of which it is impossible to destroy.

From this essential totality of impression arises the phenomenon of synaesthesia. Synaesthesia is a name for the experience of a sensation proper to one of our senses arising from a different one. It is not uncommon to speak of sounds as having colour; or to refer to colours as being loud or quiet; some perfumes seem to have an equivalence to a note in music; some flavours we believe we could express by drawing a shape on paper. If we recall that our childhood image was originally a total one, we can readily see that the mind, having created an image out of the sensations supplied by the eye and ear and nose and so on, when later supplied with data purely visual, may set in motion an equivalent set of odour, sound, and touch reactions. The mind, for all that it, too, has separate parts with separate functions, is a unity, and a stimulus in one part will not leave another without a tremor. It is not our eye that sees, nor our ear that hears; it is our mind which, receiving pulses along the nerve tracks from these organs, creates from them the image and the sound.

Synaesthesia is often apparent in a child just at the point when he is beginning to dissociate an object from its background and to distinguish his own sensations from the object that aroused them. Sensations are, as it were, floating and ready to be attached to any apparently appropriate object. A common instance is the child who calls everything he is forbidden to touch 'hot', and Professor Vernon in *Psychology of Perception* tells of a child of three who said that the number '5' looked 'mean' and number '4' looked 'soft'. The use of 'hot' is perhaps no more than the transference of the idea 'forbidden' and not strictly synaesthetic at all. Another child said that an irregular quadrilateral looked 'cruel', and yet another was so terrified by the 'evil' appearance of a twisted tree-stump on one of his picture bricks that it had to be hidden. To the developed mind synaesthesia is a common experience. Dr Johnson quotes Dionysius as saying that 'the sound of Homer's verses sometimes exhibits the idea of bulk' and goes on to ask 'Is not this a discovery nearly approaching to that of the blind man, who, after long inquiry into the nature of the scarlet colour, found that it represented nothing so much as the clangour of a trumpet!'

There is yet another possible cause of this apparent interchangeability of the senses. Our sense organs are capable of a certain range of activity only. There are sounds we cannot hear and colours we cannot see. These limits to our senses establish a scale. In sound there is at one end of the scale the highest note that the human ear can perceive, at the other end the lowest note. In colour there is the hue that lies below the deepest red and the hue that sings unheard above the sharpest violet. In brightness there is the intensity that damages the eye, and the darkness in which differences of illumination are no longer perceptible. There

1 MICHELANGELO: *The Creation of Adam*

2 MICHELANGELO: *The Last Judgement* (*detail*)

'. . . that great master . . . to catch the slightest of his perfections, would be glory and distinction enough for an ambitious man.' Sir Joshua Reynolds on Michelangelo

'As for Michelangelo, he lived to paint the dyspeptic over-trained athletes who fill his Wagnerian Last Judgement.' Bernard Berenson

3 RAPHAEL: *David's Triumph over the Assyrians*
'The Scripture Histories . . . painted by Raphaelle, scarcely dare I say that we could not
endure to look at them.' Goethe

4 ROGIER VAN DER WEYDEN: *Columba Altarpiece*
'. . . they paint with a view of extreme exactness . . . without reason or art, without
symmetry or proportion, without skilful choice or boldness.' Michelangelo

5 FRANCESCO GUARDI: *Venice*
'He trusts to mere artifice and manner—and a
very light manner at that.' Henry James

6 JAN VAN DER HEYDEN: *A Dutch Quay*
'. . . his little picture lives and speaks and tells
of perfection; while those of Guardi are as
torpid and silent as decay.' Henry James

7 J. M. WHISTLER: *Valparaiso, crepuscule in
flesh colour and green*
'. . . pleasant things to have about, so long as we
regard them as simple objects—as incidents of
furniture and decoration.' Henry James

8 SIR JOHN MILLAIS: *The Boyhood of Raleigh*

9 EDOUARD MANET: *Dejeuner sur l'Herbe*
'. . . it would not hold its own at the Hôtel Drouot or the Christies of a hundred years hence, if it were not already safely embalmed in the mausoleum of a public gallery.' R. Sickert

is room for a sort of parallelism here which leads to an idea of equivalence. The high-pitched squeak of a bat has a light-violet colour equivalent. The deepest boom of the basso-profundo is dark and rich and purply-red. This is all very well when we are aware of the full scale of our sensations and are, as it were, operating along the extent of the scale, but this is something that we rarely do, and, as the markings of our scale are only clear at their ends, we are left with a very uncertain notion of the vital (because most in use) middle ones. Imagine, for example, a picture painted in a high tonal key and in a narrow range: its highest reach may be white, its lowest a pale chocolate brown. Such an arbitrary limitation of scale is common and the mind when faced with such a picture will without difficulty accept the scale; but unless we transfer our temporary sense of scale from this picture which has imposed it to our ideas of sound we will very properly represent the deepest tone of the picture, light brown, by the deepest tone in a full sound scale, the low boom of thunder. If, however, we turn to a picture so painted that its lowest tonal note is black and its highest light brown, then, if we have not contracted our sound scale in a similar manner, we may find the equivalent of our light brown not in the voice of thunder as before but in the squeak of a bat. If there were a key to guide us and ensure that we remained in the same propor-tionate scale with all our senses, it might easily be established what colours were the equivalent of what sounds and what shapes smelled of what odours; but generally, if we are honest, we are reduced to a very much simpler formula—this sound is darker than that, this taste is redder than the other, this shape is more blue than yellow, this flavour is more sharp, this more dull.

Nor are these two explanations more than partial, for there is yet another. William Empson has described language as fundamentally a system of gestures with the tongue and he illustrates this by comparing the gesture made for the word 'huge' with that for the word 'wee' and goes on to say that all such sounds carry suggestions associated with the gesture required to make them—size or shape, movement, pressure, up, down, forward, back-ward . . . This directly relates language to the sense of touch. Sight we know is informa-tive because we can interpret its sensations in terms of touch. Is it not probable that those parts of the brain which bring order to our sensations of colour and smell and taste do so by motions or energies which are parallel to those of touch and thus seem to shadow them?

The Task of the Receiver

Nothing is very simple, although we often pretend that it is for otherwise most activities would be impossible to us. Vision is certainly not simple. It depends upon the existence of an object which modifies light; upon the process by which these modifications are conveyed to the mind; upon the mind which gives meaning to its sensation. All are necessary for the act of vision, but the mind alone gives meaning.

The mind organizes the sensations it receives. But this does not mean that the mind is free to organize them in any way it will. There are a number of possible meanings, and there is no meaning; but there is not an infinity of possible meanings. The way in which we organize what we see depends upon our experience: in other words, our minds, the organizers of sensations, are themselves the product of sensation and they organize in accordance with observed experience.

Descartes's 'I think therefore I am' gives ground for belief in the existence of a self-governing personality, but 'I think' is not a simple matter either. Sensations are the raw material for thought. Thought itself is a complicated sensation and cannot come into existence without a reservoir of sensual experience. The new-born child has a potentiality for thought, but no experience upon which to employ it. As its experience increases so it organizes its sensations into a world of increasing complexity. These experiences are to begin with all first-hand, sensations of touch, heat–cold, hard–soft, wet–dry. Upon these opposites it begins to raise the structure of a perceived environment until it relates an object, warm, soft, and dry, with a sensation of light and certain vibrations of sound. And when the child has learned to recognize the reappearance of the object which combines these sensations in a certain proportion and to react to it with the sound 'Mama' it has taken its first step upon the road of language, that capacity which, more than any other, will distinguish him as man, the creature who makes meanings. He will also be beginning to think and in the Cartesian sense 'to be'.

Professor Vernon describes an experiment in which observers were kept in a completely silent room. It was found that at first they experienced sleepiness, then disturbance of thought which began with loss of concentration and which progressed 'in some cases to complete disorganization. Thoughts became incoherent, and the observers developed erroneous ideas about their own bodies including feelings of unreality and depersonalization. These were accompanied by growing anxiety leading to states of panic such that they were compelled to give up the experiment.' A rather more complicated experiment was carried out at the University of MacGill in Canada. Here the unfortunate subjects were kept in a small room where they lay on a bed; they could hear nothing but the unvarying buzz of machinery; with translucent goggles on their eyes they could see nothing but a blurr of light; and they could touch little because they wore long cuffs which came down over their hands. Some of them were able to stick it out for five days; others could not endure more than two despite the very high rate of pay they were receiving. At first they slept a great deal, but later they were unable to sleep except in snatches. 'They became bored and restless, and could not think in any concentrated fashion about anything. In fact, when their intelligence was tested, it was found to have deteriorated. They frequently suffered from visual and auditory hallucinations, and their perception of their surroundings was impaired. Objects appeared blurred and unstable; straight edges, such as those of walls and floors, looked curved; distances were not clear; and sometimes the surroundings moved and swirled round them, causing dizziness.'

We do not know the intellectual resources of those who were subjects to this ordeal, but, whatever they may have been, the lesson is fairly clear . . . the personality is the creation of perceived form and without perceived form the personality disintegrates.

The mind is master, but its mastery at first is only potential, not actual. The conductor controls the orchestra, but he cannot conjure music from an empty orchestra pit. The mind to fulfil its destiny of organizing needs sensations. Our perceptions cannot work in a vacuum. Only the mind diseased can touch an object that is not there, or hear a voice that has not spoken, and only then because it has experience of objects and of sounds which it can draw upon and simulate.

The mind that creates order is itself created by sensation and sensation depends not only upon the proper functioning of the senses but upon objects 'out there'.

These objects may be presumed to be, in so far as they exist at all, a constant factor for all of us. A goat may eat nails, we may eat nails; our digestions may cope differently with the problem, but that does not alter the material nature of the nails.

The object is common to us all; the machinery by which we perceive it is not. The blind man cannot have the same ideas of objects as ourselves; nor in a lesser degree can the far greater number of men who are colour-blind; and what subtle variations of visual capacity may there be which we have no particular reason for distinguishing? Provided a man can tell a dollar from a penny, or a table from a chair, do we, in our normal activities, inquire whether he sees it in colour or not? If he recognizes what we recognize, we do not question that he sees as we see: indeed, up to a point we have proof of it if he acts appropriately; but beyond that point we have no proof and require none, because for normal purposes recognition of an object is all we need to expect from our fellows or, for that matter, from ourselves.

We cannot very well deny that the question 'Why do I like this and you like that?' may in part be answered by pointing to the differing sensibility of our five senses. But the blind man and the deaf man are exceptional, the man whose senses function unimpaired has a far greater area of community with his neighbour than not; their differences are small, their similarities are large.

So, if the object we perceive is common to us all, and the channels by which we perceive it have so much in common, how is it that we make something so very different of it?

Our minds are in part the creation of our sensations, and in a hasty moment we might conclude that, as we see the same objects in a similar way, we have similar minds. And so, indeed, up to a point we have. But beyond this point there is more to be said. Have our minds initially the same potential? There are some who believe, because they wish to believe, that all minds are equal in capacity. These same people presumably believe that all men are physically capable of running a mile in under four minutes. The rest of us believe that individual beings have varying capacities and as one child is born with long legs and one with short, so one is born with a mental capacity greater than the other. This variable potential is obviously one source of difference in individual judgements of value.

Yet another lies in the range of sensations which are fed to the developing mind and give it a bias. Let us take the simple opposites, warm–cold, full–empty, dry–wet. The child who is generally warm and full and dry will regard coldness, emptiness and wetness as objectionable departures from the norm; the child who is commonly cold, empty, and wet will come to regard these as the conditions of its being and their opposites as brief and transient delights. But although the experience of these hypothetical children varies so greatly they are experiences of similar sensations not of different ones; both children experience the opposites, though in differing proportions.

It is idle to assume that any two people see the same object in the same way. Vision in its full sense is the child of experience and as every vision is itself an experience it follows that every vision is unique and unrepeatable. Vision is an organic process, not a static fact.

But although it is mistaken to suppose that we all see the same objects in the same way it is a reasonable mistake to make; the contrary assertion, that we all see all things in a totally personal way, is not reasonable. We are certainly individuals, but not as individual as all that. The element of constancy in human experience is necessarily very strong.

The variation between individual human beings can appear great or small according to the field against which it is seen. In a wide-varying pattern of phenomena such as mountains, bicycles, human beings, and horses, the similarity between humans and horses is emphasized; but in a pattern comprising only humans and horses it is their differences which are apparent. The change is one of scale. Where a variation is seen in relation to other much greater variations it appears small; where the larger variations are excluded from view it can seem enormous. Such values are relative and we must remember that though all men seem alike to the statistician they seem very different to themselves.

On the normal scale of life human beings have more in common with each other than they have differences. This they recognize by living together in communities. We are born helpless and dependent, we mature at approximately the same age, we suffer similar physical and mental pangs, we have similar physical limitations, we are subject to social relationships, we love, endure the decay of our powers, and die. Yet despite this community we are potentially and actually individuals and all this that we do, in some measure we do alone.

2. The Gathering of Light

There is no light in nature. We live, and walk, and do our work in un-utterable blackness. Our usual saying is that within the skull all is dark, but in reality that is the only place where there is any light. Nature is lightless. The lightning flashes darkly, the thunder roars silently, and all things are without temperature. It is mind that has given nature her beautiful light and colour, her cheering noises, her genial warmth, and her fragrant odours. Nature is a blank and incomprehensibly dreary desert, but as we spend all our time living within our bony skulls, we rarely discover the truth.

ROLAND ROOD, *Colour and Light in Painting*

VISION depends upon light. Without light the sensation of vision cannot be directly experienced. The mind is a compulsive organizer and can simulate vision in darkness and raise ghosts, but it cannot see without light.

Light is a sensation in the mind caused by the sensitivity of the eye to certain electro-magnetic waves, waves of energy. But the eye only reacts to a very few of the wavelengths which transmit energy. The ascertainable range of such wavelengths is said to extend over seventy octaves whereas our vision covers only one. We are not far from being blind. Our built-in optical apparatus with its limited range consists of nerve-ends which react to the stimulus of these energy waves and which transfer their reactions along a complicated communications system to the brain. The brain receives these reactions as a sensation which it identifies and disposes according to its previous experience. The brain's activity has three distinct stages: the sensation; the recognition of the sensation; and the action taken as a result of it. The sensation itself is a means not an end. The biological end is the action the mind takes.

There are many phenomena which we cannot experience because we lack the right equipment. The universe no doubt has material sufficient to keep fifty senses busy if we had them and had the mental capacity to organize their messages into a meaningful pattern. The world is abuzz with the unperceived. Sometimes, as with radio, we make for ourselves apparatus which converts stimuli which we cannot sense into ones that we can.

The visual apparatus we are born with is designed to gather light waves from a wide field and to direct them so that they are reassembled on the retina in a relationship corresponding in two-dimensional form to that which their sources occupied in space. We normally see the human eye as a slightly protuberant elongated oval with pointed ends, rather

13

like a rugby football. This is its window, the cornea; but the whole eye is more or less spherical and that part of it we see is no more than a segment of its outer surface. The most important part of the eye is the retina, a very sensitive membrane which accepts the stimuli offered by the light waves. This covers about half the inner surface of the eye furthest from the window. Light rays enter the sphere through an opening in the iris. The iris is the coloured part of the eye and is composed of muscle which governs the size of the opening, contracting and expanding automatically, its reactions set in motion by changes in the amount of light reaching the retina. The pupil, the dark circle in the centre of the visible eye, is the opening. Behind the iris and in contact with it is a soft bi-convex lens which is attached to the outer-casing of the eye by a minor muscle. It is by altering the tension applied by this muscle that we alter the shape of the lens when we wish to focus at different distances. The eye must necessarily have depth in order to give room for this lens to focus on the retina (Figure 1).

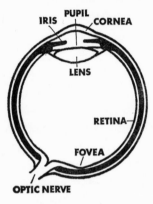

FIG. 1

Briefly, the cornea is the visible part of the eye and is the part which receives the light; the pupil is where the light is given access to the lens; the lens in turn projects an inverted image on the retina at the back of the eye. From that point the optic nerve and the mind take over.

There are four ways in which we can try to ensure that the retina receives a sufficiently clear-cut image; by automatic adjustment of the lens; by moving our eyes in their sockets so that the image is thrown directly on to the most sensitive part of the screen; by turning our heads; and by physically adjusting our distance from the object by advancing or retiring.

All this is a very simplified account of the eye and its components, but it does enable us to discuss some of the limitations and idiosyncrasies of our visual apparatus.

Firstly, rays of light can only enter the pupil if they strike the protuberant cornea at an angle which will permit them to be directed through the opening of the iris. As the eye is approximately spherical we might be inclined to suppose that the visual field is very nearly circular about the point upon which the eye is focused when we look straight in front of us. But this is not so, for each eye has physical limitations due to its position in the head. Light rays can reach the right eye more or less unimpeded from the right, but the nose raises the horizon on the left of it; the contrary is true of the left eye. Thus the extreme ray which can enter the right eye from the right side does so at an angle of about 104° from the optical axis; but the last ray which enters it from the left can hardly do so at a greater angle than 60°. Each eye individually has thus a lateral field of about 164°, but they have a combined field of about 208°. Vertically there is also inequality. Light may enter our average eye from above at an angle of about 70° from the optical axis because of the barrier at our brows; whereas, from below, the cheek-bone presents a lesser obstruction and the possible angle is about 80°. Because our eyes are horizontally, and not vertically, coupled we gain no advantage in vertical range by using both eyes and our field vertically cannot exceed 150°. This makes up a fairly extensive field, but the eye is an imperfect instrument and our vision is not equally effective over the whole of it.

From Energy to Sensation

The critical point in all this gathering of light is at the retina, for it is here that the process of turning energy waves into sensation is begun. The retina consists of about 100 million nerve cells or receptors, and of about half a million neuron-ends, the terminals of the system of communication between the eye and the brain. Broadly the receptors and the neurons work together on a trigger principle. When we squeeze the trigger of a gun we release a spring which in turn releases the stored-up energy in the cartridge which drives the bullet up the barrel; it is not the energy we applied to the trigger which drives the bullet, but the energy that was stored in the cartridge awaiting release. So it is with the receptors and the neurons. The sensations we experience are not those of the energies that reach the receptors from the world of exterior phenomena, but of the energies already lying stored within the nerves. The energy of the activated receptor upsets the energy balance of the neuron and thus instigates a disturbance in the nerve fibre which is propagated along the line until it reaches the central nervous system. As when we fire a gun it does not matter whether we squeeze the trigger heavily or lightly, provided we squeeze it *enough*, so it does not matter how strongly the receptor is stimulated, provided it is stimulated sufficiently to set off the nervous disturbance. The gun either fires or it does not; the neuron discharges its energy to the brain or it does not. The energy we experience is already within us, but it is selectively released by energies outside us. All sensation depends, not primarily upon our sensitivity to stimuli, but upon the amount of energy stored in our neurons.

When a gun is fired it cannot fire again until it is reloaded; there is a time immediately after the neuron has discharged its energy-sensation to the central system when it cannot be activated again however violently the receptor may be stimulated. After this negative period there follows an interval during which the neuron may indeed be stimulated, but only if the stimulus is greater than was necessary to set it off before; in this it is unlike the gun, but only briefly. After a short interval the neuron recovers its former condition and is ready once more to react to the original trigger pressure. There is even evidence that just before the neuron reaches the stage of complete recovery it will react to a lesser stimulus than normal. There are several ways in which a stimulus greater than that required to 'fire' a neuron can be made to register on our nervous system. A receptor violently stimulated may continue in a state of sufficient activity to fire the neuron again when it recovers from the first discharge, even when the stimulus has been withdrawn, rather as though the trigger of an automatic pistol remained stuck down although the finger had released it. This means that a strong stimulus will be appreciated for a longer time than will a weak one, but it does not mean that it will be felt as a stronger one. This is achieved in another way.

There are in the retina not only neurons connecting the eye with the brain but lateral ones that connect one part of the retina with another. In this way a violent stimulus in one spot is communicated to others, so that more neurons are activated; this is as though when we pull the trigger of a gun too violently other neighbouring guns were to fire in sympathy. Although this ensures that we get a spread of the sensation spatially (it is, for example, the reason why a bright object appears larger than a dark one) it does not intensify the sensation. But if we accept that the neurons are of different powers and of differing trigger sensitivity we can easily account for the varying intensity of the sensations we experience. A weak stimulus will activate only those most delicate neurons which are the ones least loaded with sensation-provoking energy. Such a weakly stimulated field will consequently provide only a faint sensation and one that does not persist. A strong stimulus will, on the other hand, tend not only to spread spatially owing to the lateral neurons, and to persist temporarily owing to after-effects of the stimulus on the more sensitive receptors, but to activate more neurons and more powerful ones so that the sensation experienced will itself be stronger.

The Mechanics of Adjustment

For the apparatus of the eye to function efficiently in the realms both of violent stimuli and of faint ones an adjustment is necessary. When we pass from a lighted foyer into a darkened cinema the immediate sensation is of total blackness, but gradually our eyes become accustomed to the change of illumination and we find that we can see reasonably clearly. Equally when we go from darkness to light the first impression is dazzling and for a short time we are unable to distinguish anything but the light itself. In each case a period of adjustment follows. The time taken depends on the degree of illumination and the age and health of the subject. The average eye becomes to a large extent adjusted in three minutes, but may not be completely so for half an hour.

The mechanics of adjustment depend largely on the nature of the receptors in the retina. There are two types, named after their appearance, *rods* and *cones*. They make contact with the neuron not, in fact, directly but in stages through bipolar cells which in turn connect with a second set of conducting neurons. As there are two hundred times more receptors than neurons, each bipolar cell has to serve a number of them, and each optic nerve cell in turn serves a number of the conducting neurons. In the centre of the retina there is a small area where this does not apply; here the receptors are very small and very densely packed, and each one has its own appropriate bipolar cell and optic nerve cell which it shares with no

II Max Ernst: *Le chaste Joseph*

other receptor. This favoured spot is called the fovea, and light pulses received there give rise to the clearest vision of all. The effect of this is rather like a gear system differentiated according to the part of the eye.

The distribution of rods and cones over the retina is not even. The fovea and an area immediately around it contains only cones, no rods: but as the distance from the fovea increases so does the number of the rods increase until in the outermost parts of the retina the rods are greatly in the majority. (Figure 2.)

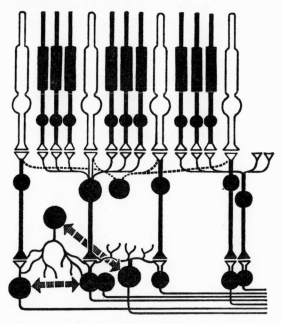

FIG. 2

These rods and cones not only have a different appearance but clearly do different work, although there is still some doubt as to exactly how they do it. The rods contain a bluish-red pigment, the *visual purple*, which bleaches when it is exposed to light but which gradually regains its colour in the dark. Light waves cause a chemical change in this pigment; in darkness an appropriate chemical change restores the original substance. The more visual purple the rods contain the more sensitive they are to light. Thus when we go from darkness to light our eyes are at maximum sensitivity and we are dazzled; the visual purple bleaches rapidly in order to bring the sensation down to tolerable limits, and to facilitate this the iris of our eye instantly contracts, narrowing the pupil, so that less light enters the eye. When the visual purple has been reduced by bleaching to an appropriate level the iris relaxes, admitting more light until a suitable balance has been obtained. If we now return to darkness a reverse process takes place, and we see nothing until a return of the visual purple increases our sensitivity to the point at which the low stimuli of near darkness can be appreciated.

The cones, however, contain no visual purple and therefore in the fovea, which consists only of cones, light and darkness adaptation scarcely takes place at all. As the rods are more sensitive to dim light than are the cones, it follows that in very poor light we should get a better image from the outer parts of the retina than we can from the normally more sensitive fovea. This we know in practice is true and probably accounts for the experience we have all had that an object known to be stationary, when we stare straight at it in the darkness, appears to move, for the eye is automatically trying to transfer the image to a part of the retina where it will be clear, and the involuntary movement our eye is making we attribute to the object.

Although no one has yet been able to discover any chemical in the cones which reacts in a similar way to the visual purple which is in the rods it is generally agreed that some such chemical must be there. The unknown substance has a very distinct characteristic, for, whereas the visual purple in the rods seems to react to brightness only, whatever is in the cones reacts to hue.

The Quality of Sensation

All this so far might have been understood and agreed by a person who was totally colour-blind from birth. But light can give rise to sensations not to be perceived by such people. Light, we must remember, is an energy wave of which the properties are both the length of the wave and the energy or force of it. Brightness and colour are properties of the sensations to which energy waves give rise when they act on certain organs. The rods, reacting in a varied degree both to the length of the waves and to their energy, initiate the sensation of brightness. The cones, however, do not appear to be much concerned in conveying a sensation of brightness, but only of hue.

What we perceive as white light is an energy pulse of mixed wavelengths. If we spread out those wavelengths so that they can be perceived separately (which we can easily do by passing them through a transparent object composed of a material that will bend the rays, for long waves conveniently bend at a different angle from short ones), we will experience a visual sensation quite unlike brightness. The longest waves will give us the sensation which we call red, and the shortest will give us the sensation violet. Between the red and the violet the sensation will change by imperceptible stages through orange, to yellow, to green and to blue. Beyond the red and beyond the violet there are many more energy waves, but these are not experienced by the human organism as visual sensations.

Transition from one colour to the next in the spectrum is continuous: there is, for example, no point at which yellow becomes green or at which green becomes blue. We are now in a subjective world in which the very words we use to define our sensations have marginal differences. In attempts to establish experimentally the point at which the average observer makes the change from one colour to the next it was found that individuals would vary as much as 10 per cent in one reading from another. The confusion is added to by the limitations of our vocabulary. Many arbitrary colour terms exist, but we only agree generally

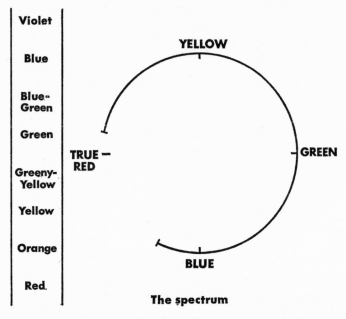

FIGS. 3 AND 4

in the use of the names of the six broad divisions of the spectrum. Yet it is possible in certain conditions for the human eye to distinguish in the spectrum 250 hues, a distinction which, because we lack the need for it in our everyday life, we allow to go to waste.

At this point we are still conceiving hue as a property of light and can therefore think of it as appearing as a sort of measuring stick with red at one end and violet at the other (Figure 3). In the mind, however, where these sensations truly have their existence, the progression is circular, for there is a point between violet and red and linking them to each other, where the mind experiences purple (Figure 4).

Brightness has, as it were, a single dimension, it may be greater or less; hue on the other hand has two dimensions, it may vary from red to violet, but it may also vary in depth or intensity of hue; this dimension we call saturation. The sensation of vision is a fusion of stimuli of both rods and cones when both are working, and therefore we commonly see an object with three purely visual qualities . . . brightness, hue, and depth of hue.

For their better understanding let us suppose that any hue we care to choose, say red, is set in parallel against a line of brightness which diminishes from white at the top to black at the bottom. It is not difficult to conceive that we could establish a succession of reds which, once it were distinguishable from black, would proceed in equivalent brightness until it lost its identity in white. A totally colour-blind person would experience these two parallels as alike, for they have identical brightness. Let us now suppose a third parallel set

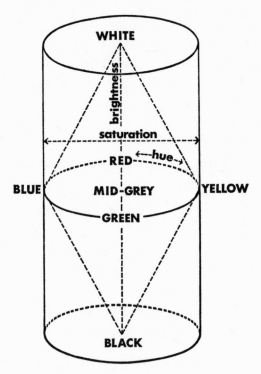

The psychological colour solid

FIG. 5

up, of which the constant is a more intense red. It will still be possible to produce a series which runs from near white to near black and which to the totally colour-blind person will appear exactly like the other two; but to a person of normal vision all three lines are distinct, and though hue and brightness remain the same in the third parallel as in the second, they will be distinguishable because of a difference in saturation. For those who can conceive these things figuratively there is a diagram known as the Psychological Colour Solid (Figure 5). In this figure both saturation and brightness are read vertically; the central axis is brightness; the solidity of the body represents the normal hue circle. The axis of the double cone represents therefore a hueless transition from black to white. A line parallel to the axis and close to it would represent a hue of little saturation passing from darkness to brightness; the further from the axis the line is drawn the more saturated the colour becomes, but so much the less is its brightness range, until with every hue the point of maximum saturation is absolute at the middle point of brightness and it can only be made lighter or darker by dilution. This figure has the advantage of revealing at a glance that the greatest range of saturation is in the middle area of brightness, but that the greatest range of brightness is at the central axis, where there is a total absence of hue. It is also clear that every hue can be matched for brightness at some point along the brightness axis, but that every degree of brightness cannot be matched by a comparably bright hue.

We have already recognized that white light is the sensation which we receive when all the wavelengths that give the idea of hue are received simultaneously. Sometimes, however, these energies of different wavelength reach us combined in proportions unlike those which make up white light. The rules of their behaviour are fairly simple.

If we combine yellow light and blue light in equal proportions they cancel out their quality of hue and meet on the brightness axis, appearing there as grey. If the proportion of yellow in the mixture is too great the result will be on the yellow side of the axis and we will see a weakly saturated yellow. If the blue is the stronger we will experience a weakly saturated blue. When two hues by equal mixing cancel out in this fashion they are called complementary. Every hue has its appropriate complementary hue. Hues that are not complementary will, when mixed, produce a third hue, but cannot produce a neutral grey.

If, again making use of the fact that hues as we experience them can be plotted circularly, we make a diagram in which yellow is diametrically opposite to blue, and red is on the same diameter as a bluish green, we can interpolate all other hues so that each is opposite to its complementary. The centre of our circle will then represent a neutral grey, and the circumference a full range of hues at their maximum saturation. On this diagram it becomes clear that if we mix two opposites (complementaries) in equal proportions their saturation is nil; that the more unbalanced the mixture is, the stronger the saturation will be; and that the saturation of a mixture will always be less than if there had been no mixture at all.

The same principle applies exactly even when we mix two hues which are not complementary. We may draw a line between any two points within our figure and on that line will occur the point at which the two hues form a third. The position of the third will depend upon the proportions in which the original two are mixed. We must think of hues as exerting a pull rather than a push, thus a strong red stimulus will drag a less strong blue into a meeting-point that is more nearly red than blue. Our diagram is two-dimensional and therefore can only be read in terms of one degree of brightness which is set at the centre. If we imagine it to be a solid as in Figure 5, we can also plot the way hues will combine if we mix one of, say, strong saturation (and therefore of moderate brightness) with one of considerable brightness (and therefore of lesser saturation). In this case brightness exerts the greater pull and the third point, the hue at which they meet, will be displaced in the direction of the brighter. (Figure 6.)

This diagram also shows how by making use of only three hues we can combine them to form any other. For example, if we mark our circle with R for red, G for green, and B for blue, and join these points we divide our circle up into three arcs: RYG, GB and BR. By

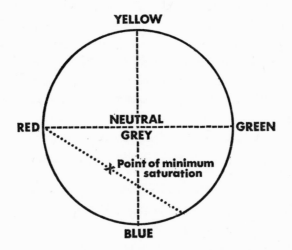

The mixing of coloured light

Fig. 6

mixing the stimuli from R and G we will achieve a hue somewhere in the line RG; likewise by mixing G and B and B and R we can by altering their proportions form a hue at any point on those lines. If we now adjust these three hues we can so balance them as to meet at any point we choose within the figure R G B. Every hue can therefore be obtained from the mixture of three only, *but* these hues will be at relatively low saturation, and we cannot obtain the most intense hues in this way.

The laws for the mixing of lights do not apply to the mixing of pigments. Surface colour, as we shall discover later, has different characteristics.

Thresholds of Sensation

We cannot remind ourselves too often that when dealing with vision we are concerned not with absolutes but with sensations the character of which depends, within certain limits, upon other factors than the immediate stimulus, for example upon the proportion which the stimulus bears to the general level of our experience.

In our discussion of the way the stimulus of light activates the neural receptors we used the analogy of finger-pressure on a trigger; the amount of pressure required represented the amount of energy necessary to excite sensation by the firing of the energy-laden neurons. The minimum amount of energy necessary before the human eye can see is very small. But even this minimum varies according to the part of the retina involved. As a figure of absolute sensitivity is only to be established against a background of darkness, it is not the centre of the eye which yields the lowest figure, since that is largely composed of cones which are comparatively inactive in the dark and require more light to stimulate them; it is in the outer parts of the eye, where the rods, which are extremely sensitive in the dark, are in the majority, that the greatest sensitivity is recorded. Here the energy required to activate the optic nerve is a thousandth part of that very small amount which was necessary in the centre. The power of the faintest star which is just visible out of the corner of the eye is about 100 million millionths of a watt. When one considers how inadequate is the illumination provided by a sixty-watt electric bulb the sensitivity of the human eye seems surprisingly great. If, indeed, our star can be perceived in a fifth of a second, as is thought likely, then the retina is about thirty-thousand times as sensitive as a good radiometer.

Although we can perceive so small an amount of energy, this does not mean that we can, over the whole scale of visible light, distinguish gradations of this intensity. The stimuli for average good vision lie between two million and 200 million times the lowest illumination which the centre of the eye can see; but we cannot distinguish 200 million stages of luminousness. In fact, experiment has shown that between darkness and the maximum brilliance which the eye can stand there are only 562 steps of just noticeable difference. If we assume that all these steps are of about the same magnitude, it seems that we can only distinguish, in the upper range of vision, changes in brightness which are about 350-thousand times as great as that first brightness, 0.272 micro-watts, which the centre of the eye was able to register in the dark. But all the stages are not of the same magnitude. When the strength of a stimulus is increased, the sensation we experience follows a law of diminishing returns: differences that are noticeable at small intensities become unnoticeable at large ones. The candles fade as the daylight creeps through the windows, and when the sun shines on them they appear to go out.

The human eye is sensitive to all wavelengths that lie between 800 and 365 millimicrons; on either side of that band we have no visual sensations. We are not equally sensitive even to these wavelengths; the retina, for example, responds more readily to yellow and to green than to red or to violet, and will accord to these a greater brightness reaction. Even this irregularity is not constant. A chart of the relative sensitivity of the rods and cones shows that the cones reach a peak of sensitivity at the greenish-yellow hue, while the rods give an extreme reaction to the yellow-green; furthermore the rods are less sensitive than the cones to the long waves, red and orange, but more sensitive to blue and violet, the short ones. When we are in conditions of low illumination the rods are more active than the cones; it therefore follows that the blues and violets will appear brighter in poor light than in good.

As daylight fades not only do the hues of the landscape steadily lessen in saturation until all is grey, but the brightness of flowers in the garden alter in relation to each other; whereas at noon the geraniums were brightest, at dusk they are outshone by the delphiniums.

Nor, as the rods and cones are unequally dispersed in the retina, is our normal daylight vision of even sensitivity. The object that we fix with our eye appears clear and in full colour because the image is reflected on the fovea which is all cones; but other objects on the outskirts of our field of vision are received by parts of the retina which have many rods and few cones and consequently there is a weak colour reaction to them.

Light acting on the eye reduces the eye's sensitivity; the stronger the light, and the longer the stimulus is continued, the greater the loss of sensitivity. If we look fixedly at any object for a few minutes it will gradually lose brightness. In normal living we rarely have cause to do this, but if we make a conscious effort to do it we find a decided inclination to blink; we are instinctively trying, by a brief snatch of darkness, to renew the visual purple. If the object is coloured, not only will the brightness decrease as we gaze, but the saturation will lessen as well and the object will move towards greyness. In the normal process of vision we are, by exposing the retina to light stimuli, constantly losing sensitivity, and by changing the nature of the stimuli we are constantly renewing it. There is a continual balancing of which we are unaware until particular conditions, such as a snowy landscape, make us acutely conscious of the need for a complementary swing of the pendulum.

One side effect of the process of adaptation is the creation of after images. If we look hard at Figure 10c for about a minute and then transfer our gaze to a sheet of white paper, we will see the same image, but in reverse brightness like a photographic negative. What has happened is that the area of the retina which formerly bore the whole image has become desensitized, while that which bore the black comes to the new stimulus of the white paper with full vigour; consequently the previous brightness relationship is reversed. As the sensitive area loses its sensitivity the image fades, but it is not so much because the black or negative image becomes white as that the whole ground becomes of an undifferentiated greyness and the contrast is gone.

Similar after-images appear if we fix our gaze on a coloured object and then transfer it to a white surface. In this case the after-image appears in a colour complementary to the original. A ripe lemon will, for example, give a blue after-image, and purple grapes a yellowish-green one.

Positive after-images also occur, but these are of a different origin. A lit candle passed quickly before the eyes will appear to leave a trail of light behind it. This is because the receptors have been overstimulated and are still sufficiently active when the neurons have recovered from their first discharge to fire them again.

Weak stimuli give rise to neither positive nor negative after-images, but they have their own peculiarities. If, for example, a very small object is poorly illuminated we may not see it, yet if without changing the strength of the illumination we enlarge the area of the object it will become visible. This is due to the lateral neurons, mentioned earlier in this chapter, which appear not only to spread the area of a sensation but to reinforce it. A similar thing happens with colour. Strong colour may be experienced over a large area, but if the same stimulus is confined to a small area the saturation will be progressively lessened until, when the area becomes very small, the sensation of hue is lost altogether and the spot appears to be grey.

We have already noticed that even in normal lighting the other parts of the retina are less able than the centre to produce the sensation of hue, but what happens as the image is moved further from the centre of our field is not a straightforward and gradual loss of hue but a selective loss. Reds and greens tend to disappear before yellows and blues. Thus a ripe orange will appear yellow if the image is taken towards the periphery of the retina, and turquoise will appear blue rather than green. Strong bright colours continue to give a hue sensation (though a lessened one) well out towards the edge of the retina, whereas weakly saturated dark ones quickly turn to grey.

Congenital total colour-blindness in which people see only in terms of brightness or tone is exceedingly rare; partial colour-blindness in which reds and greens appear as yellows and blues is fairly common. From this, taken in conjunction with the facts of peripheral vision, it has been concluded that in some ways yellow and blue are more basic to human vision than are red and green.

The Modification of Light

So far we have traced, without going into much detail, the way light rays are turned into sensation producers. All this has been somewhat abstract; we have been in a world of sensations rather than meanings; it is as though we had been trying to understand the workings of a radio set without reference either to a listener or to a transmitting station. The next step is to consider how the light rays are modified by the matter on which they fall.

Light behaves in a consistent fashion. Because it does so we are able to interpret one light sensation in terms of other light sensations; this reliance on the belief that what has happened frequently will happen frequently again is the basis of all human behaviour. We turn out the light and walk down the darkened passage in the confident belief that the passage is still there. All day long we perform such acts of faith. We soon learn what data are sufficient to found our lives on. If we have no faith in the consistency of our sensual world we will at best go mad from uncertainty, and at worst never become conscious creatures at all. If, on the other hand, we have too much faith, disaster will overtake us, because our actions will at some time be inappropriate, as if, for example, we continued our walk into the lift shaft at the end of the passage. Material success in life normally goes to those whose faith is as great as the data will permit, but who then spare no effort to ensure that the data are as they suppose them to be—to the man who backs his skill at golf, but does not omit to cough when his opponent is addressing the ball.

Light waves hitting a surface will, if they cannot penetrate it, bounce off at an angle similar to that at which they struck it. When light from a point source strikes matter its reflected ray will reach us if our eye is situated somewhere on its path. On the consistent observance of this law all meaningful vision ultimately depends. (Figure 7.)

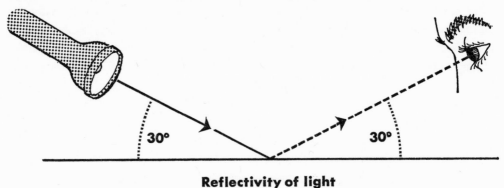

Reflectivity of light

FIG. 7

Matter not only reflects light; it can also have the quality of absorbing it. White light, as we know, is composed of energies of various wavelengths; matter can treat these waves selectively, and by absorbing some but not others can upset the balance which creates white light. When, for example, our beam of light strikes a surface that we call coloured, say a red carpet, a great deal of the green component of that light is accepted and absorbed by the carpet, whereas the red component is rejected and reflected; in a sense red is the one colour which a red carpet is not.

In practice light does not normally spring from a point source, and even with a strong primary source such as the sun there is always a great deal of diffused light as well. We do not see points of light, we see areas of it.

The perception of area depends upon the idea of distance. Distance is an idea which arises from movement.

When we see a horizontal line our idea that it is long is based on the fact that we can only focus all points along it in the centre of our field of vision by moving the eye from side to side. If our bodies were a permanent fixture and had never moved, so long as our eyes could be swung in their sockets, we would still have a notion of breadth. As it is, the idea is greatly extended because we can further our inspection of the horizontal by swivelling the head, and can extend it further still by turning our bodies around. A continuous horizontal line becomes then the circumference of a circle of which the fovea of our eye is the centre.

The notion of height is similar, but not identical. A vertical line we can also fixate by moving our eyes up and down, but their range is now much less than when we moved them horizontally. Furthermore we much less frequently turn somersaults in order to follow an upright line back to its starting-point than we revolve laterally to pursue a horizontal one. The result is that although we have no difficulty in conceiving a horizontal line as one that, if protracted, would circumscribe *us*, we do not easily conceive a vertical line in this way. Surely, we say, if a vertical line passes over the top of our heads and down the other side and under our feet and up again, it loses its verticality and becomes, certainly at its apex and nadir, horizontal. This depends upon our point of reference. If the movement involved in tracing the line with the fovea of our eye is the criterion, the line that goes upwards before our eyes is certainly the same line as that which passes over our heads and under our feet. But it is not the only criterion. There are two others that contribute to our concept of breadth and height, and the first of these is the law of gravity.

We are aware that our practical ideas of a horizontal line are not entirely dependent upon our eyes but upon measuring devices. There are various ways in which we determine whether a table is level, or that a picture is hanging straight, but they all involve reference to the vertical. And a vertical line for practical purposes is the line of pull between the earth's gravitational centre and all matter coming within its range. We have, therefore, admitted into our idea of verticality another centre than that of our own eye, the centre of the earth. The line we see as a vertical one is a compromise between these two. We conceive it as being straight from distant space to the heart of the earth; in order to see it as such we must admit the idea of distance *from* us, for never are more than two points on its extent going to be equidistant from our eyes.

Given these two ideas of height (extension above and below our natural centre of vision) and breadth (extension on either side), we are able to construct any two-dimensional shape about the centre established by our fovea.

The Idea of Distance

As soon as we come to a three-dimensional shape or form we have to introduce another element: our centre itself has to be mobile. And so, being able to walk our bodies about, it is. When an object is distant from us our concept of that fact is based upon the effort involved in transporting our centre towards it or away from it. The muscular effort that turns our eye from right to left is replaced by the muscular effort to advance or withdraw the cornea of our eyes. Our sense of distance is based upon this and upon the similar experience of advancing and withdrawing our hands or other principal organs of sense.

But, and the *but* is essential to the matter, we learn that certain sensations follow this process of advancing and withdrawing, and by deduction based upon these sensations we learn to interpret certain signs. The signs, eight in number, are these.

The first is that the farther an object is from us the smaller it appears to be. Thus, if we know the size of the object when it is close, we learn to estimate how far off it is in accordance with the diminution in size of its image on our retina.

The second is the loss of clarity in the image when far off due to interruption of the light rays by dust, smoke, and water-vapour. This lessens brightness, saturation, and the distinction of detail. It also changes hue in the direction of blue and purple.

The third is when the outline of an object is incomplete because another object intervenes between it and the eye and thereby plots its relative position.

The fourth clue is the varied way in which light reflects from surfaces of differing inclination; and the way in which the object casts shadows.

When we accommodate our eyes for comparatively near vision we do so by contracting the ciliary muscle. We know from experience what state of contraction is appropriate for objects at various distances; consequently a particular state of tension will imply a certain distance of focus. This is our fifth clue.

The sixth is in the activity known as convergence. Other muscles come into play in order to synchronize the vision of our two eyes. This only occurs over comparatively short-range vision, but within those limits the movement of the muscles which direct the eyes will be related to the distance of the point upon which we have made our sight converge. The nearer our targets the more steeply we shall have to angle our eyes.

Our seventh clue, also applicable to short-range sight, is our capacity for stereo-vision. If we hold a pencil up before us and open and close each eye alternately it is apparent that left and right eye record quite different images. And yet when both eyes are open and in convergence the image that we see is one and not two and there is no apparent contradiction within it. The left eye sees something of the left facet of the pencil, the right eye sees something of the right; by synchronizing the image both right and left sides of the pencil are visible at once and we are conscious of the sensation that what we see is three-dimensional. Indeed, we *know* that many things are three-dimensional from evidence of the sort we have just mentioned, but objects within stereoscopic range look as though they are so in a very different way. The extent of the difference is evident when we use the old-fashioned stereoscope, a viewing device whereby two photographs of a scene taken at slightly differing angles are co-ordinated. Naturally we should read such a scene, even when it is beyond human stereo-range, as three-dimensional, but when seen stereoscopically we believe ourselves to be seeing a third dimension which normally we only assume; the photographs look like a model.

The last clue is the phenomenon known as parallax. If we look out across a field of view in which there are objects at various distances and we move our heads from side to side we find that the relationship of near objects to far ones alters. If we look at a near object, all far ones seem to move in the direction in which we move our head. If, on the other hand, we focus on a distant object, then it is the near object which appears to move, but in a direction *opposite* to that of the head. We are, in fact, moving the foreground over which we see our object, or the background against which we see it; and the nearer the near object is to the eye the greater will the apparent displacement be.

We do not make much conscious use of these methods of determining distance; they are in use all the time, but they are subconscious and automatic and few of us are aware that they exist. Nor are they of equal importance. For practical purposes the most important is the fourth, the way in which surfaces reflect light.

Solid into Image

By long practice as children we become familiar with the reflective properties of surfaces which are inclined to us at differing angles and we learn to interpret them in terms of nearer or further off; up and down. The angle of reflection is the chief means by which we translate the two-dimensional image which is formed on the retina into a three-dimensional concept.

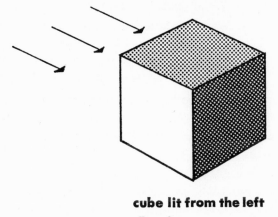

cube lit from the left
FIG. 8

Let us suppose a cube like a child's brick is lit from one side. If we view it from the opposite side the left surface will appear bright, the side partially exposed to the light will be of a slightly different brightness, and the side hidden from the direct light will seem dark. By the difference in the quantity of light reflected from these surfaces we are able to see that the object has three sides inclined to each other in such a way that experience of similar objects leads us to assume that three other identical sides exist. So true is this that we are all able to accept that Figure 8 represents a solid cube lit from the left when in fact it is a piece of paper which has printed on it three particular quadrilaterals in differing shades of grey. We might indeed interpret it in a variety of ways. We might suppose the shape it represents to be lit from the right instead of from the left, whereupon we will accept it as a three-sided concave figure rather than a six-sided convex one. If we do not do so it is because we are accustomed to this sort of symbol for a convex object. But in the interpretation of vertical air photographs where no clue is given to the mind as to the nature of the objects represented we assume that the source of light is opposite to us and that shadows fall towards us; so that should the print be, in fact, presented the other way round we will read as valleys what are in fact hills, and vice versa.

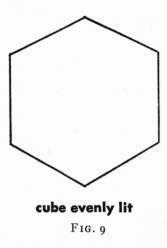

cube evenly lit

Fig. 9

Let us go on to suppose that this cube were to be lit by separate sources of light in such a way that every surface reflected exactly the same quantity of light to the observer, what would happen then? The figure then becomes as that in Figure 9. The surfaces, no longer differentiated, no longer appear to be inclined in different planes and we can no longer see that the object is three-dimensional at all. This visual trick is one that has played its part in the natural selection of animals; many creatures are dark on their backs, lighter at the sides, and lighter still on their under-parts; this 'counter-shading', or shading in a sense contrary to that which natural illumination gives, has the effect of flattening out the appearance of the creature and thus making it less visible to its enemies. The same principle is sometimes employed in military camouflage. (cf. Plate 13.)

Let us now go further and place our evenly lit cube against a background made of the same material and lit so that it reflects to our eye exactly the same amount of light as the cube itself. How shall we represent what we see? Only by a surface of uniform tonality. Can we say that the cube is invisible? Certainly not. It is visible. It is there and we can see as much of it as before. But we cannot distinguish it; neither its parts from each other, nor it from its background.

What comes of this is the factor which in one way and another will throughout the whole of this book signify more to us than any other, the factor of contrast. Seeing means little to us unless we can distinguish; distinguishing means the ability to separate an object from its background.

The Object-Ground Relationship

The establishment of an object-ground relationship is essential for meaningful vision, but there are circumstances when we cannot achieve it. The effect then is that we find ourselves looking into a formless envelope of light: we can see, but we cannot locate what we see, because there is no evidence to tell us the whereabouts of the surface. In normal life this rarely occurs. A snowy landscape, if sufficiently featureless, is one example. A cloudless blue sky is another. Some cinemas (I am thinking of that in Williamsburg, U.S.A.) light their empty screens in a way that gives the same effect. The power to distinguish an object-ground relationship depends upon our ability to make a distinction of sensation, a distinction which can only be of brightness, or of hue, or of saturation, or of all three in any combination.

Visual distinction is greatest when the two extremes of brightness, black and white, are opposed. The opposition of hues, if they are of the same brightness, produces a much less readily appreciated distinction. In this case the opposition of complementary hues will lead to stronger distinction than the opposition of hues which are close on the colour-circle. Some part is played in this by the influence which one colour has on its neighbour. For example, a grey can be made to appear black if it is shown against a background of white, but it may seem almost white if shown against unrelieved black. Hues are similarly affected. A hue will normally arouse in its neighbourhood the complementary sensation. If red is shown against green, our reaction to both is intensified. If a neutral grey is placed on a red background, it will become tinged with a bluish-green; if against a blue ground, the grey will acquire a yellow hue. In each case the effect is to increase the difference and to make distinction easier.

That our eyes should perceive an object as being in but separate from its environment is so essential to the act of vision that we do not realize that with all visible objects the process of disentanglement must take place, and does take place, whenever we use our eyes. In Figure 10a, where a simple circle of black is printed on a white page, everyone will read the area contained by the circle as the object and the surrounding white space as the background. But why should not the area confined by the line be the background and the area outside it the object? The first answer is that the mind, though incorrigibly active, is at the same time incorrigibly lazy and the area enclosed by the circle is simpler to comprehend than the area outside it. Secondly, because we have an easy mental ticket, or word, for the enclosed space we are prepared for it, whereas the space with a hole in it has less practical importance in our daily lives than a circle and we have no ready-made word to fit it. Thirdly, since objects which we know by touch to be separable from their surroundings are almost always visually circumscribed, we are apt to assume that, if light differentiates objects from their background two-dimensionally, there is differentiation in the third dimension also unless we know to the contrary. For this last reason if we see a containing line we are inclined to read, all else being equal, the space inside as a positive object and all outside as the negative surroundings from which we could physically subtract it.

Sometimes, when the spaces on both sides of the line are equally bounded, where both are equally easily comprehended and where we can as readily give a name to either, ambiguities occur. However long we look at the circle in Figure 10a we will not find that our reading of it alters, but if we look at Figure 10b where the circle has been evenly divided into eight segments we will, after a moment's concentrated looking, perceive that these segments have been resolved by our minds into an upright cross. If we continue to look we will find that the reading has changed into a diagonal cross, and after yet another brief period that it will turn back again to an upright one, and so on . . . much to the irritation of those who dislike finding that bodily functions which they had supposed under their conscious control are not. In Figure 10c, where four of the segments have been blackened, the phenomenon is

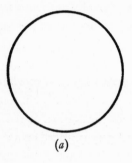 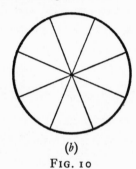 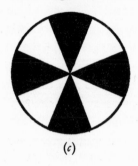

(a)   (b)   (c)

FIG. 10

more marked. We switch steadily and involuntarily from reading the white cross against the black ground to reading the black cross against the white one, and back again. The difficulty in both figures is that the mind has insufficient evidence to determine which cross it should read. Because of the law of gravity the cross with a vertical axis might be expected to have a slight preference as being the more stable and the more likely to be an object, but if so the preference is certainly not enough to stabilize our reading. Also in Figure 10c, because we are accustomed to read black on white positively as print, we should expect the mind to accept the black reading without ambiguity; but it does not do so, for no sooner have we fixed on it than the white segments push into the field of our consciousness and they in turn compose the cross.

The first cause of this swinging interpretation is physiological. When we expose photographic film the image that results is the product not only of the brightness of the light but also of the length of time the plate is exposed to it. This is not so with the human eye. It is indeed possible for the eye to be exposed to light for so short a time that no conscious image reaches the mind, but this time is very short indeed, a fraction of a second in normal conditions. Once the image is established further exposure does not increase the intensity of its contrasts, but, as we have seen, rather the contrary, for the image tends to lose in power. But within almost any field of vision there is great variety and the eye is able to flicker over the field, refreshing itself with contrasts, so that always one part of the field is

10   11

10 PICASSO: *The Three Dancers*

'I was Member of Parliament for Fulham, where many artists live. They agreed with me that art should be judged by the amount of satisfaction it gave the viewer. I fail to see what satisfaction this particular fabrication could give.' Baroness Summerskill

11 ST GEORGE HARE: '*But this was in the olden time . . .*'

12 *The Borghese Vase*

14 *Ganesa*—a Hindu god who is sometimes represented riding in a chariot drawn by a mouse

13. *The Aouchi*, like many other creatures, is light on its underside and dark above. This shading, contrary to the effect of natural illumination, has the effect of flattening the appearance of the creature and reducing visibility

seen in terms of the other, and the eye does not lose its sensitivity. Where our field is an unrelieved monochrome with no tonal variation, as on a snow-covered plain, the result is virtual blindness. Just as our sense of smell quickly becomes satiated by the perfume of violets, so our eyes become insensitive if exposed to an unmodified stream of identical stimuli. We already know that when we look fixedly at an object our eye automatically refreshes itself by moving away from the stimulus as it receives it, and returns only when in a condition to react positively to it again. We are not normally aware of what is going on because the mind, having determined which is the object and which the background, keeps its attention fixed on the object while the eye flickers over the ground; but where the ground for some reason (as with our crosses) competes equally with the object the mind, back at its automatic game of creating meanings and establishing likenesses, finds itself dragged from one object to another of equal importance and is aware of a process which would otherwise escape it.

All distinctions are initially recorded on the retina as shapes or outlines. If the distinction is sharp and the contrast between the two surfaces is strong, our minds, though accepting the enclosed area as an object, will tend to read it by tracing the outline. If, on the other hand, the line of demarcation is so blurred that, although we know a change has taken place, we cannot say at what point it occurred, we will tend to read the object as a bulk and its centre of gravity will be more significant than its outline.

Bulk, which is a weight plus size notion, is not properly applicable to a shape which has only two dimensions, but only to forms that have body and are thus susceptible to the law of gravity. Nevertheless, because nearly everything that has importance for us does have body, we attach three-dimensional characteristics to what we know are merely surfaces, and even to sounds and flavours, so that these, too, we think of as having bulk.

We are now passing the bounds of pure sensation and are already becoming involved in the world of ideas. Those physiological processes that gave us feelings of brightness, of hue, of saturation, concerned only the eye itself and a small appropriately receptive area of the central nervous system. As soon as we accepted the notion of extent we admitted the idea of area and of body. These new experiences are vastly more subjective and important than the simple sensations of vision, for they bring us into the world of movement and up to the threshold of the world of meaning, to a world in which we can function as men.

Two sensations imply proportion, an awareness of the ratio that one stimulus bears to the other; so that we cannot admit the idea of two sensations unless we also admit a third idea, that of duration. If we are to consider the composite stimulus red-and-blue, then the point must come when the red ends and the blue begins. The red will occupy one area of the field of view and the blue another. If the sensations are not simultaneous but successive, then the duration will be of time not of space, but it will still contain a fresh dimension none the less.

Obviously we are now able to experience very complex visual relationships indeed. It has been estimated that there are 128 just noticeable differences of hue in the spectrum and that there are twenty-eight just distinguishable differences in the purples which lie outside the spectrum. This gives us a choice of 156 different hues, but these hues can be distinguished in about twenty different degrees of saturation running from the first perceptible sensation of hue after neutral grey up to the greatest saturation possible. There are also 572 degrees of brightness perceptible between white and black. Because we can distinguish neither as many hues nor as many saturations at the lightest and darkest ends of the range as we are able to in the middle we cannot multiply the number of these hues, saturations, and brightnesses together to find out how many colours can be discriminated by the human eye; but an estimate has been made and the result is formidable. Any one hue may be perceived in about 2,000 differing qualities, which means that we can distinguish in all about 300,000 different sensations of colour.

This, one might have thought, was enough, but when we try to consider the implications of the relationship red-and-blue we find that we are concerned not only with the sensation red and the sensation blue, but also with their interaction, for the red has become a different red because the blue is there. Yet another ingredient we must remember is the step itself, or degree of change in sensation, involved in progressing from one to the other. As any blue and any red may appear in 2,000 different guises this step may be any one of four million degrees. Nor is this the end of the matter, for we have still not taken into account duration or area, and since the number of just perceptible differences of position and size which these colours may take up within the field of vision has not, as far as I know, been calculated, it will certainly be as well if we admit that the sensation red-and-blue is capable of an infinity of different values.

A visual sensation depends not upon one simple nervous discharge but upon an accumulation of them. The mind cannot respond to one; the amount of energy it releases is too small. For example, as a sensation of colour is reduced in area, the colour aspect of the sensation decreases until the red patch becomes a small neutral-coloured dot, and even this dot is the product of the repetition of many neutral discharges, not of one. The sensation of this bright red patch is built up of an enormous number of these dots each progressively, up to a certain point, intensifying and defining the experience. Equally, this diminishing characteristic is true of time as well as of space: if a light ray is exposed to us too briefly we will not be able to record it, for we depend upon its rapid recurrence before our minds can make anything of it. From this it follows that any sensation inevitably involves duration of both space and time. All sensation, however simple, if it can be differentiated, has form inasmuch as it is marked off in time or in space, or in both from the surrounding condition; but the form it takes may be simply 'brightness', or 'redness', or 'loudness', or 'pain', or whatever it may be; in other words its quality may have no tactile significance, no 'shape' other than that imposed upon it by the limits of the organ or sense by which it is conveyed to us.

Change in sensation, whether it be from red to blue or from one brightness to another, is the raw material from which the mind creates visual shape. Colour, when it is first accepted by the mind, is a visual sensation; it gathers to itself echoes of the other senses by virtue of its position in various scales, but until it does so it is and remains theoretically a sensation solely related to the eye. Visual shape is not a sensation of this sort. It depends for its existence upon other than visual experience and although it can have no visual existence except in terms of brightness and hue it requires more than this for the mind to create it; it requires particularly the fundamental sense of touch and, once it has been created, the sensation of shape takes us far beyond the simple relationship eye-to-mind and is able to involve infinitely various aspects of our existence.

No sensation is an isolated experience. We cannot detach even a single sensation like redness and say 'This exists quite apart from any experience I have ever had', because it, like everything else, is a part of our one great indivisible sensation of being. Nevertheless it seems to us that we are able to divide up the laborious process of being into chunks as though each one had an existence independent of the rest, and the very fact that we need to do this, and succeed in doing it, gives to the chosen sensation a false air of independent existence. In practice we rarely try to give independent form to single visual sensations, because in that guise they are not meaningful and we look primarily to the eye as a conveyor of meaning. We do, however, more often isolate the single experiences of sound, of scent, of taste, of touch, and try to accept them as though they were suspended in a vacuum.

Nevertheless, in practice, the sensations of which we are aware are complex ones, a symphony rather than a note, a shape more often than a brightness. We group together a sequence of sensations and speak of them as an entity. The sensual quality of this entity, table, picture, rose, whatever it may be, depends on the relationship of the modifier of energy, the object out there, with the capacity of the receiving power within us. When the eye, or the hand, or any sensually aware part of the body, is involved in a sensation it sets itself, like a railed vehicle, to explore the duration of that sensation. If the sensation changes direction, the setting of the organ of sense must be changed, too, in order to accommodate the new experience. If the change of direction is gradual the alteration of set need not be violent: if the change is sudden, arbitrary, unprepared for, the organ of sense must make an equally sudden and unexpected change, exactly as when, after driving along a motorway for many miles we suddenly find ourselves without warning in the erratic and steeply angled streets of an old town. Preparedness does in part lessen the unpleasantness of this experience; we know that we are going to be faced with the necessity of a change of set and have already, as it were, changed gear; but that mere preparedness does not make such violent changes pleasant is shown by our relief when the road opens up again before us.

Visual shape has two main aspects: outline and bulk. Every outline involves the idea of the movement of our eye along it, and the identity of ourself with it; every bulk conveys the motion of lift and effort. Arising from these are other aspects such as surface and distance. Every surface conveys a sense of roughness or smoothness to our finger-tips; if the object is near it is within our grasp, if it is far the very notion of farness contains an idea of the effort we should have to exert to bring it within reach. These are not visual sensations; the purely visual sensations of brightness and hue tell us nothing about any object except . . . its brightness and hue. We cannot therefore expect to find the essential qualities of any shape by considering only the mechanism of the eye. Shape involves a world of dimension, of position, of objects, of otherness, of world-out-there.

It is very difficult, if not impossible, to conceive of shape in the abstract. Although we may think that we have for short periods excluded from shape any representational factor and succeeded, against the mind's inclination, in not interpreting it, we cannot free it from gravity. Our world of objects is, and has always been, and despite our present excursions into weightlessness is likely to be, a world of direction and balance, a field organized by gravitational pull. A vertical line is *carried* on its base or *hung* from its tip; a horizontal line disposes the force of gravity evenly along its length; a triangle has a base and an apex; all forces are organized by our minds in accordance with the principles which in our infancy we found to be essential for the conduct of our material affairs. Outline, the silhouette of shape, is seen as a surface along which we move, and its quality is acquired from the quality of that movement. The space enclosed by the outline, on the other hand, being conceived in some sense as an object, is subject to those same stresses which govern objects. If the area is supported by a base which, interpreted in terms of familiar materials, would be inadequate to support its weight, a feeling of insecurity will be a quality of the form. If the area of the form is disposed irregularly about what would, if it were a solid object, be its point of balance, then the feeling of instability is inherent in the form. In both cases we are conscious of forces of imbalance which, if translated into terms of solids, would result in an activity in which we would become involved. A situation is before us to which we automatically set ourselves to respond. The weight is going to crush its base and we identify ourselves with that part which is actively set for a task too great for it. The residual sensation in this case may well be one of fear, or of the ludicrousness of the disproportion between the challenger and the challenged, as in the case of the Hindu god, Ganesa, who is represented as an elephant in a chariot drawn by a mouse. (Plate 14.) When a weight is perceived to be in the very act of falling, a vestigial drive is set up in us to stretch forward quickly, before it is too late, to adjust the balance. In either case, as the object is, in fact, a weightless percept, and the bulk will never crush nor the falling triangle fall, we are left in a state of permanent, if slight, frustration with a tension which cannot be discharged.

If we invert such figures, they acquire other qualities. The triangle on its apex becomes stable; but a figure with a massive base supporting an insignificant weight acquires another disproportion: we feel as though we have set ourselves to pick up a leaden weight only to find that it is made of plaster; the response is so far in excess of the challenge that a surplus tension is retained which cannot be absorbed in the end situation and Ganesa will look almost as foolish carrying a mouse as the mouse did carrying Ganesa.

The Expressiveness of Sensation

By involving the fundamental sensations of touch and movement in our percepts we gain the capacity of sensation to be expressive. Even relatively simple sensations can be expressive when they involve echoes of meaningful human activities. For example, we have seen so many hues, shades and saturations of red that the particular red which we are now experiencing is an individual red which has its own place in the hierarchy of reds: it has acquired a position on a scale which is not properly a scale of hue at all. We gain ideas of deep and shallow, strong–weak, far–near, heavy–light, high–low, qualities which depend on touch and movement for our ability to conceive them. It is the complexity of such relationships that makes it possible for simple sensations to acquire overtones of expression. Height implies effort, instability, illimitability, reach rather than grasp, and if lift is cancelled by fall, it is weightless and ethereal. Breadth is solid, enduring, stable, human, limited, tangible. Brightness is vital, active, positive and strained. Darkness is restful and relaxed.

The difficulty with these simple sensations lies in determining exactly what they express. The simpler a sensation the more doubtful is its expressive content. If our field of view is filled with white the sensation may be felt to contain an element of chastity, or of alertness, or of cold, or of infinity, or of sickness, or of celebration, and so on; and which of these the mind selects as the ingredient will determine the sort of notion that white expresses. To say, as some would, that white expresses itself, is verbal chicanery, for this can only mean either that white is a pure percept without expression, which is perhaps what they intend to mean, or that white expresses all the possible expressivenesses of white at the same time and since many of these are mutually exclusive this can only mean that white expresses that which is the common denominator of all white expressivenesses, which can be no other than the percept white.

Every additional sensation which is introduced to a percept helps to define what it expresses. For example, the totality of the composite sensation red-and-blue is not to be thought of as $a + b$, a particular red plus a particular blue, but as a movement and progression in the mind as it encompasses one sensation and proceeds to the other. This movement, according to the way the tensions involved are released and recreated, will have qualities of direction, speed, and duration. The particular type of movement may have similarities of tempo that suggest a human activity, perhaps a dance, so that the red-and-blue sensation while not actually conveying to us the idea of dance may well express an overtone of gaiety.

As all sensation is activity, the principle underlying the expressiveness of form is the movement of energy. Pulses of energy may be felt as fast or slow, constant or intermittent. Abstractly these different characters of energy are what they are and have no essential expressiveness, but they acquire expressiveness when we measure them against a fixed standard. Such standards are inherent in our physical natures. Before birth we were surrounded by the constant thud and rush of the heart beating out its rhythm, and from the moment of our birth until our death we have carried that rhythm within us. In moments of excitement or exertion the tempo is increased; in moments of repose and calm it becomes more slow. Patterns of energy, whether we perceive them as lines, bulks, areas, colours, sounds, flavours, or perfumes, in so far as we detect a rhythm in their relationships, can find an answering rhythm in ourselves and acquire in our minds a sort of glow, or significance, because of the proportions they bear to the rhythm in our blood. We are not only the centre of our universe around which all revolves, we also supply the meaning of all phenomena and the measure of all sensation.

3. Man and the Object

The mind, that ocean where each kind
Does straight its own resemblance find.
ANDREW MARVELL, *The Garden*

BECAUSE we move, and because we have the sense of touch, we are able to develop our visual sensations into an idea, an idea compounded of notions of position, of weight, of size, of material, of temperature, of taste, of sound, of smell, of function, as well as of light and colour. That idea is, for us, the object.

By the time a human being has matured his world is full of objects. Always his life has been very largely a matter of reacting appropriately to these objects, and it will continue to be so. He must dodge the car as he crosses the street; he must keep his hand from the fire; he may drink whisky, but must eschew strychnine. The more objects his world contains the more complex his life becomes and the more he must study to master the appropriate reactions if he is to survive in it.

In order to react appropriately to objects we must recognize them. Now, it is certainly true there are some things we can recognize by sensations other than visual ones: we can recognize the fire because of the pain it causes us when we touch it, we can recognize whisky by the taste of it, and the sonata by the sound of it. Those who are blind can recognize many things by touch, but most of us base our recognition on visual images because they give us advanced warning of the implications of objects and enable us to anticipate their demands. But we do not need all an object's visible manifestations for this purpose, there are so many objects, and so many aspects of them, that it is necessary for us to simplify and to codify their images on the basis of some quickly apprehended characteristic features.

The most characteristic feature of almost any object is its shape, for it is this which governs its function. A letter-box may be red, but it is not its redness which makes it a letter-box. Hue and saturation may serve to mark off a sub-genus from a genus, an individual from a species, but it is shape which gives the most reliable clue to what kind of thing an object is. This is why the blind, who have neither hue nor saturation nor brightness, recognize most things as well as the rest of us because they can appreciate shape through their finger-tips; and this is why brightness, which can most easily be organized by the mind into giving consistent information about shapes, is very much more important in the common affairs of life than colour.

Once it is clear that what chiefly concerns us about an object is that we shall act appropriately towards it, then the minimum data to ensure that result is all we need. We strip the image of everything that is not specially characteristic and we are left with a sign.

The object we know as a pig gives us certain sensations which we construct into the idea *pig*. But the image on the retina is not the pig, nor, if we subtract from that image the sensation of colour, is it any less pig; nor does it matter how much we subtract from the image so long as some clue remains that will alert the idea *pig*. Let us employ a certain mark exclusively for pig, and let that mark be the letters P I G. And if, parallel with the development of the visual sign, we develop sound signs, we shall find ourselves with a spoken language as well as a written one.

Nevertheless, as the image on the retina of the eye is not itself a pig, nor is the sign P I G a pig. The first is a visual sensation directly related to the individual object and with which we associate other sensations according to our experience; the second is a visual sensation quite arbitrarily related to the object and which represents the object only because we are agreed that it shall do so. Between these two sorts of sign there lies a whole sequence of others, each in a slightly different relationship to the object it represents.

Leonardo da Vinci wrote: 'Write up in one place the name of God, and put a figure representing him opposite, and see which will be the more deeply revered.' To Leonardo, seeking to prove the superiority of the image over the symbol, the answer was in no doubt, but we may not find it so easy to be certain, particularly in the instance he gave us, that the image is the best road to the idea. If it were we should abandon literature and concentrate upon the development of the strip cartoon. Michelangelo, the poet, would have thought differently.

The important quality for any sign is its constancy, for a sign is where an infinite number of individual facts, experienced in an infinity of ways, meet in a point. Without signs we should not only be unable to communicate with each other, we should be unable to communicate with ourselves; they are the generalizations that provide the pivot upon which our lives turn.

The appearance of objects is constantly being altered by circumstances; therefore, if we are to retain any notion that the object we are seeing so differently is the same object whose recognizable features we know, we must learn to discount automatically the circumstances that have given it variety. We look out on to the snow in moonlight and it is white; we see it under the midday sun and it is still white; yet we are told that sunlight is 800,000 times as strong as full moonlight. White is an absolute concept—can there be degrees of whiteness? In fact, the practised eye of one who has cultivated perceptual sensitivity will not see either surface as white; but for most people and for most purposes both appear white because they are known to be white. If, on the other hand, these surfaces were not known to be white, if we were to look at a patch of snow lit alternately by sun and moon through a hole in a card, and had no clue to the behaviour in other light conditions of what we were seeing, our minds would receive the stimulus of its hue and brightness unaffected by any other related experience; we should, in fact, not only see neither snow nor whiteness but we should see no surface at all, only a three-dimensional space filled with luminosity of a certain quality . . . and that quality we should not register as white. It was, I think, Ruskin who pointed out that if one were to paint a patch of green grass in full sunlight as the eye received it the result would be taken for a bed of primroses because what we know to be green we see to be yellow. What we see, the image, is the sensation conditioned by our knowledge, not the sensation alone.

This characteristic of constancy applies not only to colour but also to size and shape and movement. We know that the distant trees on the horizon appear smaller than the trees in the garden near by, but we do not realize how small their image is until we try to outline it upon the window-pane. Our knowledge of the actual size of the trees has affected our perception of the size of their image. If we look at a coin at an angle to its face and then draw what we think we have seen, the result will almost certainly be more nearly circular than the image was. The mind slews the elipse towards a circle in order to bring it more closely into harmony with our mental image of a coin. The child drawing a figure of a man represents him full-face with the two eyes, the two ears, the two arms, and the two legs, which the child knows him to have. It is the same with movement. When we are sitting in a stationary train at a platform and the train immediately beside us moves off we believe that it is we who are moving and find it necessary to look out of the other window at the stationary buildings to assure ourselves that we are not. We prefer to believe that it is we who move and that it is our background which is stable, for this is the normal state of affairs. The mind strives to bring consistency into the chaos of our visual world and some-times makes nonsense of it.

Brightness, hue, saturation, outline, form, size, texture, function, all things that we see in our object, are all variable according to the circumstances in which we see them, but as long as an identifiable clue remains we reduce them to an idea with a constant, and therefore recognizable shape.

But the shape of an object, though by far our most effective, is not our only visual guide to identity; sometimes it is the shape taken by attributes rather than the object itself which enables us to recognize it. For instance, we know a policeman by his uniform, a judge by his wig, Saint Peter by his keys, Neptune by his trident, Jove by his eagle, and Peace by her dove. A whole code of distinguishing features has been built up, mainly, it would seem, for the convenience of religious artists of the sixteenth century who were thus enabled, very simply, to alert the informed as to what they were about. But even here the recognition is of individuals or groups of objects, rather than of the genus itself.

Recognition can also be helped by the background, or situation, in which an object is seen. A bottle on a bar counter is unlikely to contain disinfectant, nor will the largest stone in a tray of costume jewellery be the Koh-i-Noor diamond: their surroundings identify those objects without putting us to the trouble of detailed perception.

Movement, which is most often seen as a change in relationships between an object and its background, can also, on occasions, be perceived without clear perception of shape at all. If the movement is distinctive in kind, then it can give a clue to what made it. The indistinguishable shapes that leap across the Australian bush are surely kangaroos; the vehicle that leaves a track with angled rather than curved changes of direction is a tank, not a lorry; when the grasses stir in an undulating pattern we recognize the snake; the log that dives is a crocodile.

Size, too, when taken in conjunction with situation, can play a part. The shapeless bulk half seen in the jungle is an elephant not an ant, by virtue not of its shape but of its size.

The Selection of Experience

Although our cluttered world of objects has been greatly simplified for us conceptually by classification, and perceptually by taking the part for the whole, there remains still far too much to cope with. We manage to bring it within bounds by the simple process of not noticing ninety-nine hundredths of the recognizable objects about us. After the distinct stages of perceiving and recognizing, we are arrived at another, noticing.

We give objects our attention for broadly two groups of reasons: because we cannot help it; and because we want to.

It is difficult not to notice an earthquake; it is easy to overlook a whisper. The principle at work here is whether the contrast of the stimulus is stronger than the general level of surrounding contrasts. In normal life an earthquake would provide stimuli disproportionately strong, but one can imagine circumstances, for example a nuclear bombardment, when the stimuli it provided would be appreciably below the general level and would escape our attention. Similarly a whisper cannot compete with the stimuli of ordinary life, but in a prison cell or during a silent vigil it would be so strongly differentiated from the surrounding peace that one could not fail to notice it. At one time I lived within a short distance of a busy railway; when a train passed the house casual guests would look at each other in startled horror, but we to whom these cataclysmic events were an unavoidable part of our daily life were usually not aware of them. Nor is it always just the difference in intensity between the stimulus and its background which forces itself on our attention, but often a distinction of kind rather than dimension. A tulip growing in a rose bed is noticeable, not because its shape is a more violent stimulus than a rose bush's, but because it is out of pattern.

It is really not possible to consider objects apart from their grounds, because no object can have a visual existence without one, even though it be no more than vacancy itself. Nor, as we have seen, can an object have a meaningful visual existence if it modifies light rays in exactly the same manner as the ground it is on. To be indistinguishable from one's surroundings is to put on a cloak of invisibility.

With simple grounds, the idea of figure-ground relationship is straightforward enough. We focus on the figure, or object, perceive it with maximum clarity and intellectually *fix* upon it. Yet the ground does not disappear; we perceive that also. It is not a question of all or nothing, but rather of two quite different levels of vision. But grounds are rarely simple monochromatic expanses; they are more often, themselves, a complex relationship of objects. When we focus our eyes on a picture that has been hung against a patterned wall-paper we do not resolve the wall-paper into a monochrome; we can see, even while we look at the picture, that the background against which it hangs is an assemblage of steamships, lighthouses and sea-gulls. We have, then, not two distinct levels of vision only, object and ground, but a third level also, one at which we are able to differentiate within the ground itself. Nor, it seems likely, is our capacity to distinguish a diminishing recession of object-ground relationships limited by anything other than a physical inability to see them. Nevertheless, these distinctions do diminish very rapidly, and their relative importance diminishes equally steeply: the distinction we make between the picture and the wall-paper is a far more important one than the distinction we are marginally making between the lighthouse and the paper sea it stands in; and this in turn is a more important distinction than that between the alternate large and small waves of that paper sea.

When looking at an object on a complex ground we can certainly see that ground, but the extent to which we are aware of it is another matter. There are two main considerations: the first is purely perceptual. The simple rule would appear to be that the stronger the stimulus provided by the background, whether in saturation or in brightness, the less we are able to discount the ground when looking at the object. If we look at a white cat upon a Persian rug we may go a long way towards shutting out the rug from our conscious minds, because the visual stimulus of the cat is the greater; but a Persian rug upon a white carpet would be less likely to hold our undivided visual attention, because the competition of the carpet is too intense. A second rule is that when hues of equal brightness are concerned we can more easily exclude a complementary background than we can a background which is close in hue to the object. This means we can more closely fixate a red spot on a green ground than the same spot on a yellow one; we can shut out the green ground more easily than the yellow. This second rule also provides the exception to the first. White is the most positive of light stimuli; black, in theory, is entirely negative; but being complementary they obey the second rule, not the first. It is easier to exclude awareness of the ground when we see a black spot on a white ground than if we see it on a grey one, although we are also more likely to be caught in an involuntary swinging interpretation.

Even these simple rules are subject to other considerations. We must extend our idea of background from the immediate physical field in which the object is seen, to include all our related experience. For example, if we were accustomed to see a red spot on a yellow ground, but had rarely, or indeed never before, seen it on a green one, it is likely that for some time at least the green would compete more clamorously for our attention than the yellow. Even the simple sensation of red on yellow becomes in this way a dynamic, variable, personal experience and our whole life is seen as a palimpsest of backgrounds, contributing something, although not necessarily anything of great significance, to all our perceptions. But before we build too much on the variable nature of human reactions to phenomena let us quickly make clear that there *is* a norm based upon the physiology of man, and that to this norm deviations will, in healthy circumstances, tend to return. Once the human mind has discounted the surprise of finding red on green in the instance we have just considered, the pattern of its attention would become based upon the simple rule that complements exclude one another.

Organization by Interests

In its simplest form a background is an undifferentiated monochromatic expanse against which an object appears isolated because of the different way in which its surfaces reflect light. Here the mind seizes on a readily apprehended difference in sensation in order to build its object-ground relationship. But though the distinction of the object from its immediate ground is always based on perceptual factors inasmuch as we cannot make it without them, there are other sorts of object-ground relationships which are more truly conceptual. That even in the simplest cases the concept enters into the mind's decision as to which is object and which is ground, we have already agreed; but when the ground itself is a complex one which contains differences of hue and brightness which might be separable we then have to disentangle the distinctions which interest us from those which do not. Having done so our field of vision becomes organized into (1) the interesting feature, which advances with a spring to the forefront of our consciousness as soon as we disentagle it, and (2) the remainder of the field which recedes to a secondary state of awareness.

On being exposed to a visual field the mind first strives to organize it in accordance with its previous experience. It seeks for some form it can recognize so that the sensation it is now undergoing will be placed in relation to the totality of its sensual experience. It achieves this by working on the form presented to it in an effort to make it fit over one of the great repertoire of established forms with which its experience has equipped it. What we are trying to establish is not simply 'It's a collar-stud', but 'This is a collar-stud on the carpet'. We are distinguishing the object from the background and in the same act we are giving the background a character which relates it to the whole of our experience.

The Emergence of Pattern

Whereas the organization of the object seems to involve its recognition, the organization of the background is at first purely formal; recognition, though almost always implicit, comes later. Disposing of uncertainties is the mind's first and greatest task; thereafter it has other responsibilities, but this it must do if it is to be mind. Recognition, which is based upon the notion of consistency, that what has been before will be so again, is the first step in the elimination of uncertainty. But we need to eliminate uncertainty from the background as well as from the object. This we can do by 'The collar-stud is on the carpet', but because the carpet exists in a subordinate stage of our awareness we are content that it shall have a formal consistency only. It need not be consciously recognized as carpet, but only visually apprehended as a pattern of sensations to which the collar-stud is extraneous. The mere fact of establishing which is object and which is ground gives to the background the unified character of secondary status; but if we are to see it as a whole, as a single concept, as 'background', we will be at pains to resolve it into a form which has coherence. This form, or character, or element that provides consistency, is what we call pattern.

Pattern arises from the tendency of the mind towards repetition, towards constant criteria, towards stable standards, towards the need for a certain sequence of cause and effect, which provides the central psychological fact of our lives. Without repetition and consistency we cannot live at all, for there would be no law. Everything that comes within the range of our sensory apparatus must either in some way be fitted into the logic we have established, be excluded from our awareness so that we can pretend it does not exist, or be accepted and assimilated and the logic be adjusted to contain it.

Visual pattern may be of shape, or of hue, or of brightness, or of saturation, or of sentiment; its essence is that there shall be a rhythm perceptible within the field of view. Once the nature of the rhythm has been established and the mind is accustomed to it, anything which breaks rhythm will be distinguishable, any object which destroys the harmony of the pattern, or which checks the smooth run of the mind over the accustomed and expected ground, will be noticed. There are, then, three courses open to us. We may elevate the inconsistency into the role of object against background, thus removing it conceptually from the plane of the offended pattern; this is the normal process. Or we may reorganize the pattern to account for it. The mind finds it so necessary to impose order that it does not hesitate to extrapolate if that is the only way in which it can discern the workings of a law. In this way it can turn even heterogeneity into pattern, one against which any duplication of shape, or brightness, or hue, is instantly distinguished. Finally, we may try to ignore the irritating inconsistency and teach our senses not to respond to it. Some minds are so strongly disposed towards this constancy of response that they will not observe a break in the pattern, but will simply misread it as a conformity. When this book is printed I will myself read the proofs many times, so will professional proof-readers employed by the printers and by the publishers, yet within a month of publication several mis-spellings, word-omissions, duplications and so on will have become apparent. We will all have been to some extent the victims of our familiarity with the pattern of the language. We know what should be there and we will read it as though it is.

The more complex the pattern the easier it is to overlook an inconsistency. An experiment in which a pack of playing cards was recoloured so that the diamonds were black and the clubs red resulted in some at least of those who were tested not observing anything wrong. The pattern of a pack of cards, although familiar to most of us, is a fairly complex one and the mind is well able to lose in it what it wants to. But even here there are limits to the tricks we can play upon ourselves. The urge to constancy would need to be very great indeed to accept a coloured postcard of the Mona Lisa as the Ace of Hearts. Yet in everyday life we frequently meet with people who are interpreting facts as they want them to be and not as the evidence suggests they are. Politicians are particularly adept at such forms of self-imposed deceit, but we are none of us free of it and when we indulge it to a very obtrusive degree society calls us mad.

A great deal of our perceptual activity takes place at a level slightly below that of full consciousness. So well able are we to operate at this state of awareness that many of us can drive a motor car on an accustomed journey in such a way that at the end of it we cannot recollect any single conscious observation or action we have taken on the way. Eye and hand act in fluent co-operation while the conscious mind is elsewhere building castles in Spain. We seem to be capable of not one or two or three distinct levels of awareness, but rather of progressive degrees of it. An object can be seen, recognized, and discarded, without the conscious mind becoming involved in the act of oblivion at all. Or, if it is not to be discarded but acted upon in some routine way, it can still be done with the minimum of mental involvement. The pen with which I write, the paper, the paper-clips, the ink, the blotting-paper, I must not only perceive and recognize but must also accord to them just sufficient of my conscious mind to find them when I need to use them. But it is idle to pretend that this involves any great degree of awareness. In familiar surroundings, and with familiar objects, very little conscious attention suffices to initiate the activity upon which we are set. Do we notice the knives and forks when we sit to a meal at our own table? We would notice if they were not there, or were arranged in an uncustomary order, but otherwise they are so deeply grooved a part of our existence that we see and use them automatically without considering what we are doing. This automatism is not so marked in less familiar surroundings. We just notice the equipment of a friend's table; we are slightly aware of the the knives and forks in a restaurant we do not frequent. But even this degree of heightened awareness, heightened because we are alert for signs of phenomena which we must meet with a special reaction, is not of the same order as when we are actively looking for an object.

It is inconsistency within known patterns which enables interpreters of air-photographs in wartime to detect military installations. Human activities tend to create on the surface of the earth types of mark which are consistent with the purpose of that activity; if another type of activity is suddenly introduced, as in war, fresh marks appear which are of a kind essentially, although perhaps only slightly, different from those that were there before. Because they are 'out of pattern' they catch the eye of any observer who is familiar with patterns seen in this way. For example, cattle released from a milking shed will in a short time establish a network of tracks across a field, whereas troops billeted in that same shed will make quite a different network. The trained interpreter is alert for contradictions to the peaceful patterns of the earth, but his consciousness of these is partnered by his awareness of those special types of pattern which he associates with military activity. He is looking for the marks made on the ground by armoured vehicles when they laager; for the fan-shaped scorch on the grass that forms before the muzzle of a gun after it has fired; for the regular spacing of dots on the road that betray a disciplined convoy. These signs, well known to him, have become positive meaningful shapes which, as he already has the explanation ready made, harmonize, not with the peaceful pattern of the ground but with the pattern in his mind.

In circumstances of search, the mind is astonishingly exclusive; if we are looking for a collar-stud we do not notice diamond watches and tin-tacks which, if we allowed ourselves to see them, would merely impede us. Our awareness of an object's visual identity is now at its height.

The Sources of Emotion

In so far as our perception of an object is merely a signal for us to do something, to catch it, to jump out of the way, to eat it, to forget it, and so on, we conserve our effort. This principle, if there were nothing to check it, would become a running-down process leading ultimately to the development of a creature of automatic responses. Biologically it would be a step downward upon the ladder of evolution towards organisms which respond to stimuli but, so far as we can detect, have no awareness of themselves. But mind, once it has become a storehouse of data, is able to lift our reactions beyond the range of immediate stimuli into the field of events which have not yet occurred and which are still far from being able to provide material for sensory perception.

It is a monstrous simplification to assume that the mind is a store-house of sensations presided over by the power of reason. Reason is the faculty that plays with sequences, that interpolates, extrapolates, and variously combines and divides. Its processes are induction and deduction; its ideal territory is measurement. But the sensations that we gather through our finger-ends, through our eyes and our ears and our nose and our palate, and which we experience briefly in the dark of our heads and then store there in some fantastic code-system, are material for other activities as well as for measurement.

The first of these other movements or functions of the mind is emotion; love, hatred, fear, doubt, amusement, all that great armoury of affective states which to most of us are the very substance of life. Emotion, although it is an effect following upon a cause and is as much a result of sequences as is anything else, is largely independent of reason. It is easy to reason about the causes of love and fear, but it is not possible to reason ourselves into those states. Reason is concerned with quantities; the emotional faculty deals in qualities. The distinction is rather like that which exists between tone and hue, in which tone identifies whereas hue distinguishes; or like the palate which, by-passing recognition, merely signifies pleasant–unpleasant, sweet–sour, accept–reject, in contrast to the labelled bottle, *caviare* or *strychnine*, which calls upon our experience and our knowledge.

The function of the palate in the survival of the organism is evident. Too many fatalities would result if we had to gain all our knowledge of what was edible or not from digestive experience. The appearance of things has very little to tell us of their food value—we are granted merely a moment of acceptance or rejection. We must swallow and die, or spit it out and live. This is why we have evolved and retained a sense of taste. Likewise with odour, which is the quality of unseen airs, we can normally rely upon neither sight nor sound nor analysis before the breath of them is in our nostrils, and if we do not instinctively find their noxious qualities displeasing and stop our breath the poison will be at work in our lungs.

Taste and smell and sight and sound and touch are particular and immediate sensations directly dependent on the stimulus of certain nerve-ends. Love and hate are not sensations of this sort; the seat of their activity is deeper in the mind where sensations are given qualities which upon their first acceptance there do not belong to them. Nevertheless, although our affective reactions to them take place at a different stage, it is reasonable to suppose that the function of this sort of delayed palate is similar to that of smell and taste, that it is part of the guiding apparatus of the organism on its way through time and space. As this function could be performed just as well at first impact as it is with the simple senses, there must be some reason why our emotional valuation is delayed until the sensation has already been received by the mind and is lodged there. The answer is that the emotional reaction is concerned not with simple sensations of one type—this smell, this colour, this line—but with complex sensations formed by the fusion of different sensory perceptions. Two things which may be harmless in isolation may become toxic when fused. If the fusion takes place within

15 *Rose 'Pink Supreme'*
'Rose is a rose is a rose is a rose.'
Gertrude Stein

16 *A Spider's Web*
At what point does a work of nature become a work of art?

17 *The Architecture of the Caddis Fly*

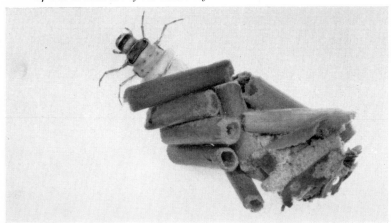

III Naroccio di Landi (Sienna): Madonna and Child (gilded wood)

the mind at a stage beyond that which records simple sensation, then this is the first place at which an automatic response can be made, so that we experience sweet or bitter, accept or reject, in the more developed form of love or hate, embrace or kill. We do not love (unless we misuse the word) a simple sensation, though we may like or dislike it. We do not hate or fear a hue or a line unless and until those simple sensations have become complex ones for us by the addition of associated ideas; then indeed they may pass into the inner recess of the mind where the deep emotions play—but not until. Emotional states are automatic responses to composite sensations.

We need not be surpised that this system does not invariably and automatically produce the right answers. Apart from the fact that so exceedingly sensitive a mechanism can easily become disordered and give the wrong signals, the suggestion that it should always be right presupposes that the right answers are known. We plan machines to perform certain operations, for example to imprint letters upon paper, their function is defined, for we have laid it down. But what is the function of the machine that we are? And who has laid it down? The emotional system has evolved as a device that keeps the organism upon the paths that lead to survival, but it has only evolved so far and is still in process of evolving. It may be that in certain conditions of life the emotions are a handicap and not an advantage. If so, natural selection will eliminate them. If circumstances change, then the use to which we put emotions may change also. They may become vestiges of a practical function for which they are no longer required, and will gradually wither; or they may become, being independent of function, cultivated for their own sake.

Mechanisms are not concerned with ultimate rightness. They are concerned to perform immediate and finite functions. If our palate is well adjusted, we dislike the flavour of bad fish and spit it out, but our palate is only concerned with leading us to the rejection of bad fish, it is not signposting the way to the higher Ethics, to the Eternal City, or to the fulfilment of the Will of God.

Operating in much the same area of the mind as the emotions is that curious faculty that we call the imagination. The imagination is essentially creative, it is the energy that fuses sensations together so that they become new entities. Within it takes place the unconscious coupling which gives birth to visions and dreams, to the *Odyssey* and to *Macbeth*, to Botticelli's *Birth of Venus* and to Beethoven's Fifth Symphony. In its minor manifestations it is wit and gives birth to the *mot juste*, the diner's tale, the unpremeditated aside. Just as two chemicals may join to become a third, and just as the mating of creatures brings to independent being another creature, so the mating of ideas generates others, parented indeed, but dissimilar to its parents and unique. The chemical and biological analogy can be carried further, for just as certain substances cannot be brought to fuse at the appropriate level, and as some forms of life are genetically incompatible, so some ideas can be juxtaposed, but will never fuse. Such a mule-alliance is not the work of the crucible of the imagination but of the cooler, more conscious region of fancy; the apparent new entity is not an entity at all but a piecemeal construct in which no fusion has taken place.

We commonly speak as though it is the ability to reason that separates man from other creatures. It is not certain that other creatures do not possess this in some degree, but that they possess imagination is far less likely. If one faculty rather than another sets man apart from the remainder of creation it is the imagination. To the extent that he possesses it man is a creator, not of life only, for most other creatures are potentially that, but a creator of ideas.

Reason, Emotion, and Imagination, all operate to some extent automatically. In certain conditions they become spontaneously engaged, but above them, exercising a loose and frequently inadequate suzerainty, is that fourth function of the mind, the Will.

The Will is most nearly identifiable with that part of our mental apparatus which we call the Soul. All things are me but my Will is most me. Ideally the Will governs the remainder of the being; in practice it hardly works out like that. The Will is generally better at controlling the body than the mind. By the Will we may initiate those muscular contractions which end in raising the arm, opening the hand, turning the head. The Will may take us to China or Peru, it may take a horse to the water, it may seat the artist at his easel, the writer at his desk; but it is a great deal less competent at commanding the reason, less competent still to control the imagination, and least competent of all to control the emotions. What the Will can do is to set the stage for those other functions to take over; its control is indirect, but, with practice, it can be fairly effective. The Will is the most mysterious of the varied capacities of the mind.

4. Reality and the Idea

Words are the daughters of earth, and things are the sons of heaven.
DR SAMUEL JOHNSON, *Preface to the Dictionary*

WHAT things are we cannot know. We know so much about many of them that it is reasonable to say that we know what they are *to us*. But this is their significance, it is not them. Their significance is all we know, and that we have given them. But we cannot claim to have created them, because to some extent they have determined their own significance. The boot is rather on the other foot: it is they and our perception of them which have created us. But once *we* are we can then re-create them in terms of each other and it is this re-creation that we know and call the objective world.

Let us suppose that the actual object is before us which has been photographed in Plate 15; not the photograph, because that is an image even further from the object than we are ourselves, but the three-dimensional thing itself whatever 'itself' may be. We distinguish the object from its ground; we inquire of our sensations and, according to their report, we decide on its size, distance, form, texture, weight, probable behaviour, relevance to our present situation, its capacity for stimulating other senses, and so on. At some time, very early in this analysis, we have crystallized the whole experience in the idea to which, were we asked, we should give the name 'flower'. In fact, our analysis and perception probably went no further than was necessary for us to alert the idea, for, unless there is some special purpose to be served, the mind is content with the minimum of data. The word 'flower' is one form in which we can re-create the idea, it is a form which allows those who use the same group of signs as ourselves to have a fairly precise notion of what this particular, strange, expandable, intangible, word-creating idea may be likely to contain in the way of generalized data. Or, it may be that the idea is a more precise one than 'flower' can itself convey, one which requires an elaborate and clumsy formula to indicate its range: 'this is a cultivar of the genus *Rosa*; it is known as "Pink Supreme"; it is a member of the group known as Hybrid Teas; this actual specimen I plucked in the garden half an hour ago from the fourth bush on the right beyond the lavender hedge; it is from the bush I planted three years ago in the rain to replace the one that was eaten by the children's pony.' Now, indeed, we have plotted a visual sensation (which, after all, is all we have experienced) in relation to many other sensations of various kinds, and our idea reaches back with invisible threads into the pages of scientific knowledge, to Linnaeus, to the English rose, to the roses of Damascus, to the rose of Sharon, into the sequences of our personal history, of horses and holidays and mountains and seas, and it could reach out, in truth it does reach out if we choose to follow it, sending its filaments into our entire lives, to every nerve's end, into every experience, every memory forgotten but not lost, into everything which has ever gone to become us. And this is that rose's identity . . . for us, but for no one else. But it is not the rose.

Ideas are complex sensations which take place in the brain. They are like those paper flowers they make in Japan and which we find in our Christmas crackers; we drop the shapeless little foetus in a glass of water and it blossoms before our eyes, sending forth branches and leaves and flowers, its potential is made actual. It would be very easy if we could say that an idea was all that we perceived about an object plus all that we know about it, so that it became percept-plus-association; but it is not as simple as that. These things go to make up the idea, but the idea is not them, not in any shape or form, any more than the cow in the meadow is grass and water and sunshine and cattle-cake. A cow is a cow, a rose is a rose, and the idea of a rose is the idea of a rose. The idea of a rose we may know, but a rose is something we may never know, for its very being as a rose is for us bound up in its existence as an idea. Only a rose can know a rose by being a rose.

More than half our trouble with ideas is that we can only interpret them and discuss them in an extended form. What emerges from this process is not the idea itself but a succession of ideas which, although they were potentially contained in the original, were not the essence of it. When we read a poem packed with visual imagery how clearly do we actually visualize?

> 'Quinquereme of Nineveh from distant Ophir
> Rowing home to haven in sunny Palestine,
> With a cargo of ivory,
> And apes and peacocks,
> Sandalwood, cedarwood, and sweet white wine.'

Do we see the five banks of oars rhythmically entering the water? Do we even know how they were arranged? Do we know the shape of the prow, smell the cedar-wood, feel the caressive smoothness of the sandal-wood? Does it spoil the image that we dislike sweet white wine? Or do the words hardly mean what they say at all? Have they just an aroma of meaning, half caught at, half doubted, like a perfume that passes us in the street?

How much of any of this is actually formulated in our minds? No doubt we could answer these questions if challenged, but does the effect of the poem depend on our doing so? Is it not rather that what we delight in is not a quinquereme, or even the remembered image of one, but the idea of one? And is not the idea of one when alerted in our minds by the symbol (or word) quite different from the idea we would have if the boat itself were before us?

The idea of a quinquereme does not for many of us include a distinct visual percept unless we make an effort to give it one, and then perhaps if we do, it will become not a synthesized idea at all, not a creature of the imagination, but a construct, a creature of the fancy.

But we are going ahead too fast. It is not the word rose and the idea which it alerts that concerns us at this moment; it is the object rose which is before us and which becomes the idea rose as we look at it. The idea which is created in the presence of the perceived object is not identical with that which is created in the presence of the symbol. There is not one idea *rose*, there is an infinity of ideas *rose*, but since we are not equipped to distinguish infinity in any respect we categorize them, and we can make a very clear distinction between our idea in the very act of perceiving the object and our idea when our perception of it is in the past. The primary idea rose, when it is freed from its perceptual rigidity, becomes the secondary idea rose from which much of the perceptual element has been winnowed away.

What, then, is the connection between our idea of the object as we perceive it and the object itself? The link is that stream of energy which we are experiencing as sensation. The energy reaches us as it does because the object, the modifier of energy, is what it is. This energy, modified in a particular way which we recognize, fuses with the secondary ideas already present in the mind to create a fresh sensation, a primary idea. While we are in the presence of the object (and by 'in the presence of the object' we mean aware of the object in a positive sense, for we could be in its presence without awareness) we are actually enduring the creation of a primary idea. Once the stream of energy ceases, because the object is removed or because our senses are no longer reactive to it, the idea becomes a secondary idea and takes its place in the whole bundle of secondary ideas which are stored in the attics of the mind. If the primary idea was a particularly strong one then it will play an important part in amending the secondary idea and in the creation of further ideas; if it is a weak one, very similar to others already acquired, its identity will be lost in the secondary idea and will make no measurable contribution either to it or to any new primary one.

The idea rose, though not the same as a rose itself, is, we must acknowledge, the partial product of an object, of a something 'out there', which will continue to exist, though we do not; but there are many ideas which seem at first glance to have no tangible percepts behind them, that are not the creation of an object-out-there. When we speak of grace, honour, wisdom, neatness, accuracy, freedom, boldness, discipline, gaiety, solemnity, clarity, skill, our ideas are clear enough, but it requires a moment's concentration to realize that what we have done is to take one aspect common to a number of secondary ideas and to elevate that aspect to the level of a separate idea. We cannot physically remove the redness from the rose, nor extract the gaiety from a child's laughter, nor separate a soldier from his honour; yet in the world of ideas, of sensations which take place within our minds, we can do just this and because we are able to detach aspects from ideas of which they are really an inseparable part we can also attach them to objects of which they are not properly a part at all. By doing this we can, if we wish, give courage to a rose and gaiety to a sea-wave, we can make the mountains skip like rams and the little hills like young sheep. This makes the world of ideas sufficiently complicated. Now, indeed, the saying of Somerset Maugham that 'yellow may be a horse and cart' comes close to expressing a truth.

Abstractions like these are the greatest bearers of value, for it is by conceptualizing such aspects that society has evolved its most effective patterns for behaviour. Once learned in childhood such values are not easy to forget; they remain pregnant with praise or blame. We may think very poorly nowadays of courage and chastity, but it is difficult to disembarrass ourselves of our learnt value for such attitudes.

Just as, when we are considering pure perception, we found that what we were concerned with was not a state but an activity, not a being but a becoming, so it is with ideas. Form presupposes formlessness, honour dishonour, courage cowardice; these things are what they are because their complementaries are what they are. They are dynamic concepts, held in perilous being by the exertion of a contrary force. An idea present exists because of the unseen presence of ideas absent. There is a sort of object-ground relationship in ideas as in vision.

If this is so the idea *rose* depends for its existence upon the idea *not-rose*, and what we are experiencing is not simply the fusion of what we see with what we know, but the tension between the is and the is not. Once the tension is past and the conflict of creation is decided something has gone out of our joy in it. However exquisite our pleasure in contemplating the rose, we cannot indefinitely do so; once the idea has been created and the energies which went to form it have reached their point of rest the savour goes out of it and we must replace it by other stimuli which will in turn give rise to other primary ideas. We may certainly return to the object because of some quality that it has, and refresh the primary idea by re-enacting it, but we cannot hold what is, in fact, a process indefinitely.

Man as a Maker

If the way in which we perceive natural objects is so complex, what of objects which man has made? Is there any way in which a man-made object is less 'natural' than one shaped by wind and water? It is certainly very difficult to see why there should be. Man is, after all, himself one of nature's phenomena and what he creates is no less the creation of nature than any other consequence of the impetus of life. At what point can we say that the decisive change of kind occurs? A bird is 'natural'; is its nest? A beaver is 'natural'; is its dam? A caddisfly is 'natural'; is its encasement? In what essential way does the web of a spider differ from a steel-girder bridge? Or the corridors of a mole from the arched palaces of kings? (Plates 16, 17.)

Man's earliest artifacts were tools with which he extended his mastery over matter. The

first standard of value in such an object is that it should fulfil its purpose. A striking implement that was easy to handle, that crushed the things it was intended to crush, but did not
itself shatter, was good. These qualities were generally found to belong to a certain shape
of stone or wood; the eye learned to recognize the appearance of balance, weight and
strength, and regarded the appropriate visual characteristics as a guarantor of the tool's
efficiency. The simplicity of this scale of values is deceptive, for in order to create a tool
having all three qualities which a striking implement should possess we must compromise
and accept a head less well calculated to crush if it is to remain reasonably easy to handle.
It is the tension produced by conflicting needs which dictates all functional shape. The
more multifarious the needs, the more complex the compromise and the more variable the
solutions. Nevertheless, however many needs we attempt to satisfy in one entity, there is a
tendency for the shape which results from the conflicting tensions to crystallize and for us
to regard any deviation from it with suspicion or disapproval. Once we have with difficulty
established an ideal compromise shape we can recognize it with little effort and react
towards it automatically; it now gives the minimum of trouble and we can employ our
released energies on the task of still further reducing the frightening uncertainties of life. If
circumstances change we may indeed modify the ideal, but unless we are psychologically
ill we do not seek to destroy it and start all over again, save, of course, when we find that in
the passage of time it has come about that we are using a constant shape for a purpose which
has quite altered.

But not only does an implement have a purpose which gives us one set of values, based
on efficiency, it is also a thing *made* and its shape is a record of the activity, which went to its
making. We see the cooking-pot first as a container of a capacity proportioned to its strength
but secondly as a gesture of the hands that worked in the wet clay to make it. We also are
makers and modellers and merely by looking at the pot we partake in the act of its creation
and in the matter from which it is made.

From this point onward our simple purposeful creations rapidly acquire qualities that
are not related to utility. The striking tool which is larger and heavier than normal expresses
(or reflects or echoes) the superior strength and status of the man who wields it; the clumsily
shaped handle is inferior, not solely because of its failure to conform to the established
optimum form, but because it embodies the shortcomings, the poverty, the carelessness,
the lack of skill, of the workman who made it. Moreover, on top of this expressiveness, there
is that which accrues to the implement from our knowledge of its history: this is the club
that crushed the skull of a rival chieftain; this is the cooking-pot in which the annual mid-
summer ceremonial feast is traditionally cooked.

Although perhaps at first each man made his own tools, it eventually became apparent
that some were more expert makers than others, and the product of the most highly skilled
came to be recognized by some characteristic modification of the form in which the magic

of its greater potency was thought to reside. Such tools were bartered for, fought over, and acquired value and conferred status upon their possessors. Others who were unable to acquire the authentic product of the inspired workman tried to imitate its magic by copying its appearance. The modification of the standard form which was personal to the magician-maker was clearly the feature in which the magic resided and in order to acquire the properties of the good tool this and this only was what the copyist concentrated upon. His mind being set upon this peculiarity he emphasized and enlarged it; if the excellence of the original lay in a slight deepening of a curve which provided better balance, the copyist was likely to reproduce the curve in a meaningless and exaggerated way; possibly a real advantage was revealed by such a distortion, but more often it merely impaired the efficiency of the tool. As a tool it was a failure, but as magic? In this simple way the battle-hammer became the ceremonial mace, and the axe flowered in such splendour as the halberds of Cardinal Scipio Borghese's Guard. (Plates 18, 19.)

The imitation of the superficial in an effort to achieve the essential has always been with us. The witch who until recent times (and, for all I know, still) made a wax doll and stuck pins in it, not only relieved her feelings but believed she caused pain in those parts of her enemy which corresponded to the wounded wax. The second-rate actress who throws a temperamental fit because Bernhardt used to; the second-rate painter who fails to wash and drinks more than is good for him in the name of Modigliani and Gauguin; the poet who affects starvation, drugs, and suicide; the innumerable geniuses *manqués* who adopt promiscuity, homosexuality, perversions and unbalances of all kinds, in the desperate hope that these paths will lead to the elixir of life that they so desperately wish but which is not theirs, are all practising sympathetic magic.

This, though the main channel by which utilitarian shape becomes decorative shape, is not the only one. The second channel is that of excess vitality. At first the difficulty of making these tools and learning to use them was so great that no energies were left over. As, however, the work by repetition became more easy the energy required for it was less, but the energy was still there, the tension existed and demanded release; naturally this release was most simply found in repeating the learned and familiar action. If that complete action were repeated precisely, the consequence was merely a stock-pile of tools, but if one gesture gave more pleasure to the worker than another, because of the physical release it gave, then the shape which the gesture recorded was liable to become amplified and to develop its own life—not from any portentous 'will to form', but simply from the excess vitality of its creator, a movement akin to that of a child hopping its way back from school, or to the grace-notes of a bird whose heart is overfull of love and delirium of the sun. A tool produced by an exaggerated gesture might be deficient in utility, but each time the creator saw it he would feel anew the pleasure which the gesture gave him; and others, unequal to his skill, would, on beholding it, feel within themselves his vitality and disciplined control. Is the step so far from the tool that pleases because it works well to the tool that pleases though it will not work at all?

As excess energy and time were required to create the useless form, so excess energy was needed to delight in it, and excess wealth was needed to possess it. A man needed to be rich before he could afford to use one axe in battle and another on parade, one set of pots for cooking, but another for the mantelpiece. In this way yet another value was imposed, a social one. The elaborate and useless object, particularly if made from some far-fetched and rare material, argued wealth in its possessor, and wealth being power, the respect which is due to power rubbed off on the useless object, and it became a symbol to the greater number of all that is desired and unattainable. To the owner also it symbolized his power and as such became one of his household gods, and thus acquired even greater value in his own eyes and in those of all who came beneath his shadow.

Foremost amongst man's tools was the building, the vessel made to contain himself. This was perhaps the most important artifact of all, for whereas the axe was an extension of his hands and the cooking-pot an extension of his belly the house he built was the extended husk of all himself, not a practical tool only which kept him warm and dry and secure from beasts, but a barrier against space and eternity, the guarantee of his identity, the diagram by means of which he anchored himself in chaos and gave himself a pivot from which to move the world. His house was his other self and upon it he hung his trophies. It acquired far more than utilitarian status in his eyes: when he was within it he was in a world of his own making; outside the storms raged, but inside was the still centre of his turning world. Its appearance held a significance beyond its physical functions, so that while its outside proclaimed to his enemies his strength it was to him a welcoming gesture, and, like the frame of a picture or the socle of a statue, set aside a world of his making, a world wholly of man, where light and heat were at his command, a world of art.

To the outsider the house he never or rarely entered contained a kernel of mystery. The exterior became a symbol for what he did not see, the façade *was* the house, the inside was a dark hall, a nothingness in which a god dwelt, visited only by initiates. So the work of art became turned inside out, and the outside of a building instead of being conceived as the skin surrounding and dominating a space of stillness, became an expression of qualities which had no formal existence within. Buildings created for an esoteric ritual became sculpture, specialized vessels which, with a splendid accumulation of ornament or a disciplined elegance of form, were really reliquaries in the small heart of which lay the shrivelled spirit of a god. (Plate 21.)

The form of the original utilitarian object is governed by three things: by the purpose which it is to serve; by the nature of the material from which it is made; by the manipulative capacity of its maker. A storage jar is the form it is because the material from which it is made, if it is to contain, can most easily be shaped by human hands in a particular way. The physics of storage and the structure of the hand are nearly, but not quite, universal factors; the material from which the vessel can be made is not.

The herdsmen who drifted in hordes to and fro over the great central Asian plains developed as their material the hides and horns of animals; those people who settled in river valleys turned naturally to the modelling of clay and use of reed and thatch; the inhabitants of forest used timber and bark; while in those places in which leather, wood, and clay were scarce people were driven by necessity to the carving of stone. These materials dictated the form of every object made for use, and inexorably as the optimum form for tool or untensil was evolved so it became the acceptable concept, the ideal, the standard of what such things should be, to the society that grew up to the use of them. But out of these objects valued for use grew those objects esteemed not for their utility but for their magical properties, their symbolic quality, their power of conferring status, and finally for the curious sense of delight, of communicated skill and vigour, which the mere contemplation of certain objects could confer. In this way all artifacts of a community tended to develop a family likeness, a likeness based on its primary material and on the developed and transmitted skills of those who worked it. Thus each tribe evolved its peculiar sense of form, its concept of what was proper, and, as they learned to see the form of a tapir as right for the tapir and the gazelle's form as right for the gazelle, so they felt certain that their cooking-pot was the correct form for all cooking-pots. They did, in fact, set up an ideal cooking-pot of which the value lay not in its utility but as a fixed form in their minds. Again, in so far as the cooking-pot became an irrational ideal form, men were able to perceive it divorced from its functions and once more they were able to partake of life in an uncommitted way.

Across the sunny panorama of local formal certainties established in this way stretched the shadow of the movements of people. Drought, the exhaustion of pastures, the disappearance of soil in flood and dust-storm, the increase of communities beyond the capacity of neighbourhoods to sustain them, drove people to change their habitat and with it, sometimes, to change their basic material. Generations of artificers in stone, finding themselves deprived of stone but possessed of clay, would try to impose, so far as they could, their old sense of form upon the new material. It might even be that for a while several technical tricks of the old trade would linger in the new and help to give a further bias towards the old. But the old form in the new material was a hybrid and had eventually to give rise to a new type, a product of the conflict between the sense of form of the artificer and the possibility of form inherent in the new material. When these migrations of peoples involved the enslavement of existing inhabitants the picture was further complicated. The influx of a warlike race of otherwise inferior technical accomplishment, upon a peaceful and advanced community, would be likely to result in the enslavement of the technically skilled and the continuity of their sense of form, so that it is not unusual to find in these circumstances that the conquerors became the culturally conquered. If, however, the invading race were of an alternative high culture the result was a strong conflict of forms which commonly had as its consequence a class structure in which the indigenous culture persisted in a degraded shape amongst the suppressed population, while the forms of the dominant people became the taste and style of the aristocracy. As communities, by conquest and by trade, became more and more involved, so the hybrids resulting from the competition of their forms became more complex expressions of human history and their artifacts became not only tangible records of their makers' actions but records of the evolution of the race.

The Use of Appearances

At first sight it might seem that we are able to distinguish between objects which the agents of nature make for a purpose and those which they make to please the senses; but only at first sight, for though the lion's leap is an efficient physical fact directed to a certain end, the display dance of the bird of paradise, or the musical proclamation of a cockerel on a dung-heap, which are both designed to please the senses, are just as well directed to serve in the chain of drives and incentives which urge on the biological purpose as is the onslaught of the lion. The difference lies slightly perhaps in the performer's attitude, but principally in the audience's reaction. The lion leaps on his prey and thinks nothing of the leap, nor feels anything of the leap, but only regards the achievement of his purpose, the satisfaction of his drive. The dancing bird, however, is unlikely to know his purpose; he feels, as we sometimes feel, the drive to dance, and the cockerel feels, as we often feel, the drive to proclaim, but the awareness that the dance and the fanfare are means to an end is not inherent in the action; there is a sense, both to performer and to audience, in which dance and song exist for their own sake alone. The dancer and the singer are demanding admiration for what they do; they are dealing not in functions, actions, or objectives, but in appearances.

Animal life makes use of appearance in several ways. The dog whose hair stands on end, the cat that arches its back, the toad that inflates itself, the caterpillar that turns its top segments bright pink and heaves them up like a face, are all instinctively adjusting their appearances to impress enemies with the idea of their ferocity and size. The warrior from Nigeria with the tattooed face, and the guardsman with his bearskin in Whitehall, are doing the same thing. (Plates 22, 23.)

That an increase in size has an intimidating effect upon an enemy and an encouraging effect upon oneself is reasonable enough, for size implies weight and strength; but that colour should have a similar result requires explanation. . . . It is known that some creatures, probably the majority, have no colour vision at all, and it may be that the effect which we are considering is really one of brightness contrast rather than of hue, and that the hue difference is accidental. The caterpillar, yellow-and-black striped like a wasp, cannot be anything but conspicuous to its enemy the bird. Does the biological value of its coloration lie in some warning inbred in the predator to beware of strongly contrasted objects? For example, is the pigmentation itself evidence of an unpleasant flavour? Or does it not rather lie in the simple association of caterpillar with wasp? The wasp is conspicuous so that birds may distinguish it from less fiercely armed flies; it loses nothing by being easily seen, for it has no prey that will flee from it; the black-and-yellow caterpillar, innocent of other protection, is in this way guarded by the wasp's sting. Similarly the caterpillar that changes the colour of its leading segments and then displays them is not fearsome to a bird because it has gone red, but because the change of hue has emphasized certain tonal contrasts; the impression it now gives is that of a large-headed creature, unlike a caterpillar, and potentially dangerous.

Conspicuousness is important in giving the impression of power, for if a creature does not seek to conceal itself we argue that it is demonstrating from strength and has no need to skulk in the shadows. It is immaterial whether it is conspicuous by its size, hue, tone, form, or behaviour; if we want to impress our neighbours we can display in any or all of these ways. At heart all such display is imitative and would have no value if we did not know from experience that things which are large, brightly coloured and noisy are also dangerous. As we develop a more sophisticated approach to these matters we are inclined to discount the bearded loud-talker as a charade and to watch more warily the small man who remains quiet, because we have learned that we suffer more often from unseen and furtive perils than from those which obviously declare themselves. The creature that makes a great display of its powers does so in order to avoid having them tested; we would all prefer our enemies to run rather than fight.

The obverse of this intimidatory show of strength is the recessive colouring and behaviour of the majority of creatures. Whether prey or predator, and most are both, they pin their chance of survival on being unnoticed. Some move by night, or cling to hidden ways, creeping close to the ground; they live still and silent lives, and escape attention altogether amongst the general background of sand and stones. Others pretend to be what they are not: the stick insect and certain caterpillars freeze in the presence of danger and look like twigs of the herbage amongst which they are feeding; the leaf butterfly passes for a leaf; many creatures feign death. Commonest of all are those social animals to whom the background is not earth or sky or water, but the great scurrying mass of their fellow creatures, and for whom the strongest chance of survival is to be an indistinguishable part of the great host which prodigal nature has produced in the hope that at least some members of it will survive repeated holocausts. Of this sort is man; and those who dress to be like their fellows, who wear the uniform of their class and nation and creed, are practising instinctive camouflage behaviour. This is the motive power of that great social instinct, conformity.

As usual, whenever there is a force operating in one direction there is another force which works in a contrary sense. For his protection the social animal may seek to be indistinguishable from his fellows, but in many respects, and particularly sexually, he is in competition with them and it is then that he will use display to gain his personal advantage. The peacock flaunts the magnificence of his tail; the stallion arches his neck and paws the ground; the soldier polishes his brasses, shines his boots and presses his uniform; bird, beast, and man show in their bearing and their gait the acute tension of their virility. Opposition is intimidated by his arrogant asumption of superiority and melts away, while the female of the species, admiring the garments, the plumage and the gestures of the male, is, in fact, fulfilling the biological purpose of selecting the most vital male, the bearer of the strong seed of life, as her mate.

It is generally true that life produces to excess everything that is vital to its continuance; then, by a system of counter-measures, it siphons off, holds in check, or finds another use for, the unneeded residue. The tensions of vitality find their release in displays which serve a selective biological purpose, but the instinct for display itself, if inhibited for any reason from performing its function, can be cultivated as an end in its own right, or at least as one in which the biological end is more remote. The ballet-dancer at Covent Garden does not specifically perform his or her dance to find a mate, nor do we attend the performance to choose one, but the heart of the matter for both dance and audience is the display of strength and skill which holds up for our delight man's virility and power. The display has become detached from its purpose and we are experiencing the sensation of living without direct involvement.

One day perhaps the distinction between a work of art and a work of nature will not seem to have been worth making. As our powers of perception and of understanding increase so categories mean less and individuals mean more, but in so far as categories are still useful and give us insights into the nature of individuals we must attempt them. All works of art are works of nature, but they are a moderately distinct genus within that all-enveloping family; their distinguishing characteristic is that they are primarily concerned with appearances, not functions. The genus of appearances is itself divisible into three sub-genera: appearances which are produced by creatures other than human for evident biological purposes; appearances which are produced by man for biological purposes; and appearances which are created by man for the sake, apparently, of their appearances and which have no ostensible purpose other than that inherent in our perceptual reaction to them.

This classification, for all its evident truth, contains apparent difficulties. If the creation of a work of art is the using up of a superfluous drive which would otherwise find a harmful release, then it *does* serve a purpose. Secondly, the classification so far seems to take no account of objects of undoubted utility which we yet seem to see as works of art. We admire the web of a spider and a great steel-girder bridge, the meanders of a river and the rotundity of an earthenware pot, the skeleton of a leaf and the mechanism of a watch. These admirations seem to be similar. Indeed, they are similar if we bring to them an admiration innocent of immediate purpose, if we admire them for their appearances. Our admiration may arise in part from our consciousness of how admirably fitted they are for their purpose, but that is not in fact the reason for it; we have no purpose when we admire them and therefore, for us, they have none at that moment. Appreciation, admiration if you like, there undoubtedly is for a machine that performs its task efficiently, but here it is the performance we admire, and the appearance of ease and economy of effort in the performance. The work achieved may demand our approval, our astonishment even, but not the sort of admiration we have in mind, for that is disinterested and is reserved for appearances.

So it seems that the distinction is not solely in the object, nor even in the artificer of the object. A sunset, the nest of a weaver-bird, the Taj Mahal, can all be seen with a wonder which is much the same in kind. The essential factor lies in the way they are looked at. But the farmer who sees the sunset as the presage of tomorrow's weather and nothing else; the ornithologist who sees the nest of the weaver-bird as a potential repository for a bird's eggs; the tourist who sees the Taj Mahal as a romantic curiosity; these are not involving themselves in art. (Plate 26.)

It follows that even if an object is created with a purely functional intention it may become a work of art if we strip it of its function and regard only its appearance, and, conversely, an object created as a work of art ceases to be one when it is regarded as an object of utility or of commerce.

When both natural and man-made objects are seen as works of art it is tempting to suggest that a clear distinction can still be made between them because in the second case we are conscious of a relationship with the man who made it. But even this distinction does not stand up very well to scrutiny. The element of communication in some works of man is decidedly small and it is not always that element which is the chief source of our pleasure. It is often the fortuitous qualities that come from nature and not the calculated ones from man that are the cause of an object's appeal. It commonly happens that the chance bruises and incrustations of time have added a quality, perhaps not at all of a specious kind as those who are committed to finding always a simple answer suggest, but for the very reason that they have modified a work of man in the direction of a work of nature. A Shang bronze gains greatly in quality from its patina; those few pieces of old porcelain which chance has preserved kiln-fresh have a brash unsympathetic air; and the resurfacing and regilding of old furniture that goes on daily to furnish the lavishly appointed salons of the capitals of the world has resulted in a destruction of subtle beauty as wholesale as any perpetrated by the Goths. The truth appears to be that although with a certain adjustment of mind we can, and do, appreciate works of nature very much as though they were works of art, we are also able to appreciate works of art very much as though they were works of nature. There is a whole area of appearances which cannot be said to be wholly one or the other.

The essence of the sort of pleasure we are discussing is that we should experience the sensation of living without being encumbered by direct involvement. In a world of objects which we know only through our senses we find ourselves too easily concerned in aspects of them quite other than their sensual presence. The world and its affairs thunder by and over and on, and the perceived object is gathered up or abandoned according to its relevance to the headlong rush of change, and in the process the appearance of the thing, the immediate sensual apprehension of it when there is but the object in its material presence on the one hand and the unique mind on the other, is almost totally lost. Art is a simple device by means of which we are lifted out of the realm of things to which we have to react responsibly, and find ourselves at a level of consciousness where our perceptions exist for themselves alone. The artist not only selects the aspect from which we are to regard appearances, a selection which we may or may not approve, but, more importantly, he prepares us to receive it by insulating it from the world of affairs, by putting his picture in a frame, or his statue on a socle, or his play on a stage, or his garden behind a gate. This also is the reason why poets use rhymes, and inversions, and rhythms more marked than in everyday speech. These devices are the spring by which we leap to the level of a spiritual life.

Our existence on the simplest level is a matter of our physical presence sharing space with other physical presences; but our lives, as we experience them, are spent amongst the mental equivalents of these physical matters. It is by means of these mental equivalents that we are enabled to control the material presences. There is a physical world, and there is an equivalent world created by our senses, and this is the world in which we live. This world of equivalents normally exists in frequent reference to the physical world; presumably in the lower forms of life the reference is continual and as complete as need be, but man who, notably amongst creatures, has discovered that he can adjust the material world very successfully by developing his freedom of manoeuvre in the world of equivalents, has developed the capacity of reducing his reference to the material world to a minimum, and living very largely in the world of ideas.

Once man has acquired the basic experiences from which he is able to construct ideas (and this he has done only through his sensual experience of matter) he feels himself to be superior to that very matter from the experience of which, and with a view to the control of which, his very self has been created. This is the source of his sensation that man, like God, is a spirit, something that is beyond and above matter.

There is not one level of awareness; there are many. Nor is there simply a world of solid objects and a world of ideas. The world of solid objects we can never know, that is beyond our reach for ever; we can only know it by its equivalents, in its relationships to us. These relationships can be very various, can be constantly changing, and are susceptible of infinite enlargement. The function of our sensual experience of objects is to enable us to adjust our own material presence to theirs; it is in the highest degree purposive. The process of perceiving, noticing, recognizing, categorizing, forgetting, has been evolved to enable us to complete the hazardous obstacle-race of our lives. Right! we say. We are essentially aware creatures; that is our strength, and if this is what our lives consist of we demand at least a little time in which to be aware of them. When life was hard and we strove night and day with the necessities of it, fighting the earth itself for our barest needs and fighting our enemies who competed for those necessities, there was no time or energy to spare to be 'aware' of life. Surviving took all our time. Our joy consisted in the satisfaction of our various hungers; a full belly was a heaven hardly won. But now that we are temporarily on top of that problem and our satisfaction comes easily and we neither starve nor fight, and the struggle to avoid these evils occupies a relatively small part of our time and energy, we have a surplus of both and we must dispose of them. Some of us at least propose to use them in savouring the very processes by which we have come to be what we are; we wish to touch, and see, and hear, and smell, and taste, for the sake of the very joy of doing these things; we wish to reason, and to count, for the pleasure of reasoning and counting; we wish to perceive relationships for the sake of the pleasure we gain from exercising our power to perceive them; we wish to create new relationships to satisfy at one and the same time our sense of power and our sense of curiosity. This is the life of the senses, and of the mind; it is also the life of the spirit, for which we have been enfranchised from the needs of the body; but, because in the time of our necessity we were purposive creatures we may also, if we are inclined, put what we do to a purpose; but when we do so we readmit to the mastery of our lives our greatest enemy, time.

Art is the key to certain aspects of this mental life, but not to all aspects. We may enjoy the experiences of the senses without the intervention of art; those who lie in the sun on the sand, oiled and beautiful saurians, habitually do so. Or we may enjoy working with ideas which are remote from sensual experience; this is the playground of the pure mathematician which has its appropriate pleasures. In both these ways can be achieved, briefly—for that is all experience makes us hope for—a sense of timelessness, but in the first the mind is set at a position of rest and is hardly involved save as a registration centre for those simplest of sensations, warmth, well-being, and the sound of the sea; while in the second the mind is everything and the material world has receded beyond apprehension. In the second case, the activity of the mind of the mathematician might, if we could experience it, be of great beauty, and although it might, in the moment of its activity, have views beyond the perceptible elegance of its sequences, even here, one can conceive that for those with the necessary faculties its workings upon an abstract problem of nice complexity could be as exciting and delightful as the grace-notes of a singer.

The state of mind that we call happiness is one of absorption. It involves unawareness of self and results either from a transference of consciousness from ourselves to something outside ourselves, or from a concentration upon some activity of our own senses which amounts to the same thing. We speak, for example, of losing ourselves in a book; or it can

IV Cezanne: *Mont Sainte-Victoire*

happen when we stand motionless, entranced by the fall of sunlight on a leaf, or when we hear a child's voice from a distant street.

Life is a great stream of consciousness in which there is no present, only a fast-diminishing past. It is as though we were in the rear of a train and saw everything only at the moment it was behind us; we have no sense of what is before us except in terms of what has already gone by. Art is one way in which we seem for a moment to grasp the present; it is a way of achieving undiluted awareness.

5. The Call of the Image

Hamlet
Do you see yonder cloud that's almost in shape of a camel?
Polonius
By th' mass, and 'tis like camel, indeed.
Hamlet
Methinks it is like a weasel.
Polonius
It is back't like a weasel.
Hamlet
Or like a whale?
Polonius
Very like a whale.

WILLIAM SHAKESPEARE, *Hamlet*

REPRESENTATIONAL art springs from a source quite different from that of the objects we have been discussing. Man-created shapes cannot have evolved by way of tool-making alone. To believe that they did so we must believe that men gradually came to recognize in the shapes they made for use a similarity to the natural shapes that they saw about them and that then they played with the novel idea of imitation. It is true that Leonardo da Vinci recommended the development of pictorial images by letting the imagination work on chance shapes, and that the famous eighteenth-century English drawing-master, Alexander Cozens, made the evolution of haphazard ink-blots into landscapes the basis of his instruction, but this is the counsel of sophisticated minds already overfamiliar with representational art, seeking to obtain freedom from a too rigidly conceptual attitude to creation.

There are innumerable examples in the history of art in which representational form has progressively developed into decoration from which all representation has been drained away. The archaic dragon-forms of China that are lost in a sort of repetitive Greek key pattern, and Apollo in his chariot on the drachma of Alexander the Great which ended as five meaningless lines on a Celtic coin, are extreme examples of how it is the representational element which is recessive and the purely formal which is dominant. It is scarcely probable that the reverse can have happened, and that before the mere notion of created images had ever entered their experience, men could have perceived likenesses where formerly they had seen only shapes. There is, however, a school of thought which believes that some of the earliest and finest palaeolithic cave-paintings came into being in this way and that such

66

things as the bison of Lascaux sprang to life first in the artist's mind from a fancied similitude discovered in a chance stain on the rock. Even if this were so, such a shape could only have been resolved into representational form by an unsophisticated mind if that mind were already conscious of the image of the object *as an image* and not as a material thing.

A remarkable feature of some early cave-paintings is that the best of the animals portrayed in them are shown in poses which are instantaneous and which the civilized eye is normally unable to register. We only see in this way at moments of sudden and unexpected danger when our startled systems increase the supply of adrenalin, our perception becomes extraordinarily clarified, and time for a while stands still. It is not difficult to imagine that the paleolithic hunter, unhindered by much of the conceptional lumber we drag around with us, would often, in the most tense moments of his chase, experience a clarity and timelessness such as we only know at those rare crises when our motor car skids out of control, when the climber's rope begins to fray, or when we have left the saddle and are descending—how slowly it seems—in an inert parabola. In moments of enforced rest, when the herds have moved away, when in the long darknesses the unused strength pines for an outlet, the image of the exquisitely apprehended moment is projected by the mind of the hunter, and he feels again, as he sees the bison at the charge or the deer leaping transfixed, the intensity and timelessness of living. This is the moment at which the representational image is created. And yet to describe it in this way is to oversimplify the process. The child who explained her drawings by saying, 'First I think and then I draw a line around my think', was almost certainly not correctly describing the way in which she produced a picture. When we recall a motor accident we say that we see it vividly in the mind's eye; the impression of vividness is certainly there, but if we search our consciences we have to admit that the memory has the vividness and the impression of a dream; we did not see every detail clearly as the car turned over, we saw more than usual and that is all, the gaps of vision were still there. Few painters, if any, create a fully developed mental image and then set it down; writers and those whose medium is words do not think in words; words are the things that come off the ends of their pens, or the tips of their tongues. The cave-dweller, when he saw his bison in the flesh, was involved in a complicated perceptual experience of which movement was the essence; in his fire-lit cave the idea which that perception had become, when it reached a certain point of intensity, set in train a reverse process, and as movement had generated the idea so did the idea in turn generate movement, and the circular drive sequence, object-idea-object, gathered way and resulted in the drawn creature on the wall. (Plate 28.)

Something of this same attempt at the vicarious satisfaction of unfulfilled longings by the creation of images is to be seen on the walls of public lavatories. It is to be presumed that the agony of sexual deprivation was unknown to the dwellers in Lascaux and Altamira, so that they had no need to picture on the fire-lit walls of their caverns the intensity of that particular desire. If the drawings of the deprived male population of our modern towns is of a lower standard than that of their remote ancestors, it is nevertheless a great deal better than most of them could manage of any subject upon which their imaginations were not so desperately engaged. The *graffiti* of these youths are the living evidence of the origin of representational art. Vassari recounted of Filippo Lippi: 'He is said to have been so amorous that when he saw a woman who pleased him he would have given all his possessions to have her, and if he could not succeed in this he quieted the flame of his love by painting her portrait.'

The answer to the questions: Why are some of the cave paintings, by our modern standards, so good? And how is it that the hunter was able to immobilize the creatures of his memory at a point of movement which we today cannot perceive?—is surely that primitive man was far less engaged in a conceptual world and far more intimately involved in a perceptual world than we are. His eyesight was probably no better than ours, but his mind was a better, because a simpler, recipient of visual sensations. There was less in his world which he needed to leave unnoticed or to forget, his mind's mechanism for filing and storing and discarding concepts was rudimentary compared with ours, he could see totally whereas we see for the most part in shorthand. Moreover, it is probable that he was not greatly handicapped by our analytic way of proceeding. If today we draw a bison we are very liable, unless we have been trained to do otherwise, to draw its head, its shoulders, its hindquarters, its tail, its legs and so on, until in sum we have our bison; but it is probable that our remote ancestor had very much less clear-cut notions of the parts than this; he probably had no words for head or back or tail; what he saw was not the sum of a bison's parts, but a bison, total and indivisible. Words in particular have a way of limiting and defining concepts. That is, in part, their function. But the result, though convenient, is a falsification of our experience. Things do not exist in the tight little boxes which our words have made for them. Those who have no words are without many ideas which are common among us, but they retain ideas of completeness which we have destroyed.

The reproduction of the image of an object can become established as the representative of that object. This matter of representation is a difficult one. A photograph may represent a king, but the sense of the word 'represent' becomes rather different when we speak of an actor representing a king on the stage. Both stand for the idea king, but in a different way, for the photograph represents an image which we accept as a statement concerning the man we know as king, whereas the actor may be most unlike the image he purports to represent, but because of our conscious suspension of disbelief his words and gestures stir in us sensations of regality. No one mistakes either the photograph or the actor for the king, but if, in the case of the actor, sufficient verisimilitude is observed, then this is exactly what may happen. When Richard, raging at Bosworth, slew three knights who were dressed in the arms of Henry Richmond, their representation of Richmond was of a different kind from an actor's or a photograph's. An ambassador may also represent a king, but he does not look like the king; he has qualities unlike those of the king; he is not mistaken by anybody for the king; he is a man to whom are accorded certain powers and to whom by virtue of the honour that is paid him an aura, a quality of pseudo-kingliness, becomes attached. But this mystical quality is no quality of the man himself; he may, indeed, be a person of impressive character, but his peculiar flavour is that of his post, not of him; and very often he, like the king himself, is a very commonplace sort of fellow indeed.

The essential factor, that which establishes if any representation at all takes place and, if it does, of what kind it is, lies in the spectators' action of acceptance. The image created may not in any way resemble the object it represents; all that is required of it is that it shall be accepted in place of the object. A currency note represents certain purchasing power, but only because we are agreed that it shall do so; intrinsically it is a piece of ill-designed but well-printed paper. A forged note may be better printed or better designed on better paper, but if it is not accepted it can purchase nothing.

Representation, the substitution of one thing for another which is intrinsically unlike it, is a way in which we are able to satisfy certain needs and desires which are otherwise difficult to fulfil. It is convenient that ambassadors should represent kings, and that paper notes should represent purchasing power; to that extent the representation is a utilitarian matter, but it is extraordinary that it does not end there. The child who takes to bed a bundle of fur-felt and sleeps with it in her arms projects love, adoration and loyalty upon this doll. But what does the doll represent? Her mother? Is it not more true to say that the doll is a substitute rather than a representative? That it fulfils the child's need to love rather than that the child loves it because it represents her mother? And does not a trace of this same fulfilment of a psychic need colour our reaction to the ambassador and to the five-pound note? Are they just useful fictions? Or are they, too, partly substitutes? Do they not start by being the one and then gradually assume some quality of the other?

When the hunter outlined his vision of the bison on the wall of a cave he was not trying to assuage his hunger for food; if that had been his purpose he would have chewed an old bone rather. Hunger was the reason for his pursuit of the beast, but it was not the cause of his joy in the pursuit. That joy arose from the exercise of his prowess, from the intensity of his awareness of life, and it was that which he hungered to experience. He drew, not to satisfy his hunger, but to give form to the tension created in him by the intensity of his idea. A certain degree of deprivation sharpens the perceptive faculties and intensifies the image-making portion of the brain, the imagination. A hungry man conjures up the vision of fantastic banquets of baked meats, but it is not his hunger for food that he is trying to satisfy with these fantasies, it is his hunger for the pleasure of eating. A starving man has no such visions, his need is too great. The biological purpose of this unusual intensity of feeling and of the mental imagery stimulated by it is to ensure that man obtains his material needs; he is directed to food by the visions, he is enabled to capture it by the increased acuity of his perception. If he now goes out, hunts, kills and eats, the biological purpose is fulfilled, but if he does not the drive remains in mid-air and some fulfilment must be provided for it. He draws his fulfilment on the cave or lavatory wall; his physical needs remain unfulfilled but his imaginative needs have been given their satisfaction.

The fulfilment provided in this way, by representation, is of a different character from the actual physical fulfilment which would follow if the deprived man ate or coupled. The smooth inside of the stomach, whose contraction causes the pangs of hunger, will not long remain quieted by a picture of a rump steak. What has happened is that the nervous tensions of the drive have received their quietus on the level of nervous life, but the cells of the stomach have not received their sugar. The stomach continues, then, to send its messages, the nervous system transmits them, but the fulfilment the system receives does not silence the demands of the stomach, with the result that the drive remains in being and the fulfilment remains in being and instead of a process of change (a lessening of the sense of hunger as the stomach becomes satisfied), there is an apparent changelessness. The river runs and runs but remains in the same place. We, for an appreciable time, have the experience of life without time, without change, without us.

The genuine created image is more than a representative: it is a substitute, a satisfaction of drives on the psychic level; transitory sensations in this way are caught and isolated in timelessness.

Man the Image-maker

Man has been defined as an image-making animal. It is a poor sort of definition, but it really does seem that man alone among creatures deals in the strange hinterland of the spirit where appearances, divorced from objective reality, are given a reality of their own and become potent.

It would be simple if we could assume that there were two worlds, one of objective and the other of imagined facts. The division is too simple by half and at the root of many misunderstandings. The two worlds run together at so many points that the more closely we look at the division between them the harder it is to see. That there is an objective world we know, but the form in which we know it is subjective. Every object is a bottomless reservoir of meanings. D. H. Lawrence wrote so much that he could scarcely avoid writing some things that were partly true, among them, in an essay called *Art and Morality*, he has some good sentences on this very point:

'And if apples don't *look* like that, in any light or circumstances, or under any mood, then they shouldn't be painted like that.

'Oh, *la-la-la*! The apples *are* just like that to me! cries Cezanne. They are just like that, no matter what they look like.

'Sometimes they're a sin, sometimes they're a knock on the head, sometimes they're a bellyache, sometimes they're part of a pie, sometimes they're sauce for the goose.

'And you can't see a bellyache, neither can you see a sin, neither can you see a knock on the head. So paint the apple in these aspects, and you get—probably, or approximately—a Cezanne still-life.

'What an apple looks like to an urchin, to a thrush, to a browsing cow, to Sir Isaac Newton, to a caterpillar, to a hornet, to a mackerel who finds one bobbing in the sea, I leave you to conjecture. But the All-Seeing must have mackerel's eyes, as well as man's . . .

'What art has got to do, and will go on doing, is to reveal things in their different relationships. That is to say, you've got to see in the apple the bellyache, Sir Isaac's knock on the cranium, the vast moist wall through which the insect bores to lay her eggs in the middle, and the untasted, unknown quality which Eve saw hanging on a tree. Add to this the glaucous glimpse that the mackerel gets as he comes to the surface, and Fantin-Latour's apples are no more to you than enamelled rissoles.' (Plates 30, 31.)

Among the points which Lawrence ignored was the essential one that although there are many more facets to reality than the camera, the target of his attack, can record, there are also many intermediate stages between the image of the apple which we receive on the retina and the idea of the apple floating in the mind, and that life may be concerned with any of these stages. Fantin-Latour took his stance not far from the retinal image; Cezanne somewhat further off; Lawrence, because his medium was the word, much further still. There are not two worlds, that of reality and that of the mind, there is an infinite progression of worlds beginning at one end with an apple we can touch and taste and smell and see, and ending at the other with an unformulated appleness of which we are not even aware. Lawrence was asking that a picture should do the work of a word. It can do very much more, and it can do very much less, but it cannot do, nor should it be asked to do, the same. (Plates 34, 35.)

In any case an image may exist not only as an imitation of an object but as a good solid object in its own right, asking from us precisely those advances and retreats that all solid objects demand. A portrait statue of a statesman is not only a representation of that man, it is a piece of marble or bronze which occupies space, and which can incidentally carry out many of the functions of non-representational objects. It may be a paper-weight, a door-stop, a hat-stand, or a weapon; it can also be, and this is what we call it, an object of art, and as such may be purchased, stolen, hired out, loved and mourned over, fondled and dusted, exactly like any other object. Mental images are formed from statues or pictures in a way no different from that in which the mental images of their material originals were formed; there is still the same relationship of image and solid and we still have to organize our physical as well as our psychological field to take account of it, but there is now a vital change: the statue has two identities, its own material presence as a statue and its represented presence as a man, and the play between the two is at least one source of our delight. It is not a question of 'is' and 'is not' simultaneously—the image is not unreal, it has two realities.

Not only does the distinction between image and reality wear thin when the image has solidity of its own, but it is an equally difficult distinction to make in the opposite case when an image which exists only in the mind becomes effective in human affairs. Is a vision that leads to the building of empires less real than the bones of a mammoth in Siberia? The idea of glory is more real in its consequences than a concrete slab, and a mental image of a man with his throat cut may prevent us from going down a lane at night. Reality and materiality are not interchangeable terms; if an image has material consequences we can hardly afford to debate whether it is directly derived from a material presence or not, and if matter has no relevance to our lives at all how real is it? If we consider more closely we will find that it is the belief in the image that leads to the activity and that without faith the mountains will not move. Man confers potency on the image by his belief in it. He gives it reality. But if it should happen, as it frequently does, that at some point the belief becomes impossible to square with other experienced phenomena, the mind is faced with the need to reconstruct its terms, a painful and dangerous task which can involve a long journey backwards in experience, rewinding the thread of life until we reach the point at which our belief parted company with the evidence, or, alternatively, of forcing our way onward, ignoring or denying the existence of all those phenomena which challenge our illusion. However heroic it may be to pursue the former course, discretion will sometimes recommend the latter; with good fortune to aid us we may complete our lives with our illusions intact, which is a better solution than suicide of the personality. But, though we can create reality, we cannot be, as some argue, the sole arbiters of our reality. Few of us can move mountains, though we may go some way towards discounting them; objects out-there are fully potent in our affairs without any mental effort of ours and we can make them impotent only by losing our power to perceive them; our belief that the tiger is made of paper will not prevent him devouring us if he is not.

In any event, why the image? What is it doing in our human lives, and how does it come about that we set so much store by a feature which, so far as we can tell, the remaining creatures of the earth do very well without? There must surely be something in the way in which we live that either requires a capacity for image-making or else produces the ability to make images as a necessary by-product of some other activity, a sort of industrial residue. What is the relationship of the pleasure we take in the image to the pleasure we take in art? Can art exist without it? Is the image the essence of the thing? Or does it merely obscure the nature of that essence?

There are two sorts of reality: that which is outside us and of which we can know very little save that it is there, and that which is inside us of which we are steadily learning more. The subjective reality relies for its existence upon our capacity to separate the qualities of

19 *The Halberd of Cardinal Scipio Borghese's Guard*

A tool produced by an exaggerated gesture may be deficient in utility, but each time its creator sees it he feels anew the pleasure which the gesture gave him; and others, unequal to his skill, on beholding it, feel within themselves his vitality and disciplined control. Is the step far from the tool that pleases because it works well to the tool that pleases although it will not work at all?

18 *A Paleolithic Axe-head*

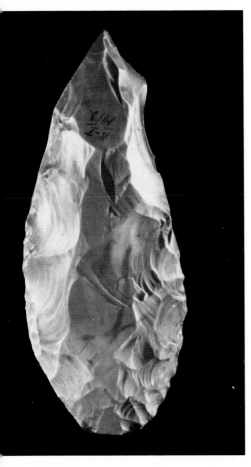

20 *King's College Cambridge, The Gibbs Building*

21 *A Temple in Mysore*

Animal life makes use of appearances in several ways. The dog whose hair stands on end, the cat that arches its back, the toad that inflates itself, the caterpillar that turns its top segments bright pink and heaves them up like a face, are all instinctively adjusting their appearances to impress enemies with the idea of their ferocity and size.

22 *North Nigerian*

23 *Grenadier Guardsman*

24 CANOVA: *Hercules and Lica*

25 *Etruscan Warrior*

26 *The Taj Mahal at Agra*

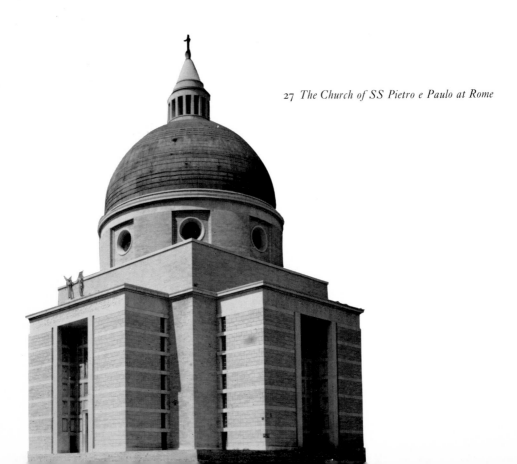

27 *The Church of SS Pietro e Paulo at Rome*

things from the things themselves. We can conceive of love and hatred, ferocity, wildness, courage, wisdom, hope and charity, not merely as qualities of people that we love or hate, or of lions that are wild or ferocious, but as abstract spiritual conditions, in fact as qualities of us. In the same way we can conceive of redness and roundness apart from things that are red or round.

The capacity for turning percepts into concepts is the base upon which man has raised his mastery of matter; it enables him to generalize and to deduce and is the foundation of his ability to reason. Economy of effort, one of the two great principles governing the operation of the mind, leads us to carry this power of separating the inseparable to the point of extracting an essence, or taking the part for the whole. Because the power to conceptualize is there, and is being constantly developed further by men, it exists, like other vital principles, in excess and must find release for its excess in play. Separating the redness from the apple is the same sort of mental feat as separating courage from a soldier; and to separate the visual image from an object out-there is a complicated exercise of the conceptualizing faculty.

These notions of separateness, or concepts, exist in our minds without our being aware of them; we only become aware of them when we give them form. It is as though the mind were a seething cauldron of unformulated ideas, working like yeast below the surface of thought, or stagnantly evolving, unsuspected, below the scum of daily life. The fact that images and memories and longings which we did not guess at exist in the deep of our minds we nightly discover in our dreams. In conscious thought these forces take form, more or less under the control or direction of our will; we dip into the dark, knowing the sort of thing we are looking for, but ignorant of its precise nature. If we are to know it we must define it, trim its edges, relate it to this and to that, give it form in stone, in paint, in sound, in words, or even in less than words. Only then does it become an idea; before that it is nothing, mere energy, as light is mere energy until the eye and the mind make it what it is. If the quality is perceptible to the senses, as redness or roundness are, we may realize it in a form which approximates to the original form from which we abstracted it; if this is difficult, we may use instead another sense which seems to us, because of certain parallelisms, to image the quality we desire to realize more essentially. We may, for example, express the quality of redness with red paint, with a geometric form, with a word, with a chord on the piano, or merely with a visualized image, and the realized idea will be different in each case, though all refer to the same original and can lead the mind back to it, but without one or other the notion of separate redness cannot be felt to exist. Equally, even if the quality has no basis in the perceptual senses we may still give it presence by materializing it in any form at all, provided we can teach ourselves to treat that form as a sign for the quality. In this way the separated qualities of things may be made apparent by associating them with some other thing: courage may be materialized as a flag, and love as a winged boy. If, however, we so accurately reproduce the visual manifestations of the thing that the image is indistinguishable from the substance, then we have not realized the separateness of its visual appearance; all we have succeeded in doing is to realize 'it' in all its unique and unfathomable 'itness'. While we are deceived all is well and we will accord to the image precisely what we are in the habit of according to the object and no more, but, as this was not what we were after, we experience that odd sense of disappointment which is ours whenever, looking for an image, we are faced with a simulacrum. The Mahometan who said to the painter of a fish 'Are you not afraid of creating a body without a soul?' expressed exactly our sensations before a perfect image. No man painting a picture or carving a stone has ever believed himself to be creating a human being. When Pygmalion's statue of Galatea stepped down from its socle he failed as a sculptor because the image and the object had coincided; it left its half-way world between idea and thing and became only thing. The thing no doubt was very good, but it was not an image.

The purpose, then, of the image is quite simply to give form to our ideas, and it is because man is an idea-producing creature that he is also an image-maker. In so far as man is content to be without ideas and to live on the plane of direct interaction between himself and things out-there he needs neither pictures, nor statues, nor music, nor language, and his life, like the beasts', will be good with the goodness that belongs to that sort of life, but it will not be the life of homo sapiens.

The images which words and pictures and music arouse in the mind are drawn from the resources of the mind itself. We cannot read who do not know a language, we cannot understand an idea unless it is already dormant within us, its materials waiting to be reconstituted. It may be that we could not write the plays of Shakespeare, but they would be of no value to us unless they were already within us when we read them. Our joy is in finding such stupendous resources of understanding in our own being. When writings are concerned with ideas that most of us do not have, even in embryo, such as the more extreme of the mystical works of Swedenborg, or of St John the Divine, or of William Blake, they have little power of revelation and succeed only in giving an impression of portentous noise; the door is flung open with great ceremony, but there is nothing in the room.

The artist makes his ideas real by giving form to them; he exercises his power to distinguish appearances from things by detaching them from the things of which they were part and giving them a separate identity. But what about the observer? He also, merely by seeing or hearing the completed work, exercises himself in the process of making concepts and takes part in the revelation without having had a great share in the effort of making it. The observer can only see what it is in him to see, and he must make some effort of spirit, if not of will, to see even that; he must acquire the technique of seeing, but he is spared the long years of mastering the technique of making, and in particular he is spared that greatest struggle of the artist, the peculiar stress of attaining personal poise which is the prerequisite of the art of creation.

The Actor and the Audience

As the representation differs in kind from the original image and has different qualities, so does the significance of the representation appear differently to the man who makes it and to those who perceive it. The huntsman who drew his bison on the rock obtained his release from the act of drawing, not from contemplating it afterwards. Jean Paul Sartre wrote: 'No one paints to create art or to make it. The artist simply paints.' That it was so in the time of the cave-painters is shown by the way one image is drawn across another; that it is so in historic times is suggested by the lack of interest many creators show in the fate of their work. The painter sells his picture and forgets that it was ever his and the writer obtains different satisfactions when rereading his work in tranquillity from those he experienced when creating it in tension and stress. The art-creator may become the art-consumer, he may even contemplate and consume his own work, but he knows that seeing is not the same thing as making, and the release of the one is not the release of the other.

The image-maker's purpose is to give form to a state of acute awareness and to isolate it in timelessness. In this it is similar to the passion for possession and permanence that drives us to gather a flower, to shoot a rare bird, or to capture a butterfly. We want to have the ecstasy of the vision always at hand; it is not the flower, the bird, or the butterfly, we want to capture, but the joy we had in perceiving them. To the image-maker, whether painter, sculptor or poet, the creation of his image is the resolution of tensions, a getting rid of something, an activity, a voiding, a birth. When he has achieved it he feels weak, light, released and empty. But his satisfactions are not confined to the simple one of expelling from his system something which has grown there and is crying out for parturition. He is also delighting in his own skill, in the control of arm and hand, and in the evidence of that control which is appearing before his eyes. To the intensity of the longing that conjured up the bison is added the verve of a purposeful movement which flawlessly fulfils its purpose. And if to these pleasures is added the wonder and applause of onlookers at this magical projection of an image which they recognize, it is little wonder if the attempt should be repeated, both by himself and by others less gifted than he.

The spectator (what adequate word is there for the man who looks at a work of art?) who has had no part in the creation of the image comes to it quite differently from the artist. If the artist is a maker who also observes what he makes, the spectator is an observer who in idea makes what he observes. He recognizes the image and embarks upon the experiences, conscious and unconscious, which the recognition entails, but the bow of the bison's back is also the gesture of the artist's hand and this gesture the spectator unconsciously repeats in the passage of his eye.

The same sort of development occurs with the making of images as we followed in the making of tools. The creator's delight in the act of creation will tend to make him emphasize the particular feature which he most enjoyed making. It may be that he enjoyed most the swift action with which he narrowed the shape of the bison's legs; if so we may look to find this feature exaggerated because of his delight in his own activity rather than because of any purpose of expressiveness which he had. Development of this sort which grows out of the maker's virtuosity awakes in the spectator similar delights: the image becomes more and more a design of harmonious relationships, a saraband of movement, a record of pleasing gestures, but less and less an image of a moment intensely and passionately perceived.

If, on the other hand, the artist allows his mind to dwell on the great bulk of the hurtling body, then he will increase unconsciously this aspect and reduce in importance those aspects which interest him less. In this case what results from his unconscious change of emphasis is a change in the expressiveness of the bison; what the spectator is now aware of is the enormous threat of this impending mass, and not the skill of the artist in representing it.

Yet again the artist may come to be involved neither in what he feels about the bison, nor in his pleasure in the physical process of depicting it, but in the perfecting of the likeness of the image he has created, a likeness not to the intensely seen bison of his experience, but to the coldly analysed bison of his knowledge. In the modern phrase he may come to depict what he knows to be there rather than what he has seen or felt to be there. In this case the spectator will go with him in admiration of detail, and in wonder at what he may conceive to be the increased similarity of the image to the bison itself, not realizing that what he is now presented with is not a charging bison but a hybrid in which the dead bison lying still before his eyes has been resurrected in a charging posture.

If, finally, what enthralls the artist is the fact that he has made an image which others recognize conceptually as a bison, he will gradually allow to fall out of his work all characteristics that are not essential to this end. This ultimately leads to the pictogram or to the sign which the enlightened have been taught to accept as meaning 'bison'. The drawing on the wall of the cave in Lascaux becomes by this route the written word.

The sequence from matter to its representation in art appears to be like this: (1) The object 'out-there' which occupies space and by which the behaviour of waves of energy is modified, becomes (2) an image in the mind. This is stored as an idea which, when it again takes form, becomes (3) an image of the object projected by an energy within the mind. When given material form this image again becomes an object 'out-there' and is subject to (4) the perception of the spectator, in whose mind it is created as an image just as the original object was in (2), but it has now lost its quality of immediacy, of demand, simply because it is recognized as an appearance and not as a thing and by doing so it has slipped free of the burden of time.

The ingredients of a representational work of art are the characteristics of the object 'out-there', as perceived by and projected by the artist and as then perceived by the spectator.

The final synthesis is not the work of the artist who makes the object but of the spectator who perceives it, but in so far as artist and spectator stand side by side upon almost the same spot, sharers in a common culture, the synthesis made by the spectator is not so very different from that made by the artist. We speak of communication being established when what we mean is that the spectator loses himself in that same impersonal ecstasy as the artist, and that both become momentarily identified in the image.

The Appropriate Material

Each way of making images, each material and technique, has opportunities and limitations which are peculiar to itself; it is not unreasonable therefore to suppose that some aspects of our perception of the object out-there will be more satisfactorily realized in one material than in another.

For example, the actor is flesh and blood like the character he represents; we do not suppose him to be that character, but he is able to do many of the things which the hero could do—he can walk and fight, weep, whisper, proclaim, and thus he is able to be the carrier of a considerable range of those ideas which proliferate from the central idea, Macbeth or Agamemnon or whatever it may be. An actor has life as the man he represents had; he does not need to represent a living thing; indeed, he cannot, because he is that thing; all that he may represent are aspects of life which do not naturally belong to him, but of which he is the conveyer. We may say as we watch him: 'How convincing a Macbeth he is!' but not 'He looks as though he breathes and could move.'

It was this same principle that underlay Goethe's advocacy of men playing the parts of women on the stage: 'We . . . remember how the parts of old men were represented to the point of deception by an able young man, and how that actor afforded us a double pleasure. The same way, we experience a double charm from the fact that these people are not women, but play the part of women. We see a youth who has studied the idiosyncrasies of the female sex in their character and behaviour; he has learnt to know them, and reproduces them as an artist; he plays not himself, but a third, and in truth, a foreign nature. We come to understand the female sex so much the better because some one has observed and meditated on their ways, and not the process itself, but the result of the process, is presented to us.' English garden designers of the early nineteenth century made a similar discovery when they found that truly natural countryside was not, for some incomprehensible reason, a garden and therefore decided that a natural manner of planting could become a garden provided that the trees and plants that appeared there were not indigenous to the site. This is not unlike saying that a group of Chinese walking about unaffectedly in the streets of Wigan become automatically a theatrical drama. The principle that a thing cannot represent itself lies at the heart of the 'natural' garden problem also.

A statue, on the other hand, exists in three dimensions just as the man himself did, but because it lacks life it may represent and effectually convey the image of life. We can say of it 'How lifelike!' But the statue cannot represent the three-dimensional quality, because it *is* three-dimensional. We cannot say 'It looks solid', although it may, of course, suggest aspects of solidity which do not normally belong to marble.

A painting carries the process a step further. The image in a painting has two dimensions only and because it lacks the third it may represent it. How often is it said of certain paintings that the objects imaged in them look as though they could be touched? Solidity, tactile qualities, atmosphere—all these the painted image may represent because it lacks them. Two-dimensionality it not only need not represent but cannot, although aspects of two-dimensionality which are proper to the image but not to paint and canvas may be represented there.

A good deal depends upon our understanding of the word image. It can have a very wide application. An image in the sense of a reproduction of the recognizable visual characteristics of an object out-there, for example a gold-plated portrait bust of Mr Odinga Odonga, is of one kind; of another kind is an image which, while retaining recognizable visual characteristics of Mr O, also attempts, by playing with these characteristics, by emphasizing some and suppressing others, to image that essential Mr O who exists behind his visible façade. The next stage is an image which sets out to represent Mr O's essential self while utterly ignoring his visible aspects. This achievement involves making visible that which is, by its nature, invisible.

Each of these types of image has its own merits. It may be argued of the first kind that a representation of all his visual characteristics as they are experienced by an observer will inevitably introduce precisely that amount of invisible aura of Mr O which we experience when in his presence; in other words, if we are given all that can be seen of Mr O the rest will be added unto us. The advocates of the second course say that there are many things about Mr O, his tone of voice, his movements, his grimaces, his past history and future intentions which it is legitimate to wish to include in the image because of such is, after all, the total Mr O whom we know and with whom we have to deal; but that if this is to be represented by a static gold-plated lump of bronze we must be allowed to take liberties with Mr O's physical appearance in order to render our image truly expressive of the spiritual him. The third school of thought disregards the visible manifestation of Mr O altogether and says, in effect, that all which is worthy of representation is the essential Mr O'ness of him and that the artist, the creator, makes visible this essence which is only misunderstood by being connected with his material appearance. One difficulty with this latter method is pointed out by those who ask how they are to recognize such an image as being that of the spirit of Mr O rather than that, say, of Mr Mennen Williams? Such a question of personalities may, in fact, be left on one side, because the artist who has forsaken the visible aspects of what he represents is hardly likely to be concerned should the outer husk of this inner essence, which he has made manifest, be unidentifiable. But if he is concerned with communication at all he will hope that the nature of that essence, its expression, will be identified; otherwise what he has made is an image which only he can recognize. He has realized the idea, but in a form which is not self-communicable.

It is obvious enough that if a representation contains no similarity at any point to the object represented we will be dependent on signs external to the representation to effect for us the connection between the image and the idea of the object. But this connecting link is not simply the means of communication or of recognition; it is the vital ingredient that makes the image a realized idea rather than simply another thing. An image from which the sign is lacking (or which we are unable to find) ceases to be an image at all; it becomes a thing, something to which we can react sensually, practically, directly, but not imaginatively.

It is clear that the degree of communication intended must affect the choice of medium—we do not write poems in Swahili for an audience of Esquimaux—but the choice also depends upon which aspect is to be realized. For example, it may be argued that if what we chiefly want to image is the aspect of pulsating life in our model, then sculpture, which can get most near to the model in form, is best able to take the further step. If, on the other hand, it is the creation of the idea of form itself which is our chief interest, then a picture will serve better because it can suggest three-dimensional form, whereas a statue, being three-dimensional form, can suggest only particular form. The question whether it is better to be near or far in relation to the material is a question of aesthetic purpose.

What we are usually concerned with in the making of images is the particular and not the general: the statue cannot image form, because it already is form, but it can, so long as it does not exactly reproduce it, image the specific form of Mr Odinga. If it is to do this it must look like him but not too like; like, because without likeness of some aspect it is not an image, and unlike, because if it were not unlike it would not give us the essential impression of being his appearance separated from him.

In practice it is difficult to reproduce the visual aspect of any living thing with utter fidelity: even the most effective *trompe l'oeil* requires carefully chosen and constant lighting if it is to stand up to scrutiny. But it is not at all difficult to do so sufficiently well to deceive an uncritical observer. Pliny's story of how Zeuxis painted a bunch of grapes so well that the birds swooped down upon them has many parallels. Apelles is said to have painted a horse which other horses neighed at, and Parrhasis, to rival Zeuxis, painted a curtain which a fellow artist tried to lift in order to inspect the picture beneath it. The 'Fly' missal in the Royal Collection has a fly portrayed on it in order, so it is said, to deter other flies from settling there. The success of this sort of thing depends largely upon the degree of attention of the observer. There is no reason to suppose that birds, horses or flies are particularly difficult to deceive; they live, after all, in a world of direct appearances; danger in the form of movement or of the uncustomary they are certainly alert to detect, but their world is not littered with images, and the conceptual separation of appearances from things is scarcely to be expected by them. Zeuxis's birds were no more, and no less, deceived than we are when we find that the restaurant, whose door we have attempted, is closed for repairs; the birds would probably not have been deceived a second time and we would not have tried the door if we had first read the notice in the window. Inattentive humans can just as easily be tricked into accepting a contrived image in place of an object as Zeuxis's birds were. Unsuspecting visitors to the waxworks will ask the way of a uniformed dummy, but only because they are inattentive. What the mind is set to see it will in all probability succeed in seing. Many years ago I had occasion to arrange half a dozen dummy army trucks on a mountain track. Civilian passers-by on a neighbouring road took them without question for a halted military convoy, but a party of officers who were expecting a demonstration of dummy vehicles pronounced them to be false. But when a second party of officers were asked 'Which of these six vehicles are genuine trucks and which dummies?' they, between them, named each one genuine and each one false. In each case the set of mind governed the interpretation of evidence.

The *trompe l'oeil* as a decorative amusement, as a parlour trick, or as a military expedient, is one thing, but the attempt at visual deception in a work of art is quite another. Several times in the history of western art there have been determined efforts to make the sculpted and the painted image coincide exactly with the appearance of objective reality. These attempts have been checked by their inherent technical difficulty and also by the counter-influence of other theories which were held at the same time and were incompatible. One might reasonably suppose that Pliny's story of Zeuxis and Parrhasis reflected only the vulgar estimate of what those artists attempted, but not the aims of the artists themselves, were it not that the history of Greek art was one of increasing attention to faithful physical resemblances. The formalized images which were made in Greece before the sixth century B.C. and which derived from the schematized forms of Egypt were steadily modified by famous sculptors in the direction of a greater realism. A similar belief in the virtue of complete representation was held in the fifteenth century in Italy and at the beginning of the nine-teenth century in England. The early stages of such belief normally produce great art, but the more closely, after a certain point, the image approaches the initiating visual experience the louder becomes the applause of those to whom it is merely the latest trick of a conjurer; but to those who have formerly found in statues and in pictures an inexplicable pleasure there is left only a sense of emptiness, for they are no longer able to transfer themselves to the realm of realized ideas. The crowd soon ceases to applaud the simulacrum, for the crowd only applauds what is new, the trick has been performed and there is an end to it; but the artists, finding that there is no more milk in the cow, go off to milk the bull instead and decide that there is no virtue in representation.

28 *An Auroch at Lascaux: cave painting*

29 *A North American Bison: photograph*

When the hunter outlined his vision of the auroch on the wall of cave he was not trying to assuage his longing for food; if that had been his purpose he would have chewed an old bone rather. He drew not to satisfy his hunger, but to give form to the tension created in him by the acuteness of his idea.

30 CEZANNE: *Les Pommes*
'Sometimes they're a sin, sometimes they're a knock on the head, sometimes
they're a bellyache, sometimes they're part of a pie, sometimes they're sauce
for the goose.' D. H. Lawrence

31 H. FANTIN-LATOUR: *Apples*
'Fantin-Latour's apples are no more to you than enamelled rissoles.'
D. H. Lawrence

Painting, for all that it lacks the life and solidity which Mr Odinga had, represents him by means of sensations of contrasted light which is the way in which we would have apprehended the man himself. If now we should leave hue on one side and create our image in terms of two-dimensional tone, we will have moved still further from the perceived characteristics of the object out-there and our concept will have been turned into a percept one degree further from the original percept than before, and will be less physically involved in it. Yet again, if we limit ourselves to an outline image and thus acquire the power of making a line represent enclosed form our image will be less gross than it was and the perceptual similarity between it and its original will be so much less. If we drop from our means of representation all similitude to the solidity, hue, tone and outline, all that comprised our actual visual perception of Mr O, what will be left? Nothing but a sign, a sign that is either the sound we make when we say 'Odinga', or the arbitrary marks that spell out his name upon the page. And with this sign alone, because we have learned its significance, we can realize the Odinga-idea, and because we are using no single element that went to complete our perception of the physical man we are enabled to raise every aspect of that man to the realm of idea. But our retention of the sensations of perception is now very slight.

The great practical difference between the word, written or spoken, and the visual image is that we cannot read the former unless we have been initiated into the mystery of language, whereas visual images can be made intelligible to all men who have eyes.

It is in the nature of this whole problem that any positive statement seems, as one makes it, to fade off at the edges into refinements and subtleties. Although it is generally true that all men can recognize a representational image it does require a degree of common experience if the object represented is to be comprehended at all. For example, a picture of an elephant would convey very little to a person who had neither heard of nor seen such a beast; nor would the Isenheim Altar-piece be as fruitful of ideas to a Hindu as would a statue of many-armed Krishna. Yet a man who speaks only Telegu will comprehend more from a picture of the crucifixion than he will from a verbal description of it in any language but his own. (Plate 48.)

The spiritual difference between the written word and the visual image is equally great. Precise though a word is, evocative though it may be, the actual machinery of visual perception is not engaged. All that takes place, takes place now within the mind; the retina and the neurons sleep; we are in a world which has been created by old, long-stored stimuli; the accidents of energy exterior to ourselves have been totally excluded from it. Even the spoken word is further from this spiritual purity than the word upon the page, for sounds have at least a sensual immediacy of a sort, but the written word is only the ghost of a sound. We have entered now into a realm not of images but of substitutes.

A substitute is an arbitrary relationship. We may know that the word 'laut' is the sign for the idea 'sea' in Malay, but it does not enable us to discover what their word for 'land' is. A word may effectually realize an idea and satisfactorily perform its magic of poising us on the edge of reality, but in itself it tells us nothing, implies nothing; it is the realized idea not the form it takes which is fruitful of other ideas, and when these in turn are realized we have the makings either of poetry or of consecutive thought. But an image contains within itself the idea of an attribute which, having been separated from the object of which it was a part, is seen to belong to other objects also. Similarity is the instrument of our being. Without the recognition that this is of the same class as that, that this fire burns so also will the other, that yesterday ended in night and so will tomorrow, we would have no possibility of learning; each experience would be novel and unique and we would not know how to react to it, and even if we hit on the correct response, if the organism survived the process of experiment, the knowledge would be useless because the like would not occur again. Without the consciousness of similarities which depends upon the capacity to separate attributes there would be neither past nor future, memory nor hope, nothing but a chaotic waste of incomprehensible present.

That a representational image is a more universally comprehended vehicle of ideas than a word is clear enough, but it is not so clear what part communication plays in all this.

The Need to Communicate

An image comes into being because its maker cannot experience his idea without giving form to it, but having made the ideal real, why is it of concern to him whether it communicates the idea or not? He has experienced his own catharsis; why doctor others?

There are the obvious answers. First amongst them that the artist, having realized his idea, changes his relationship to his work and stands aside from it to enjoy his fellow creatures' admiration and any economic advantages that he can get. This is an adequate answer as far as it goes. A creative artist is like a loaded gun: the idea lies in the darkness of his mind like a cartridge in the breech; it may lie there for ever unless the trigger is pulled. The forces that release the trigger, the need to pay bills, the need to fulfil a promise made, the need for a sense of personal achievement, the need for applause, these are the immediate causes of the work being done, but to pretend that any of these needs are the essential causes of the work of art is like saying that the conductor who rings the bell is the engine of a bus. The essential cause in the individual who creates is the need to expel from the system a weight that lies upon it. In that sense true creative art is like a birth. But as a birth is a consequence of the desire to experience life and to increase it, so the desire to live more fully by extending the nature and significance of life is the cause of artistic production. But the need to communicate this extension of life which art has created is not part of the need to create. The mainsprings of communication lie elsewhere. From the point of view of the

Life Force, the Biological Principle, call it what you will, the need for communication derives from the need to create and perpetuate social ties. Gregarious beasts seem to manage to preserve their societies with very limited means of communication, but *homo sapiens*, with his life on many planes, owes his fatal superiority to the capacity to hybridize ideas and at the same time, by their ready dissemination, to create a homogeneous society. We learn when children to formulate our ideas as our parents do, to use their language. Naturally when we come to give birth to original ideas we realize them in forms of the type we know and, because of that, other members of our society know them also and share them. If the idea is, in fact, an original idea, the particular form in which it is realized will inevitably be an original form, but though the particular form will be new it will be built up out of those old components which have become for us pregnant with meaning. It will only be necessary to extend the general parental language of forms if its existing range is inadequate for the realization of the new idea. If the language of forms which we have inherited has been exhausted, its vitality gone, its power to re-create sensation failed, a totally new general language of form may become necessary. If such a change takes place a difficulty of communication will exist until the new language is learned, but the new language must be a consistent one, its terms must be transferable, and it must be possible to construct from its parts a variety of edifices and not one building only.

There remains another possibility on a different level. We can conceive that the idea, when it is given form and can be apprehended by the mind from which it was created, continues in a constant state of *being created*. In other words, an idea which is the product of the fusion of an infinite number of other ideas can go on increasing and evolving so long as it is part of a bigger whole, a universe of ideas to which it contributes and from which it receives, but which once it is no longer capable of giving and receiving becomes a husk or shell. If this is true the artist, related to his work as the mother to her child, surrounds it with conditions of growth, or, in the common term, communicates it so that his new idea may drive on to unite with others to form larger and more complex entities, reaching out towards wholeness, the attainment of which appears to be a fundamental drive or principle of life.

On the most mundane level the artist may desire to communicate because he is an exhibitionist or because he must pay his bills; on the social level the artist is required to communicate because the corporate body is created by community of ideas; and metaphysically the idea, in so far as it contains within it the spark of life, contains a drive towards wholeness which is a state it cannot achieve if it is incommunicable.

Yet, clear though the functions of communication may be, the degree of communicability cannot, because of that, be considered an essential criterion of value. If it were we should be in the facile situation of the grocer who, when asked if a brand he sells is good, replies that it must be, because he sells a lot of it. The *reductio ad absurdum* of this is that the more communicable an idea is the more valuable it is, which elevates a scream of pain or a grunt of pleasure above a sonata by Beethoven; and as mankind ceases to comprehend the English language, which it is well on the way to doing, the works of Shakespeare would become less and less good.

Whether communication is important or not depends upon our point of view. The painter or poet who seeks only a personal catharsis may be well satisfied when that has been achieved, but if he is not so satisfied and wishes as a completion of his work to communicate, then he must use a common idiom. If however, for esoteric reasons, the artist wants to create in a purely personal language and yet still wishes to communicate, it is, of course, quite open to him to teach others his terminology, although it may not be very evident to them why they should trouble to learn it.

Once this has been done the idea, provided that it is potentially realizable by the specta-tor and that it is something he is capable of experiencing, can certainly be communicated. This involves the use of footnotes or a more or less elaborate exegesis which, if it is able to convey the idea fully, only succeeds in showing that it is not peculiar to the form in which it was, allegedly, realized, and therefore was not, perhaps, proper to it. In any event an explanation of this sort inevitably intervenes between the observer and the image. Pater's description of the Mona Lisa is the haze through which many people see it: 'She is older than the rocks among which she sits, like a vampire; she has been dead many times, and learned the secrets of the grave; and has been a diver in deep seas, and keeps their fallen day about her; and trafficked for strange webs with Eastern merchants: and, as Leda, was the mother of Helen of Troy, and as Saint Anne, the mother of Mary; and all this has been to her but as the sound of lyres and flutes, and lives only in the delicacy with which it has moulded the changing lineaments, and tinged the eyelids and the hands.' Or, if we should stumble upon it, there is a more matter-of-fact account which explains how Leonardo succeeded in keeping the enigmatic smile on the face of his stupid model by arranging for a succession of conjuring tricks to be performed at each sitting. Through which eyes shall we see the Mona Lisa? The *fin de siècle* romantic's? Or the cynic's? Having read them both it is difficult to dismiss either from the mind when we look at the picture. William Words-worth's praise of King's College Chapel at Cambridge must be in the minds of many who see that remarkable building for the first time:

> '. . . this immense
> And glorious Work of fine intelligence!'

but if they have also heard Ruskin's description of it as a 'dining-room table with its legs in the air', or that even more irreverent one of 'a sow on her back', they are unlikely to see the Chapel quite as they did before. (Plate 32.) The mind is oddly constituted and is liable to hear a wicked whisper even when waiting for the dawn of doomsday. 'I throw myself down in my chamber', wrote John Donne, 'and I call in, and invite God and his Angels thither, and when they are there, I neglect God and his Angels, for the noise of a fly, for the rattling of a coach, for the whining of a door.' We may, ultimately, owe all meaning to other ears and eyes than ours; but immediately, we do better to be left alone before a work of art and to let it speak to us in our own voice.

A great deal of what at first sight appears to be imagery of an esoteric kind is, in fact, readily susceptible to interpretation if our minds are given the right set. Those who do *The Times* crossword puzzle have achieved a peculiar language of their own which they very well understand, but which is, for example, quite meaningless to me. It may happen that we are unable to see likenesses until they are pointed out to us and that then the similarity of image to object in an unaccustomed aspect becomes evident. If this genuinely occurs we shall have widened our capacity for discriminating differences and recognizing likenesses. Often, however, this process is carried out by sleight of hand and the alleged likeness is a false one. Being polite and suggestible, willing to please and unwilling to seem stupid, we may accept, when repeatedly told so by the artist or his commentators, that the image he has made resembles the object in such and such a respect, but though we may believe we have seen a likeness what frequently happens is that we have accepted a substitute. Once the African tribesman has been told that a forked stick with a rag tied to one arm by a bunch of horsehair means Death, that particular work of art can so effectually convey an idea as to immobilize him with terror, but a terror which becomes, oddly, not the terror of death alone but of the object itself. The trouble with this sort of thing is that there is no essential reason why this terrible symbol should not mean 'Happy Birthday!' The value it has acquired is an arbitrary projection of the observers' capacity for terror; the value is not one that the object evokes, or tends to evoke, from its own nature. The forked stick is not an image of Death, it is a symbol for it.

It is recorded that Sir Francis Galton experimentally set up the figure of Punch as an idol and practised towards it genuflection, prayer and reverence. After a time he noted that he had 'acquired the habit'. He found himself perceiving the figure as a divine being at moments when he did not plan to do so. 'The character of divinity stuck to the object.' If in this way it is so easy to make for ourselves gods, it should not surprise us when we see genuflections being performed before remarkably bad pictures or, when subject to commercial influences, we feel the urge to perform them ourselves.

But if we can, by suggestion, project our emotions on to simple objects in such a way that the object becomes a source of those emotions, why should we seek to create elaborate images when arbitrary signs will do? If men can be conditioned to be moved as deeply by an elegy as an altar-piece, or by a block of wood as either, why have they bothered with the more arduous achievements?

If there is no difference of degree, perhaps there is a difference of kind?

We know already that one sense can to some extent evoke sensations which are proper to another. A poem can paint landscapes . . .

> 'Now fades the last long streak of snow,
> Now burgeons every maze of quick
> About the flowering squares, and thick
> By ashen roots the violets blow.'

We may enjoy the words as mere sound even if they mean nothing to us, but at that level the enjoyment will be slight and superficial. Their music and the incantatory element inherent in their pattern has much to do with the evocation of the vision, but the final fact of the vision lies not in their sound alone or in their music alone but in their existence as words, as man-made meaningful sounds of which we have the clue. Yet the words themselves have no qualities of the object which they signify. They are not imitative. The word 'snow' is not white, the word 'square' has no rectangular quality. They perform their magic because of our familiar acceptance of them. No one will read Villon's famous refrain . . .

> '*Mais ou sont les neiges d'antan?*'

with the same emotion as one who learned to call the whiteness which he saw one morning from his mother's or his nurse's arms, 'la neige'. But a picture of snow is another matter. The huntsmen who cross the snow in Breughel's *Winter Landscape* are painted figures crossing paint, but the shapes of the paint resemble the shapes of men in a way that the word 'square' does not resemble a cottage garden, and the white paint they cross is white like snow, in a way that *snow*, and *neige*, and *schnee*, and all the rest of them are not. More important than this, the landscape of Tennyson's quotation is not realized in the same way as Breughel's; its degree of visualization is quite different, and a detailed description in prose of such a scene would be different yet again. We cannot compare them, for they are entities of a different order.

It is clear from this that the sensations we experience in such a case are not purely subjective, and that despite all that we bring to the occasion we cannot say that we have created the occasion. We can give to a block of wood our respect, our devotion or adoration, but the block cannot give us the capacity for these sensations nor the desire to exercise them; everything in this case must come from us in an arbitrary way. But when the wood is carved into the likeness of Christ or of Buddha it has acquired from the recesses of our past the power to alert in us sensations which were slumbering and to bring to the surface of our minds ideas that we did not know we possessed. These ideas are far more subtle and various than an intensely felt longing for self-abasement, though that may be there, too. The aesthetic emotion has many dimensions, it is not merely strong or weak.

The Image as Object

An image exists on two levels; it is both a likeness and a thing. As a likeness it draws its meaning and significance from what it represents. Chardin's picture of a loaf of bread exists in the spiritual world of bread; it draws meaning and emotion from our experience of bread, of its taste, its touch, its smell, its homeliness, its honesty, and so on. But it exists also as a picture, a pigmented surface, created in a particular way, an evidence of certain skills, aspirations and longings, a unique representative of a class, the flowering of a tradition, a voice from the past, a valuable asset, an ornament on a wall, a status symbol, the creation of a man, a French painting of the eighteenth century. As long as we recognize that both aspects exist, in other words as long as we know that what we are looking at is a picture and not a loaf of bread or an optical accident, and if, at the same time, we are aware that the picture does contain elements of physical resemblance to a loaf, then these two levels of experience fuse and become one experience. The proportions in which they are combined may vary considerably, both according to the nature of the work itself and according to the temperament and set of mind of the viewer. A picture of a loaf by Braque will be more painting than loaf, a loaf by Gerard Dou will be more loaf than painting, but in both cases the result is not our reaction to so much bread plus our reaction to so much picture; it is different from either and different also from their sum: it is a third thing. (Plates 34, 35.)

A thing is itself and nothing else. But as everything that is within man's experience can only be conceived in terms of his other experiences, each thing is a something, unique certainly, but related to all other created things if not by its likeness then by its unlikeness to them. And, although every object and every experience must be classified because it is the condition of the mind's existence that it should reduce its sensations to order, an object must also be seen to be unique if our experience is to be extended by it.

Many people do not wish their experience to be extended. The ease with which the body, the senses, and the mind, can go through the motions of activity with sufficient competence to maintain life and subsistence up to a certain standard and yet reduce the whole procedure to a routine which makes the minimum of demands on mind and spirit, is depressing to those who think they believe in the Dignity of Man. The capacity to reduce things to routine is essential to man, he must *not* notice, *not* feel, *not* understand, and *not* remember, as much as possible, in order to leave himself unburdened to cope with the challenge of new demands as they arise. The capacity to live automatically, like all capacities in a healthy organism, exists in excess and depends upon a contrary principle to prevent it getting out of hand. The principle of minimum effort is a dynamic force which is countered by the opposed force of avidity for positive sensation. Between the rocket of laziness and the retro-rocket of appetite most of us with difficulty maintain an erratic course, aware and half aware.

An image is a thing, but its very being as an image *of* something gives it also a cross-reference to another experience, not in the sense of being an intellectual progression but in the sense of its location in our consciousness. It is this ambivalence, this being at one and the same time itself and something else, acting as a bridge between the unknowable uniqueness of the object out-there and our own uniqueness, which provides the quality of the positive sensation which we experience when we experience a man-made image aesthetically: it is this quality which by its strangeness forces us to be aware of our experience.

But this is not to say that it is the only source of the aesthetic experience.

PART TWO

Taste and Excellence

6. The Need for Choice

Give me but one firm spot on which to stand and I will move the earth
ARCHIMEDES

IT would be very simple if all sensations had a positive and constant value in terms of pleasure and pain and if these values were in turn always related to the well-being of the organism. We should have nothing to do but to pursue pleasure and to flee from pain, we could leave the whole matter safely in the hands of automatic reaction. The writer of the Book of Genesis put his finger on the essential point when he removed our ancestors from the Garden of Instinct and drove them out into the Wilderness of Choice.

As far as we can tell, man is the only creature who has succeeded in taking up an intellectual position beyond himself so that he is able to ask questions about his own nature as though he were detached from it. The simplest forms of life are passive bearers of their treasure and are carried about by direct forces outside themselves, by the tides and the winds; more evolved forms are more actively implicated, for example they turn from a blue light towards a red; other creatures in their degree take a greater and greater part in manipulating themselves through the complex of phenomena which surrounds them. Some of these more-evolved organisms became able to store sensory impressions in the form of memory so that they could anticipate situations when the earliest signs of a previously experienced sequence appeared. In men this device, the brain, initially a sort of clearing-house for sensations, has proliferated, grown beyond its simple function, and produced all manner of toxic side products. As a consequence we are no longer able to adjust ourselves to the world of objects out-there without thought, choice and decision; our capacity to respond instinctively and correctly to the challenges that surround us has become debilitated. Man is now a sick animal, a mad animal, or more than an animal, according to our point of view.

Our perception of any object has biologically one purpose only: that we shall be enabled to respond properly to its fellow occupancy of space and time with us. To obtain this great end much complex machinery is engaged and an extraordinary variety of activities takes place. From the point of view of the principal biological purpose we can value all these activities quite simply according to the extent to which they contribute to this end.

This complicated organism, the human being, compounded of energies, operates by a

system of interlocking needs. A need is a sensation caused by the organism being in disequilibrium. When what is lacking is supplied, balance is restored. What we feel as a need
is a tension which discharges in behaviour calculated to supply what we lack. The type of all
human needs is hunger, the demand for fuel to drive the mechanism onward. When the
sugar content of the blood falls below a certain point the muscle of the stomach contracts;
we feel this contraction as a sensation of unease which drives us to the action which will
restore the blood's sugar content; hunger ceases when its task is done. Theoretically, for
each need there is a certain terminal situation which, if it is obtained, satisfies and ends the
need, thus relieving the tension. But what happens if we cannot supply what is lacking?
We are left with an unsatisfied tension. Energy has been generated which has failed to pass
over into fulfilment; until it has been dissipated in some other direction the mechanism
will be disorganized by the pressures set up. The hungry or the sex-starved man can think
of nothing else but his need, the whole world is distorted by his longing, neither mind nor
body is capable for the time being of answering the innumerable other challenges with which
objects out-there are constantly bombarding him. It is of the first importance to his continued survival that the balanced condition of mind and body should be restored as soon as
possible. The lion, baulked of its prey, rages. His activity is inappropriate and very unlikely
to result in satisfying his hunger, but it makes him feel better. There is a well-known story
of a man who, having run for his train and narrowly missed it, saw another bending over
and doing up his bootlace. Delivering a swift kick at this unfortunate, he cried: 'That will
teach you to do up your bloody bootlace'. Our frustrated needs are not really satisfied by
such actions, but tensions which have been denied their legitimate discharge do achieve a
certain impoverished fulfilment in this way and the organism is more or less restored to the
desired condition of equilibrium. But the original need is still unmet. If the unmet need is
vital, as is the need for air, for food, for drink, we shall die: if, however, it is not of this
immediately essential kind we will learn either to do without it or to accept in its place a
substitute satisfaction. In either case the character of the organism suffers a change, for if
any one of its needs can be made to demand a different terminal situation from the one it is
developed to create, then the organism must reorganize itself upon a fresh basis and its
ultimate destination will either be a different one or it will be compelled to approach its
destination by a new and circuitous route.

Although equilibrium is the desirable end of all activity, if an organism were in permanent equilibrium it would be inert. What we know as life is a process of psychobiological
adaptation, and without disequilibrium there can be no adaptation. Each moment of our
awareness is a condition perilously poised amongst contending forces, and the story of our
lives is the track of the route of a balancing act.

What is the general nature of these forces that beckon and thrust and forbid and generally
hustle us about, but without which we should not live? They are of two main kinds, drives

and incentives, pains and pleasures, opposite sides of the same coin. The sensation of hunger is a drive initiated by a lack. The incentive is, in the first instance, the need to escape the discomfort of the drive, and, in the second instance, it is food. But without the drive the incentive is no incentive at all. A hungry lion is driven by his need to travel great distances and to overcome severe obstacles in order to obtain food; a replete lion can lie down amongst a flock of sheep and show no interest in them. The incentive has become no incentive, because there is no drive to make it so.

Pain is a drive in its most blatant form. Our instinctive reaction to pain is withdrawal so that the pain will end and the organic damage which it signifies will cease. The incentive in a situation involving pain is not pleasure but the cessation of pain. Some people, like Locke, have argued that pleasure is no more than the absence of pain, and that the man who employed a servant to give him repeated blows on the head with a hammer because the sensation was so delicious when he stopped was on the right track. A more optimistic view would be that pain was the absence of pleasure, but though it is true that the loss of a pleasure is painful to us, nobody supposes that either explanation is complete. Commonly these two aspects of a need co-operate to produce the desired biological result: we dislike the pangs of hunger and eat to still them, but we enjoy the taste of our food and eat for that reason, too.

Pain is a drive of so particular an urgency as to differ in kind as well as in degree from other drives. It is not in itself a sensation but a quality of sensation, rather as hue is a quality of light. It is the experience we have when the neural receptors engaged by a stimulus receive injury. The nerves which carry sensation to the central nervous system have a limited capacity. Only so much water can be poured down a half-inch pipe in a given time; at the point when the pressure of the water exceeds the strength of the pipe the pipe will distort to accomodate it; so it is with the passage of sensation: an application of stimulus greater than the nerves can accommodate results either in neural protest at the attempted distortion, or in the nerve protecting itself by losing sensitivity. Sometimes the collapse is local, for example, when a limb is numbed with pain; but more often it is terminated by a collapse of the central nervous system when the organism takes refuge in unconsciousness or death. Local pain is the immediate indication to a living creature that its continued smooth functioning is in danger.

If pain is a quality of sensation, so also is pleasure, and if pain is the sign that something is locally amiss with the organism, so pleasure is a sign that the local mechanism is operating smoothly and fulfilling its function.

If the mechanism of our bodies could work in a straightforward way, on the one hand avoiding pain and on the other seeking pleasure, and if by operating this simple formula we could thread our way amongst the obstacles that litter our path and compete for our space, life would be a great deal more simple than it is. Whether it *would* so operate if left to itself has often been debated. The belief that it would and does is at the basis of the Noble Savage heresy. But instinct is not left to itself. Instead of being left in the realms of automatic reaction, pleasures are, like pains, taken into the mind and lose their primal innocence there. So strong is the pressure on us to learn to modify our responses to pleasures in accordance with theoretical values or social usage that it is rare for us to respond to them with complete spontaneity. The drive of need and the incentive of its satisfaction may once have pointed in a certain direction, but our minds have long since overruled their guidance and taken on the task of saying where we are to go and how and why.

Indeed, the mind has good reason to attempt this task, for the exceeding complexity of our situation has made the use of pleasure as a signpost to what is good for us very unreliable. That some healthy, well-organized people only like what is beneficial to them may be true, but the majority of mankind is hardly of this calibre. With many of us the pleasure-principle is either insufficiently discriminating, so that we enjoy things that are positively harmful, or is too selective so that we fail to enjoy many things that are necessary and wholesome. The two arch-types of pleasure, sex and eating, were initially purposive, but, in so far as the mind has taken over pleasure's prime task, their biological value has largely changed to that of making life pleasant and thus encouraging our willing collaboration in the work of survival.

Whether unrestricted automatic response to the sexual drive would have more satisfactory biological results than the various conventions mankind practises one cannot say; presumably we should run into the same sort of difficulty that arises in the indulgence of natural diet adjustment in babies. Here there is experimental evidence to show that if an infant is supplied with a wide enough range of foods, and is given free choice, it will automatically adjust its eating and drinking to achieve a balanced diet. The task of supplying so wide a range of foodstuffs, and the wastage involved, make it impracticable to leave babies to adjust their own diet; other drives, external to the child, such as the needs of the adult who cares for the child, or of the society of which the child is a member, conflict with the automatic one. But some of the compromises which we are forced to make as a result do not seem at all well calculated to biological continuance.

The drives of sex and hunger are relatively complex ones, whereas what we need to discover is whether there are any values inherent in sensation in its simplest form. For example, is there any sense in which the drive of light has a greater value than the drive of darkness? Or of red than of blue? Or of height than of width? Or of fast than of slow? Of constant rather than of intermittent? Of smooth than of rough? Of soft than of hard?

If there are values of a fundamental sort involved in simple sensations, a better or a worse, in what do these values consist? Do they consist in the importance, the biological importance, to us of the need?

A drive is, after all, a characteristic of the organism itself, not of a stimulus. A certain wavelength of energy which we call light cannot of itself be either drive or incentive; it is neutral in the matter. Drive can only arise from the sensation which a stream of energy causes us to experience. The essence of a drive is that it is a drive towards something, towards a theoretical situation which, when achieved, will terminate the drive.

If life is a process of psychobiological adaptation it follows that without disequilibrium there can be no life. Adaptation is certainly an essential feature of the act of vision; any simple visual stimulus is an act of unbalance which requires a contrary act to restore equilibrium. The drive inherent in the simple experience of light is, therefore, a drive towards darkness. The biological need involved in the eyes' balancing act between light and darkness is the restoration of the chemical ingredients of cones and rods to a state which will enable them to make visual distinctions, so that ultimately the mechanism of sight shall allow us to anticipate the responses required by the next situation.

Every activity is like a pendulum; a force is implicated which at once sets to work to restore the *status quo*. As the swing of the pendulum increases so the strength of the initial force lessens and the counter-force grows in strength until, at the point when the counter-force exceeds the initial force, the weight changes direction and swings back. But the initial force of displacement releases a greater force than is required to return the weight to equilibrium so that, having passed rapidly through the point of inertia, it becomes unbalanced in the opposite direction.

If we apply this principle to visual sensations it implies that what is pleasant in such a sensation is not the condition white or the condition black as terminal situations, but the tension which is present in each condition and which pulls towards its opposite, the potential blackness in white, and the inherent whiteness behind the sensation of black.

If we assume that this tension is greatest at the terminal points of the pendulum our sense of activity should be greatest at these points also. But every distinguishable sensation of light, white, black, or any grey but one, is, considered in isolation, a terminal point, so that this hardly seems to help us. To do better than this we must be able to say that a strong push of the pendulum, that is a bright white, is an activity of which we are more aware than a less strong push. Considered in isolation we can, perhaps, say this, but can we ever experience any activity in isolation?

If we could equate sensation with the force of the energy that initiated it we should be on easy ground. For example, if we take absolute whiteness as one extreme and absolute blackness as the other, there is a point which is neither light nor dark, but is mid-grey. As this must be a point of no-tension it should also be one in which we take no pleasure because it is not activity. This is nonsense, for we are aware of mid-grey and can therefore derive a sense of life from it. How are we to resolve this difficulty?

Sensations, in fact, are not directly related in intensity to the energies that give rise to them. Mid-grey may be the theoretical point of rest between white and black, but it is not a point of rest for our optical apparatus. Many neurons have to be activated in order to convey mid-grey to the brain, for as far as the brain is concerned mid-grey is a positive sensation of light, only it happens that the brain is able to conceive it as being half-way between the sensations of white and of black. The activated neurons are not at rest, they are decidedly off-equilibrium and the tension is in their need to return to it. It is only in darkness that the neurons are still.

There are, then, two distinct scales: the first based upon the centre which is created by the equal mixture of black and white, and the second based upon the point of rest from which the eye is stimulated to activity; one is founded on physiological capacity and is conceptual, the other is founded on physiological activity and is perceptual. Both scales are, within the mind, simultaneously operative, so that our idea of mid-grey is both positive and neutral at the same time, positive in so far as it activates neurons, neutral in so far as it is a point of indifference between extreme percepts; similarly, black is at one and the same time neutral, because the neurons are not activated by it, and positive because it represents the complementary of white. The simultaneous operation of different scales is a common cause of dynamically variable activity.

So, then, if we are to discover a value in a simple sensation, and if we try to base this value on the degree of activity involved *of which we are aware*, we find that there are two quite separate standards. Black is conceptually active, but perceptually negative; mid-grey is perceptually active, but conceptually negative. This, though it does not lessen, but rather increases, the range of our activity, does not make the task of distinguishing the greater activity from the lesser any easier.

But our criterion should not be activity simply, but activity of which we are aware, so that what governs the value is not degree of activity but the extent of our awareness of it. And it is clear that greater activity does not necessarily mean greater awareness.

In order to be aware of a sensation we must be in a physical condition to receive it. If this sensation is immediately dependent on stimuli from outside us, the health of our sense organs, their ability to receive and to differentiate stimuli, is one thing, our capacity to be aware of them is another; a radio set may be a most sensitive instrument but if we are asleep or inattentive its sensitivity is irrelevant.

We will, in the first place, not be fully aware of any sensation unless we notice it. We notice things either because we cannot help it or because we choose to. Seeing depends ultimately on the functioning of the eyes, but noticing is a function of the mind alone. There are many degrees of awareness. We cannot be fully aware of anything. Full awareness implies awareness of all aspects, but this is something we never achieve. We select certain aspects and are aware of them and, if we wish to extend our idea, we then select other aspects and attend to them, and so on according to our capacity to conceive of points of

32 *King's College Chapel, Cambridge* '. . . a sow on its back . . .'

33 *Palace of Sport at Rome*

34 CHARDIN: *Still Life*

35 BRAQUE: *Still Life with Bread, Lemon and Knife*
A picture of a loaf of bread by Braque is more picture than loaf.
A picture of a loaf by Chardin exists in the spiritual world of bread.

36 J. L. E. MEISSONIER: *Friedland*
'. . . if a certain number of persons have been found
to agree that such and such an enormous sum is a
proper valuation of a picture, a book, or a song at a
concert, it is very hard not to be touched with awe
and to see a certain golden *reflet* in the performance.
Indeed, if you do not see it, the object in question
becomes perhaps still more impressive—as something
too elevated and exquisite for your dull comprehension.'
Henry James

37 *A Bronze Shield*

view, but this is the end of it. All aspects can only be seen by omniscience and omnipotence.

What our criterion evidently demands, then, is not full awareness. Is it, perhaps, intense awareness?

If the discrimination of minute differences were the source of our standard of perceptual values we would esteem most highly the condition of maximum sensitivity to slight sensations. Visually this is the condition obtained by looking out of the corner of the eye on a dark night, for it is in this way that we are able to perceive the most minute variation of quantities of light. At this end of the scale, however, although we can detect extremely small variations of brightness, we are severely limited in an upward direction, for a very modest increase of luminosity in the general field will make us insensitive to the lowest stimuli. This means that if we are to retain our ability to differentiate the smallest additions we shall not be engaging anything like the full capacity of our eyes.

In order to be able to make use of the largest number of our neural receptors we need a field of general luminosity somewhat higher in the full scale. Why not at the highest level of light intensity, for here it would seem that we could utilize all our light-sensitive equipment, albeit we should lose much of our power of differentiation? It is axiomatic that the appropriate quantity of beer for a quart pot is a quart; why otherwise have a quart pot? If the eye has so many neural receptors it will surely be fulfilling its destiny by making use of them? However, maximum performance for any mechanism is exhausting. The sense of well-being of the highly trained athlete is greatest when he is running within his capacity; he feels not only ease and mastery, but he is aware of further unused resources of power. The extreme exertion when it is called for, as in a record-breaking attempt, is necessarily brief, it can often not be repeated, and is sometimes harmful to the organism. So it is with the working of the eye. Our greatest employment of visual power is in an area of general illumination that lies towards the upper limit but which is still so far within our capacity that we can operate without effort and are conscious that we could accept an intensification if it were necessary. A quart pot will hold somewhat more than a quart, but it should not be made to.

It is not the functioning of our powers in itself that concerns us but the sense of well-being we derive from the exercise of them. The question we must ask is: of which sort of activity are we most intensely aware, that which involves acute sensitivity over a narrow part of our potential, or the full employment of our resources at the cost of a lesser capacity for differentiation? The answer will depend very little on the eye but much more on the mind. No degree of brightness is, in itself, more effective than any other in making us aware, but it can become more effective according to the extent to which it alerts and absorbs our attention.

The same type of argument applies to hue. The most acceptable theory of the perception of colour is that certain neurons are responsive only to certain wavelengths. When energy of one wavelength only is present we see, for example, blue, but when red also is present two sets of neurons are activated and we see purple. When all the neurons appropriate to each hue are activated the brain mixes them and experiences white. Clearly if a greater extent of stimulation is preferable to a lesser the whole is preferable to the part and white is preferable to any of its component hues. Yet few people would choose white as the visual sensation they preferred. It also follows that any mixed stimulus is stronger than a simple one of equal intensity and that a hue created by light of several wavelengths mixed is to be preferred, as involving more active neurons, to the pure prismatic colour; in other words brown is more delightful than, say, clear blue. This view would meet with acceptance by some, but not by others.

What we gain on the swings we lose on the roundabouts. When we experience a hue of low saturation a certain group of neurons is activated, and as the hue increases in saturation more neurons are activated, so that relatively stronger impulses are sped to the brain. A fully saturated hue is activating the appropriate neurons to the limit but does not affect others at all, whereas a mixed stimulus, being in its nature less saturated, involves more types of neuron but not those most heavily charged. When the choice lies between two hues of equal saturation the more complex hue will lead to a more general stimulus of the optic nerve, but when judging between the complex hue of lesser saturation and the simple hue of full saturation our criterion of the active employment of optical apparatus hardly serves to guide us.

A different approach would be to use as our standard of value not physiological aptitude but fulfilment of function. If the function of hue is to attract attention, then that hue best fulfils its function which most positively demands attention. Although this seems to show that saturated colours are to be preferred, as being better at their job, than less saturated ones, it would only be true if we were able to see hues isolated and in a vacuum, when their function of calling attention to themselves would not be applicable. In fact, the conditions in which a hue is called upon to catch our attention are conditions of competition. We notice the ripe cherry not because it is red or black but because it is red or black against a background of green; if the leaves were of the same hue the brilliance of the ripe fruit would fail to attract us, whereas even an unsaturated colour would catch the eye if it were surrounded by saturated ones.

It is typical of the times we live in that we should try to establish visual values by experiment. To be fair, probably few of the psychologists who conduct their painstaking inquiries into the colour preferences of schoolchildren are concerned at all with the question, 'Is one colour better than another?' For them such a question would seem meaningless. They ask only, 'What happens?' They seek to provide data which, if gathered on sound principles, and if statistically dependable, are then available for the manufacturers of toy balloons and lollipops, for the advertising experts of political parties, for alienists, and, only incidentally and if they can find a use for it, for philosophers and those who are concerned to discover the key to excellence.

Democracy, which is a governmental expedient, has, as a by-product, elevated the method by which it is conducted, the expressed opinion of the majority, from being a mechanical device into being a moral principle. I bow my head when the majority of my fellow citizens choose to pass this law rather than that, not because I believe they are right but because I believe that next time I may succeed in making the majority agree with me, when I in my turn will welcome the concurrence of the dissident minority; but I do not believe that the rightness or wrongness of an action is at all related to whether ten million people have voted for it or not. Truth and falsehood are not discriminated on a majority verdict; right and wrong is not a matter of counting heads; red is not a better colour than blue simply because sixty children out of seventy-one in Illinois prefer it. This seems to me self-evident. Yet to others, the whole tenor of whose commercially dominated lives has been to assert that the customer is always right and that ten customers are ten times more right than one (in fact, rather more than ten times, for the profitability of mass-production has its own mathematics), the opposite is true. For these people, for my grocer who believes that such-and-such a brand of biscuits is best because he sells them most, the criterion of the majority judgement is a clearly recognizable one, and one which he has been taught to believe has a peculiar democratic sanctity. Fifty million morons can't be wrong is an easy cry whatever word you may substitute for morons; for mathematics, we believe, cannot lie and counting can give us some sort of certainty . . . subject to audit.

But statistics, if they have been properly achieved, may tell us something, and it may well be that a theory of visual values could have more relevance to the human race if it were based on the reactions of seventy-one children in Illinois than on the reactions of one intellectual recluse in Kent. After all, these are *human* values we are discussing and the principles upon which such values can be based must be relevant to a normal human predicament if they are to be of interest to normal human beings. But normal human beings are not average human beings; the first exist in myriads, the second do not exist at all, they are a statistician's fiction.

We might hope that experiments would show us fairly clearly if there were any innate, basic, physiological tendency for one colour to be preferred to another. For example, it has been observed that the amoeba turns away from blue light, but does not turn away from red. Various attempts have been made to discover if any similarly consistent preference is shown by extremely young children. One professor recounts an experiment he conducted with his three-month-old son in which different coloured wools were held in front of the child in pairs and the child's preference was established on the basis of the relative length of time he gazed at one colour rather than another. This gave the order Yellow 80 per cent, White 74 per cent, Pink 74 per cent, Red 45 per cent, Brown 37 per cent, Black 35 per cent,

Blue 29 per cent, Green 28 per cent, Violet 9 per cent. These figures represent the time the colour was looked at expressed as a percentage of the total time it might have been looked at. The professor freely admits that the yellow and pink were much brighter than the other colours, which makes rather a nonsense of the whole experiment. If brightness, saturation, lighting conditions, and the infant's previous colour experience, for example the colour of its cot-cover and so on, are not subject to control, how useful are the conclusions? Yet it may be significant that the cold colours (which the amoeba also turned from) should all have made low scores.

Rather more extensive experiments were conducted with children aged between six months, the age at which they normally begin to grasp with their hands, and a year. Blocks of wood or pieces of paper were placed at equal distances from the child and a record was made of which block he grasped at first. The order was Red, Orange, and Yellow, while only a few of the older children, those of nine months, reached out for Green, Blue, and Violet, at all.

Other experiments involving various groups of children from two to nine also seemed to show that red was not only the colour most easily named and matched but was also the most popular. A distinct change seemed to take place as the ages advanced: in one case, although red was the most popular colour with the younger children, amongst nine-year-olds the position was sharply reversed and blue became the favourite. Other experiments showed that the drop in popularity of red took place at about six and accelerated with age and education. Another difference disclosed that whereas most boys preferred blue to red, red being a close second, the girls, who also gave first place to blue, gave second to green, then to orange and violet, and red was only fifth.

The meaninglessness of this statistical approach becomes clear from a description of one experiment in which twenty-seven children were tested. The result gave the order red and yellow equal first, green next, then orange, blue, and violet, about equal in last place. But so far from this representing the popular order of preference among these twenty-seven children, no single child actually selected the colours in this order at all, and though, for example, orange was bracketed last in the table nearly a fifth of the children put it first.

One observed fact suggests that there is a hierarchy of sensation of hue. When blue and red of equal saturation and brightness are exposed simultaneously against a neutral background in average daylight the eye is drawn to blue. And when yellow and green are shown we are drawn to yellow. The imbalance may be marginal, but it exists and is sufficiently consistent for us to say that, except in sub-daylight when the relationships alter, blue is felt as a stronger sensation than red, and yellow than green. The immediate biological source of these differences must be in the chemical composition of our rods and cones; its ultimate biological function is to increase our power of detailed perception by the enlargement of our capacity for differentiation. The apparatus of the eye is more sensitive to one hue than to another; but that is not to say that it is preferred.

A significant series of experiments was that carried out in the University of Nebraska from 1910 to 1921, and from 1928 to 1931. Taken over the whole period red was the most popular colour with women, but blue came first with the men. More interesting is the evidence that year by year the results amongst the women fluctuated more decidedly than amongst the men, presumably owing to the dictates of 'Fashion' leaders. Men were not greatly affected by this. Most interesting of all was the discovery that red declined steadily in popularity from 1910 to 1917, that it rose sharply in 1919, but dropped back again in the two succeeding years. By 1928, when the series was resumed, red again became high in the order of preference. If would be odd indeed if the sharp increase in the popularity of red in 1919 were not connected with the celebrations of victory in the First World War, and no doubt every similar fluctuation could be tracked to its source if enough were known about the circumstances in which it took place.

Of a different sort are those experiments designed to expose variations not in preferences but in sensitivity. That some people are colour-blind we know, and it is clear that their responses to visual phenomena will differ from those of the rest of us, but how if we all react with our own individually varying sensitivity?—If, for example, all questions of preference set aside, I am more acutely aware of blue than of green, or if you have difficulty in perceiving indigo at all? If there is no consistency of vision amongst us, does it not follow that what is one man's meat may be another man's poison? If, when we stand together before a Monet, we actually experience the colours in different proportions because you fail to register the indigo altogether and because I give greater value to the blue than to the greens, can we be said to be seeing the same picture, even if we exclude all that personal associated impedimenta which each of us has brought to it?

Attempts have been made to impose a pattern on these individual variations. On the basis of majority reactions 'Normal' has been established with a small permitted tolerance. A slight degree of variation in reaction from 'Normal' becomes 'Deviant'; a still greater variation becomes 'Extreme Deviant'. Of the subjects tested 20 per cent were 'deviant' from the 'normal' in one respect or another. There is, of course, not the slightest ground for supposing that there is any virtue in 'Normality'. In a leper colony leprosy is normal. If it is better to be Normal than to be Deviant, modern man has yet to determine wherein the betterness lies.

Experiments with colour alone have so far failed to produce much in the way of general principles, but experiments with more complicated material indicate that there are distinct approaches to the way objects are seen. It has been suggested that there are 'Form Dominant' types and 'Colour Dominant' types. The basic experiment designed to clarify this notion was one in which various coloured shapes were shown briefly on a screen. In one tenth of a second some observers reported colours, others reported shapes. The question is whether these immediate reactions show fundamentally differing human attitudes at all? The biological function of colour differentiation is to attract attention, a colour is a yell, a wolf-whistle, a look-here. That my attention is instantly attracted by the roll of drums before the curtain goes up does not imply that I am dominated by loud sounds rather than by the play of Hamlet which comes after it. And yet if some people tend to linger on the note of colour and consistently try to identify objects on the most superficial visual evidence they are, perhaps, a distinct psychological type. A person who experiences blue and equates that sensation with the sky on a summer's day or a favourite party frock without waiting for those further sensations of form which would, if she gave them a chance, demonstrate that what she is really seeing is the backside of a baboon, is certainly a superficial observer, but she is also overanxious for experiences to repeat themselves in a comfortable form.

Brightness, considered as a pure sensation, is subject to the same limitations and might give rise to values as indeterminate as those of hue, but the function of brightness is more extended and its criteria could, therefore, be more involved. Since successful vision depends first on our capacity to distinguish an object from its ground, brightness is only of practical value to us when it differs from the brightness which surrounds it. But the special function of brightness is to reveal the form of the object, which can only be done if the differences in brightness are within the capacity of the eye to distinguish them.

On a dark night we can separate the bulk of horse or bush from the illuminating sky, but the intricacies of three-dimensional form are hidden from us; slight changes in light intensity may be very apparent, but they may still not be very useful if they tell us no more about the nature of the object we are looking at. On the other hand, if the light becomes very bright and surfaces are very strongly differentiated the conditions are such that the addition or subtraction of small quantities of light is not evident; and if the light becomes even greater still, shapes of objects not only become liable to distortion but the eye, pained by the violence of the contrasts involved, becomes insensitive to quite considerable gradations of difference. In this case, too, the principle of economy of effort is violated. What do we want all this light for?

It seems that if we are to avoid on the one hand waste and on the other an unsuccessful effort to pierce the gloom we should prefer a degree of brightness sufficient, and no more than sufficient, to reveal easily to us the qualities of shape which identify an object.

This is true if what we are seeking is a completed act of vision. The scientist, the craftsman, the searcher after visible evidence, requires even, bright, and constant lighting. Because such men are concerned with the biological ends which vision serves they need to see everything which light can be made to reveal in order that they may act appropriately. But we, who are pursuing more devious delights, are concerned not with the practical end of vision but with some curious quality of pleasure which we can gain from experiencing it, and this, we know, comes to us more often from the thing half-seen, the unfinished sketch, the countryside at dusk, than from the utterly completed visual statement which lies under the arc lights of a laboratory. As Corot said when the sun rose: 'Now that everything is visible there is nothing to be seen!' It is evident that although efficiency of mechanical operation may be an ingredient in our pleasure it is far from being all of it.

Sensations of colour, and of brightness, and of shape, have no absolute existence and experiments which assume that they have are doomed to fatuity. What we see is not blue or red or white or grey or circle or cube, but a blue or grey or circular *something* revealed for a set passage of time in certain conditions of light against a red (or black or yellow or what you will) background. Whether it be a piece of wood, a square of card, or a wooden brick, or a fuzz of light, *that* is what the child sees, not red or blue or yellow.

If abstract hue and brightness are theoretical concepts, so also is shape. We cannot see abstract shape. As red and blue are always a red and blue something, so a circle or a square, a sphere or a cube, cannot exist in limbo. We may and do abstract the idea of cubeness and derive from it certain principles which are common to all cubes, but the principles if they are to be realized become a thing. Even the half-formulated idea itself can never be totally freed from qualities which belong to familiar objects from which the idea is derived, but which are not, in fact, qualities essential to their cubeness. We may not, for example, think of a cube as being hard; but that hardness is a part of our notion of a cube becomes apparent when we indignantly deny that we ever think of it as being soft. However, although concepts of shape cannot be untinged by our experience of the realities behind the shape, yet there are certain physical facts underlying our perception of it which may give to a shape values independent of the thing which the shape is. For example, if a circle is so large that we cannot include all of it in our field of vision without moving the eyes, then an element of effort is present which is not there if we can encompass it in one glance. Similarly if the shape is so small or so distant that we have difficulty in being certain what it is, then a displeasing air of uncertainty and of indecision belongs to it. Shapes, then, even if they have no other values, can be too large or too small.

A great deal has been written to show that some shapes are inherently more pleasing than others. From all of this no more than one or two general principles have emerged. The most important is that the part of the mind which determines the degree of attention we give to sensations is pleased at one and the same time by the two principles of variety and uniformity. The mind is an active principle; if it is to be enjoyed it must be felt to exist and if it is to be felt to exist it must act. Variety is pleasing because it ensures the mind's activity, but if the activity involved is great, then the reward to the mind in terms of orderly fact or form must be worth the effort. The eye and the mind do not proceed in a smooth and continual progress but in a succession of jumps; it follows that each step in the progression must contain within it the promise of the next stage in the same way that any pair of treads of a stair contain the implication of those above and below them. If the promise implicit in the series is one of unvaried repetition the mind no longer has any reason to remain attentive, it knows what is to come and is bored, hence its demand for variety; but if no series can be formed, or if when formed its promise is immediately denied, then the mind in its jumping progress will continually find itself at fault, it will have to move slowly and cautiously and will frequently have to retrace its steps because it has missed the next resting-place. When we see moving pictures at the cinema we register constant movement, but what in fact is presented to us is a succession of pictures each differing from the one before it. In the old days of the film the variation between the pictures, owing to the slowness of the camera, was considerably greater, with the result that we experienced an intermittent flickering effect. If the jump from picture to picture becomes too great the mind is troubled by the difficulty of relating them, the stepping-stones are too far apart and the series does not contain within it sufficient evidence of the way in which it is to proceed. In the extreme case of the successive pictures not being formally related at all the mind will flatly decline the task of making a continual progress of them and will instead regard each picture as a separate entity, related conceptually perhaps, but not formally, to the others. Even when the mind has acknowledged that each picture is to be accepted as a unit it continues, so strong is its tendency to relate and organize, to see the picture in some sort of relationship, perhaps aesthetic, perhaps historical, with those about it—is Italian, is a portrait, is sixteenth-century, and so on.

It is for this reason that a curving line is often more pleasing than a straight one, because our attention, while held by the continued slight change in direction which gives constant promise of discovery, is never shocked by a transition for which it has not been prepared, as it would be shocked, for example, by a zigzag. Because shapes cannot exist without boundaries, however imprecisely marked, this principle is true also of them, so that it can generally be found that a shape is most pleasing of which every sequence on its surface has implicit within it a promise of progression which is born out by the remainder of the form. Such a progression at its best is felt to be both unforeseen and inevitable, it has no beginning and no end, and the mind, while never satisfied, is never frustrated, because each stage leads hopefully to another and no end is promised other than a fascinated continuance of our attention.

Progression, movement, the transference of our experience from one sensation to another, is basic to all vision. If, considered theoretically, whiteness is inherent in black, and redness in green, so that every sole experience is not really sole at all, how much more in practice, when no colour and no tone is ever seen without direct relationship to some other colour or tone, is the quality of our experience dependent not upon a positive sensation conceived in isolation but upon the relationship between sensations. And, as some transitions are easy and some are difficult because of the way in which the machine which carries them out is constituted, so the eye comfortably passes from red to green but very much less comfortably from, say, a blue-red to a yellow-red. This is the source of our sense of harmony.

Harmony and satisfactory proportion, whether of the eye, or of the ear, or of touch, depend upon the relationship of a situation with those that follow it. If we can make the transitions easily, but nevertheless find them sufficiently varied to keep the senses attentive, and if by a system of echoes the disparate parts of a sensual experience are bound together into the semblance of an organic unity, the mind finds pleasure there because this is the way in which it has been constructed to operate. As Addison wrote, 'There is not perhaps any real beauty or deformity more in one piece of matter than another, because we might have been so made, that whatever now seems loathsome to us, might have shown itself agreeable.' But the fact is that we are made as we are and that our sense of harmony is imposed by that.

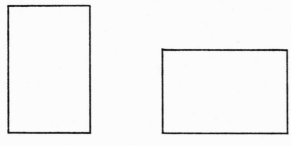

FIG. 11

It is evident that any physiological bias which seems to give preference to one hue, one degree of brightness, or one shape, rather than another, is in practice subordinated to the quality created by their interaction with each other.

Our notion of harmony contains also an implicit qualitative attitude to whatever is ambiguous. Clarity of perception is desirable if the mind is to make decisions, therefore we like clearly defined shapes and primitive colours. But we do not always wish to be involved in activities which call for decision, and if this is so we will prefer undifferentiated shapes and colours which are complex rather than pure.

It was generally believed in the nineteenth century that a special virtue resided in that proportion which is known as the golden section. It was held that a line was divided most pleasingly if the proportion between its length and the length of the longer part of it equalled the proportion between the longer part and the shorter. Equally it was believed that a rectangle constructed on this principle was more generally pleasing than any other. Experiments at one time seemed to show that rectangles of this sort were chosen more frequently because of some innate physical disposition in human beings. Apart from the impossibility of ensuring that experimental shapes are viewed abstractly and are not selected owing to some subconscious valuation based on the common proportions of tables, pictures and so on, sufficient notice does not seem to have been taken of the fact that a golden section rectangle is quite a different thing according to the way up it is presented. The optical illusion which makes a line seem shorter in the vertical than in the horizontal position applies to a rectangle as well and only an involved piece of instinctive adjustment could make our preference for a vertical rectangle identical with that for a horizontal one. Further experiments seem to show that the golden section is an average arrived at largely as a result of avoiding the ambiguity of extreme positions. A rectangle of which the sides are much more nearly equal than 1:0.65 begins to look like a square or like a figure that ought to be a square but is not; whereas a rectangle of which the sides are in much greater disparity begins to look like a column, or a track, or even like a thick line, and is in danger of losing its rectangular identity. In either case the shape acquires overtones of discomfort

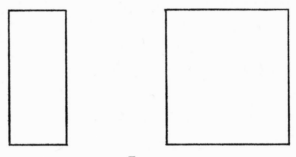

FIG. 12

arising out of the ambiguity. That in this case ambiguity *is* usually uncomfortable is because rectangular forms are not of sufficient variety to retain for long the mind's simple attention; we wish to make our decision as to what the shape before us is so that we may pass on to more visual experiences. If a sufficient number of choices is made which avoid these two uneasy extremes the average of them does, in fact, come very close to the magic figure— but this is not to say that many people actually choose it. This is a more acceptable explanation than that which supposes the mind to have subconsciously perceived the mathematical proportion of side to side and of total side to longer side and recognized in some occult way the principle of variety in uniformity (cf. Figs. 11 and 12).

The problem of the value of our visual experiences is transformed when we admit the idea of expression. Expression is the consequence of our being able to interpret one sensation in the light of others; it involves a deeper recess of the brain and is related to the personality itself. But all sensations have some such relationship. Two Chinese investigators who recognized that colour preference was an aspect of a coloured object, and that what one sees is not colour but colour in situation, asked their students to name the colours they preferred for such things as the wall of a house, an overcoat, a bed, a carpet, and so on. This reasonable approach showed that white was an easy winner.

In another experiment in America it was found that children from the countryside valued green more highly than did town children, and that white was more popular with girls than with boys because of its suitability for dress. This is enough to show that colour preferences often have a stronger social than physiological bias. The preference for white is a feature of Chinese society, not of the neural construction of a Chinaman, and experiments showing that North American Indians prefer red tell us more about North American Indian society than they do about any very significant built-in physical bias towards it in the individuals which compose that society. But none of this means that social values are the only ones involved.

7. *The Need for Criteria*

TO some extent the response to both drives and incentives is instinctive. The newly born child breathes because it is automatic to do so, not because he chooses to. He sucks on the same principle. A stimulus sets up in direct circuit a reaction. Many creatures are much better equipped than we are in this respect. The newly hatched water-fowl can swim straight from the shell; the newly born spider can act immediately and in every respect as competently as the adult spider and has nothing to learn about the responses he must make in order to survive. We, on the other hand, feel the drive, but have to be taught the response; for the first years of our lives we are dependent upon adults of our species.

If all stimuli automatically initiated their appropriate responses there would be no need of learning. Because our responses are not automatic we have to learn which are the appropriate ones. As we have to learn the appropriate responses, it is clear that inappropriate responses are possible. As we have to learn the right responses, it follows that it would be possible for us to learn the wrong ones. It is scarcely arguable that we often do. In a world of infinitely variable conditions the number of responses possible is infinitely variable. The life of the human being is one great complex response to a field of vastly involved stimuli. The more constant the world, the easier it is to learn suitable responses, for all situations will have been met frequently before and the answer to the puzzle game is known. The coelocanth, which has survived for so many million years, unchanged in form and habit, in the tepid waters off Madagascar, has solved its problem, because the problem has been without radical change since the coelocanth evolved its responses. The more variable the world the less possible is it to have a full repertoire of stock reactions to every situation which arises. For certain constant factors in our environment we have entirely adequate instinctive motor-reactions which do not involve our consciousness. We breathe and digest and void and adjust our body temperatures, within certain limits without conscious effort; only if conditions go beyond the norm do we take a conscious part in supplementing these reactions. We add oxygen cylinders, digestive pills, stomach pumps, and thermostatically controlled central-heating systems.

The extent to which our actions are no longer spontaneous varies a great deal from man to man. Clearly there are some whose lives pass from birth to death very nearly along a straight line of simple stimulus followed by simple response, a chain reaction from alpha to omega. To some extent the lives of all of us are on this plane; we are all at some time or another creatures of body; but we are also, most of us, at some time or another creatures of mind.

Because so much that is important in our lives is beyond the range of automatic reaction we are faced with interpreting the stimuli and choosing which of the possible responses we should make. Even worse than that, there are so many stimuli within our range that it is not simply a question of what responses we shall make to them but rather of which stimuli we should respond to at all. We have to assess their relative importance, to value them, to make some sort of qualitative judgements, even before we decide what detailed response it is best to make.

Once the exercise of choice became an essential part of man's existence it was necessary to establish criteria on which choice could be determined. Man's function as an individual, as a member of a family, as a member simultaneously of various not entirely compatible societies, each imposed upon him duties and needs of an increasingly contradictory kind, but from these varied functions criteria eventually emerged in the shape of customs and taboos which, coalescing into an obligatory pattern, became, with supernatural backing, formalized into religions. Standards of this kind, being the manifested will of a god or gods, satisfied so long as the contradictions between the various things which he in any one of his capacities recognized as 'good' and those things which the code ordained to be 'good' were resolved without too great a distortion; but if men in altered circumstances persisted in feeling to be good certain things which their previously established code laid down to be not good, a period of readjustment took place in which man was without a coherent pattern of choice-guiding principles. Such a period is upon us now.

Every choice implies an estimate of relative value. Brandy or liqueur? Guns or butter? Giotto or Gauguin? At the moment of choice we make a relative valuation which is true of that moment and that moment's need, but is perhaps true of no other. In a burning aeroplane at 10,000 feet a parachute is of more value than a Tintoretto.

If the purpose of perception (if purpose is the word) is firstly to enable the organism to deal with immediate problems and secondly to create ideas—complex quiescent energies which are then stored in the batteries of the mind and enable us to deal better with new situations as they arise—it would seem to follow that those sensations are best which perform both these functions. According to this line of thought it is the keen sensation that is most helpful if we have to react positively to it, and at the same time most likely to be the source of a distinct secondary idea which may be helpful in future.

Let the light be sufficient to disclose form; let the form be characteristic so that we recognize it; let the aspect from which we are to regard it be unmistakably apparent in the situation; let the reaction with which it is proper that we meet it be quite certainly known to us; given all this we should be happy. Less than this will cause doubt; more than this will be redundant. If this is true and is the whole truth, we can go on to say that, provided we do not encroach on the area of physical pain ('what if we do?' ask the masochists), all sensations which are intensely experienced are equally good, and all ideas in the creation of which we were most keenly aware are equally valuable. This argument is not negligible, but as it could end up by equating a patch of sunlight on a boiled egg with the Sistine Chapel or with dawn in the Himalayas, it would seem that other sources of value also may be involved. Our delight in the appearance of a sunlit egg is the delight which arises from the efficient performance of our physical functions. In so far as our idea of life may be bounded by physical functions this could well provide the sole criterion. With some other forms of life it does appear to be the sole criterion, but human beings who live largely in a world of secondary ideas, taking care for the morrow, have long believed that some ideas were good and some bad apart from the physical process that gave rise to them. If they have believed it there must have been some reason for them to do so, though not necessarily a good reason.

Although at first glance there appear to be many reasons why we regard some ideas as good and others as bad, they can usually be grouped together under three headings. The first of these, and the one that lies not far from the root of the other two, is the simple notion that an idea is bad if it leads to material consequences which are bad. Bad consequences are those that involve discomfort, pain, or death, without any compensating factors. Compensation takes place at a remove beyond the bad experience; an explorer endures hardship for the sake of the sense of achievement that lies beyond the mountain range; the patient endures pain in order to achieve health; the martyr endures death in order to obtain eternity; but in the absence of these or similar rewards, discomfort, pain and death, are bad, and the ideas which are likely to lead to our physical experience of these circumstances are bad also. It is bad to drive fast on the wrong side of the road; it is bad to drink methylated spirits; it is bad to disregard other people's feelings, and so on; and the ideas which encourage or permit such bad actions are bad ideas.

The second heading is the rather more difficult notion that an idea is bad when it leads to bad psychological results. To comprehend this we have to accept that the potential awareness which is the germ of 'us' has, by knocking about in a space full of objects out-there, built up into an entity which is the personality. The energy which we are has filled out and been given character by immersion in an ocean of percepts which it has soaked up and which have given it form. The principle of all being, animate and inanimate, is order. What we call the personality, psyche, or soul, is an ordered arrangement of awareness. By order we do not necessarily imply anything intelligent, consistent, appropriate, or good in any way at all, though these qualities may be present; we merely mean that anything, to exist, must have limits, for it is limitation which gives it form, and form it must have. Psychological pain is experienced when damage is being done to the personality, when it is being thrown out of form. The personality is a complex of tensions which is just as susceptible to damage as the physical body. When we experience psychological pain it is a warning that if the situation is allowed to continue the personality will cease to exist in its present form. The capacity of an idea to cause pain must depend upon the nature of the mind which receives the idea; some minds would scarcely react to a psychological avalanche while others could suffer irreparable damage from a misplaced semi-colon in a paragraph of Proust. By analogy with bodily pain a certain amount of psychological discomfort and near pain is tolerated in order that we shall be conscious of the limits of our being. These limits are vital to us, since it is they which give us form and it is in the maintaining of them that the tension of life consists. Similarly we may think it good to suffer a present psychological pain in order that subsequent greater damage may be avoided. A man may leave a woman he loves because he knows that, if he does not do so, more enduring pain, such as loss of self-respect, consciousness of distressing others, and so on, will follow. Or one may, knowing that the personality is becoming flaccid, or is losing all power of adaptation to changing circumstances, intentionally submit it to pain either with the intention of confirming its form or of modifying it. And lastly, as there are ascetics of the body who believe the spirit may be benefited by self-inflicted torment, so are there ascetics of the mind whose ultimate extension is the suicide of the personality. But some ideas, though not in themselves painful but perhaps the very reverse, we may know are passages leading either to bad physical or bad mental states. Whether we know this of ourselves, or have acquired the knowledge from the elders of our tribe, we regard such ideas with fear or aversion, barricading the dangerous path in every way we can. Conversely an idea, perhaps unpleasing in itself—for example, *pro patria mori*—may by sanctification become gratifying to the mind which has been trained to value it.

The third heading is a sympathetic extension of the other two; it depends upon the fact that an idea, neither painful because of its disturbing effect upon the mind, nor draped with taboos because of its undesired consequences, may still attract to itself by association values which do not in any way belong to it. One's attitude to a proposed currency reform might be coloured by having endured a harangue on the subject from a person with egg on his tie. Life faces us with the need to make so many value judgements that we are ready to make them on inadequate data.

In the main we conduct our lives in a haphazard way; they are really too complicated for us to do much else. We need a system of values in order to help us make decisions, but we are not too particular how we obtain our system nor very consistent in our application of it. Ideally we should, in order to make a choice, know the conditions of that choice; at some point we should determine what aspect of the object before us matters. This is self-evident when a great disparity of aspects is involved, as when we switched from regarding the Tintoretto as a work of art to considering it as a life-saving device; but unless we are made aware of the changed conditions of our choice we commonly employ inappropriate standards, as when we vote for a political candidate because he is handsome.

All objects potentially have many aspects. The same person may see the rose as a botanical specimen, as a source of visual pleasure, as an emblem of national pride, and as an object of commerce; but to do so he creates not one idea of the rose but several and he will then select that which he requires at any particular time, and according to the way it satisfies the demands of that situation he will value it. But his valuation of one of these ideas rose is liable to be touched by the value he has given to another. He may think the rose is visually pleasing when in fact his perception of it has only borrowed an aura of pleasure from its commercial value, or from his self-satisfaction in being able to identify it correctly. Art dealers are very prone to the first and connoisseurs to the second of these mis-transfers of values. As Henry James wrote in 1876 of the American purchase of Meissonier's *Friedland*: '. . . if a certain number of persons have been found to agree that such and such an enormous sum is a proper valuation of a picture, a book, or a song at a concert, it is very hard not to be rather touched with awe and to see a certain golden *reflet* in the performance. Indeed, if you do not see it, the object in question becomes perhaps still more impressive— as something too elevated and exquisite for your dull comprehension.' (Plate 36.)

Some sorts of ideas, though they may transfer their qualitative notions to other ideas, do not readily receive qualities in return. The rose-grower may think the rose beautiful because it is rare and because he can identify it, but the botanist is scarcely likely to give his idea of its identity a greater value because the colour has pleased his eye. His values depend, in so far as he is dealing with that particular idea rose which is his work, on accuracy and significance of classification, and because such qualities are readily assessed it is unlikely that irrelevant associated qualities will become attached to it. But as soon as he allows himself to admire the rose's appearance its position in his system is liable to tinge his admiration. The aesthetic idea in general is peculiarly susceptible to receiving value notions from other aspects.

We hate making choices. We are sick for certainty and search eagerly for signposts which will deliver us from doubt. It is the dislike of uncertainty which contributes so much to our instant judgement of appearances. If the object before us is familiar we know what reaction is required; there is no element of indecision, and the situation pleases us. It is likely to please us still more if the object is slightly unlike its counterparts, for then, although there is no personal indecision, we are conscious of our cleverness in having categorized the object correctly in spite of its deviations from the norm. If, on the other hand, the object before us differs materially from others to which we have been accustomed, may it not be that our old reactions will be inappropriate? We hesitate. We employ the old answer, uneasily aware that the new element is something substantial which we have not accounted for. A tension has been created, but not resolved.

38 Gazelle

39 A Malayan Tapir
Why do we think the gazelle beautiful, but not the tapir? Why did Hegel think the turbot ugly?

40 PELARGONIUM COTYLEDONIS

41 A PELARGONIUM *cultivar*

Plants of the same genus, in-breeding in isolated colonies, evolve very different characteristics. *P. cotyledonis* is found only on the island of St Helena.

V Kandinsky: Green Sound

We have strong notions of what appearances ought to be. These notions are based upon our experience of what they have usually been before, and they are, in part, socially conditioned. We have generalized our ideas of what roses are like and this generalized idea becomes what roses ought to be like. If they deviate from the norm in the direction of a slight exaggeration of some characteristic which we have been taught to admire, we may accept the deviation as an added beauty and will eventually adjust our idea 'rose' accordingly; if, however, the deviation is unexpected, if the mind is unprepared for the change because it is not merely a slight emphasis upon a valued tendency, but is so great as to represent a new form in old guise, we are shocked by it as by a caricature and instinctively dislike it until we absorb it into our pattern of what ought to be. Whether we do absorb it will depend on many factors, upon whether our intelligence approves it, or, perhaps, upon the utility of the new form, or upon our recognition of its potentiality as a starting-point for other new but desirable forms.

Fitness for purpose, or utility, is a criterion which can only properly be applied when our minds are set towards an object's function, but like other value judgements it can become transferred to the perceptive idea and attach itself to that. Because a machine fulfils its purpose with obvious efficiency there are those who believe it to be beautiful, but the beauty they see is not a beauty of form but of performance. This is the beauty of the guillotine. But to those who saw behind the smooth functioning of a machine to the blood-lust of the degraded mob it served, the guillotine was not beautiful in form but ugly. Yet neither the beauty nor the ugliness were inherent in the form, but were dependent upon which idea of the machine was dominant and how the mind was set towards it.

There is a similar, but not identical, source for the confusion which exists in our estimation of the relative beauty of animals.

Why do we think the gazelle beautiful but not the tapir? Why did Hegel think the turbot ugly? There was a cartoon many years ago which showed two humans looking through the bars of a cage at two hippopotami, the caption beneath read: 'How on earth can such creatures bear to reproduce themselves?' The point of the drawing was that one could not be sure whether it was the humans or the hippopotami who were speaking. Now, all these creatures, gazelles, tapirs, turbots, humans and hippos, have evolved through countless ages into the forms which we now behold and it is because of their fitness to survive that they have so evolved. Whether we consider that their purpose has dictated their form or their form their purpose is neither here nor there; their mere existence proves their fitness. But we do not regard their forms as equally engaging. (Plates 38, 39.)

This can be explained if we accept that all ideas, primary or secondary, are expressive; they express an attitude of us, their creators. The idea gazelle is agile, light, delicate, timid, vital, inaccessible, ethereal, grass-eating, young, and so on; the idea tapir is slow, heavy, clumsy, truculent, rooting, earthy, old, and gross. These first are very proper attributes of a gazelle, and the second are admirable characteristics for a tapir, but we do not regard these attributes from the point of view of gazelle and tapir, we regard them from our own point of view. Agility we admire in humans, clumsiness we do not; from our human aspect grass seems clean whereas roots are dirty, and the idea of digging for roots and grubs with our noses is not pleasant. The gazelle has attributes to which, if they occur in a human being, we are sympathetic, for they represent our own youth, therefore the form of the gazelle which expresses all this to us is sympathetic also; the tapir, on the other hand, expresses qualities which, while they would no doubt meet with approval from other tapirs, cannot do so from us, and our idea of the beauty of its form suffers accordingly.

Our pleasure in the form of these creatures cannot be dissociated from our knowledge that they are animals. Our minds are set to consider the gazelle as a gazelle and the tapir as a tapir. Any element of recognition implies 'set' and we cannot avoid it. Even a sunset, which has less of form and potential utility than most percepts and therefore demands little in the way of response from us, we see as a phenomen of light at play amongst the impurities of the air. Whatever type of sunset it may be we see it, and need to see it, as a sunset and not as the bloom on a decayed peach or a sore on a horse's withers, which, if we were not given an identifying sign, the flushing pinks and yellow might equally be.

The extreme contrary point of view was taken up by Benedetto Croce and expounded in uncompromising form by E. F. Carritt in *The Theory of Beauty*: 'Nothing has so stultified criticism and appreciation as the supposed necessity of first determining the genus and species of a beauty. To ask in face of a work of art whether it is a religious painting or a portrait, a problem play or a melodrama, post-cubist or pre-futurist, is as ingenuous a confession of aesthetic bankruptcy as to demand its title or its subject. The true motive of such a quest has always been the discovery of rules and canons which shall save us the trouble of a candid impression: for without rules there are no kinds and without kinds no rules.'

Now this, with all due respect to the distinction of the purveyors of it, is nonsense. Because the recognition of the nature of an object and its categorization leads frequently to a blurring of the act of perception and the production of ready-made, unfelt valuations, we can no more say that this is not an integral part of perception than we can deny that a knife-edge ridge is the only way up a mountain because most people fall off it. The problem is to get up the mountain without falling off. Not only is it not a 'confession of aesthetic bankruptcy' to know what one is supposed to be looking for, but it is a basic condition without which perception cannot take place at all. Plato was more nearly right when he wrote: 'A man who is to make no mistake of judgement about a particular production must, in every case, understand what that production is. If he does not understand what it is, that is, what it is meant for, or of what it is in fact an image, it will be a long time before he will discern the rightness or wrongness in the artist's purpose.' Croce's 'Every individual and every moment in the spiritual life of an individual has its own artistic world' is perhaps true, but his conclusion, 'and these worlds are artistically incompatible', is untrue; it would have been better if he had written 'and these worlds are indissolubly related', for then he would have maintained the integrity of the individual experience without trying to abandon the significance which experiences gain from their similarity to others. After all, the idea of categories of individuals is not a particularly difficult one; the danger lies in regarding the categories as real and the individuals as fictitious, whereas the truth is that individuals have a reality which is denied to categories, but which we can most easily approach to perceiving in terms of categories.

Because responses such as 'a turbot ought to look like this' are not instinctive but are learnt or acquired does not mean that they are less potent in our lives than those which are inborn. Many more men have fought and died for needs which they have learned from the societies of which they are members than have ever done so from instinctive reaction or from enlightened self-interest. There may be reasons for all the different codes of social behaviour we practise, but the reasons have no longer anything to do with our conformity to them: we do what we do largely because it is our custom, and it is our custom because we have watched other members of our society reacting to the situation in that particular way. According to the degree to which we make selections on personal grounds rather than as learnt responses we are individuals; if we make no personal responses but accept the values and the approved responses of our society without consideration we are members of a larger group, the herd. Because for the most part we accept many of the responses of our society and yet still do evolve other responses which are personal to ourselves we are semi-social animals involved in the sort of dilemma which all hybrid types must endure.

As values ultimately depend upon needs, a scheme of values can only arise from the needs of the personality that establishes it. The man who has formulated his need into some definable end-situation such as being President of Bongo-bongo, or of revenging himself upon an enemy, or of acquiring huge masses of currency, or of achieving sainthood, can value all other drives as subordinate to this. They will be good or bad for him in so far as they serve his end. Such single-mindedness is, fortunately, very rare. Most of us are not so simple; we are not driven by some huge deprivation to compensate ourselves by enormous achievement; we can, for the most part, satisfy the tapeworm of inferiority that gnaws at our vitals with small offerings of vanity. Our lives are more complicated, for we are by no means always sure which value ought to be subordinated to which; but life *is* complicated, and making a firm decision about priorities is by no means the same as making a right one. Bongo-bongo may turn to dust and ashes; and the annihilation of one's enemy could leave life empty; only the getting of wealth has the advantage that there need be no end to it, but this last, despite the satisfaction which it evidently confers, seems to stop short of being the path to happiness. Even those who have pursued with success the virtue of abstinence are reported to sit gnashing their teeth throughout all eternity for envy of the sins they refrained from committing.

What are most of us up to? What are our needs and our values? We sacrifice to God and Mammon. We live and earn our living. For some people these two activities are synonymous, for some they occasionally overlap, for many they are on opposite sides of the river. The way in which we combine them provides the pattern against which we establish our standard of values; sometimes we use one yardstick, sometimes another; we have many standards not one, and many values for the same object. Choice first enters the question, and with it value, when we decide which yardstick to use. The question is not 'Do we prefer this to that?' but 'Do we prefer this way of looking at it to that? Do we prefer this set of values to that?' And the answer to those questions is contained in our idea of the meaning of life.

8. The Personality in Situation

The taste of nations is different, as well in matters pertaining to the mind as in those of the body, and . . . just as . . . the Spaniards imagine and prefer a type of beauty quite different from that which we prize in France, and just as they desire their sweethearts to have a different figure, and features other than those we desire to see in ours, to such a degree that there are some men who will form an idea of their beauty from the same features that we should consider homely, just so, it must not be doubted that the minds of nations have preferences quite different from one another, and altogether dissimilar feelings for the beauty of intellectual things, such as poetry.

OGIER, Preface to *Tyre and Sidon*

JUST as it was not possible to consider the experience of hue abstractly but only in situation, for red and blue are always a red or blue *something* which has its existence *somewhere* and is perceived by *someone*, so also we cannot consider the responses of a human being as though he existed in a vacuum. Man is not a solitary animal. Among the environmental factors which help to mould his personality are other men. His dependence for mere survival upon the adults of his species throughout his earliest years reinforces in a hundred ways the similarities which he inherited. The desire of parents is to teach; in this way they progressively free themselves from the responsibilities and anxieties of their child's reliance on them. The desire of the child is to learn and to gain freedom of action; this he achieves largely by imitation so that the world of ideas which he constructs coincides at many places with the idea-world of his father, his brothers, and, eventually, of his sons. But man does not limit himself to imitation; among the many contradictions of his nature are the opposed principles of conformity and rebellion, of imitation and initiation, of security and danger. Because of this, although man is a gregarious animal, he is not a fully gregarious animal; the herd is part of his background and he is partly, but not exclusively, the product of it.

The instinct for imitation is the foundation upon which the collective behaviour of the family, the tribal unit, the nation, or the social class, is based. Formed, as it were accidentally, by the necessities of man's long vulnerable childhood, collective behaviour is retained and fostered as a form of primitive defence and becomes not merely a pattern outside the individual to which he conforms, but a part of the individual personality itself, rather in the same way as the unborn child which, though an entity, is not yet an independent entity, but one in which the life is fed by its mother's life, and is linked to her as the perambulating astronaut is linked to his space-craft. In more advanced societies the strength of the corporate pattern progressively decays, although it is increasingly pursued as a virtue in reactionary, newly emerged, and otherwise insecure communities. Such steps as the protecting of national flags from insult by law are designed to create a common loyalty and strengthen the corporate pattern. A piece of coloured cloth becomes a tribal token; respect for it is common ground in the society; it exists as a unifying principle in peace, and a rallying-point in war; it is treated as though it were a sentient entity until it forms a homing-point for man's instinct towards reverence, loyalty and self-immolation, attitudes inculcated by adults in order to facilitate the transference of their responsibility for their young to the young themselves. In the most primitive societies the crudest forms of aesthetic activity serve in the same way to cement the community. At a technical level the musical rhythm of the tribal dance exercises members of the tribe in concerted warlike action, while at the psychological level it helps to create a common feeling and purpose, and reinforces the compulsion to conform to the pattern.

The habit of acting in unison with our neighbours serves also the animal principle of protective colouration which we have already discussed. The member of the herd finds his security in being anonymous; when sheep are attacked by wolves it is the straggler, the outlier, the vagrant of the flock that is most vulnerable. The collective principle is the refuge of the weak. The great carnivores do not hunt in packs, only some wolves and jackals do so.

But human life also acts upon principles which work in an opposite sense. There is the drive to differentiate, to distinguish, and to compete, as well as to cohere, to conform, and to combine. Biologically, differentiation is the path of development, of natural selection, whereas conformity is a point of biological rest. There is no absolute value involved here. Development is not essentially more desirable than stagnation. The nineteenth-century discovery of evolution was seized upon avidly by most thinkers and has left as its aftermath the widely held conviction that change is not only inevitable but desirable. This is equivalent to a belief that it does not matter where you go so long as you go somewhere: a point of view which loses sight of the other aspect of the evolutionary discovery, the notion of natural selection, the survival of those that are fittest to survive. Biologically, unless there is need for change, evolutionary development is irrelevant. While change, or imbalance, exists, evolution serves as the method by which life carries out the essential process of adaptation to changed circumstances. In a world of sudden and violent change a form of life which is able to evolve satisfactory responses is obviously superior to one that is not.

The most fruitful cultures of life are therefore those which combine both principles; man has done this to a remarkable degree, and among men those societies which have been most successful in adjusting the two principles, of harnessing the individual to the team and of resolving the team into individuals, are those which have combined the greatest degree of stability with an adequate degree of adaptability. They have evolved the strength to maintain those territories of consciousness which have been won and have balanced it with the flexibility to adapt themselves to those changes in the environment which might otherwise make the *status quo* inappropriate. It is often pointed out that those great conservative societies, China and Egypt, failed to survive because they could not adjust themselves to changing circumstances; it is less often pointed out that they survived longer than any others. The Commandment *Honour thy father and thy mother that thy days may be long in the land* was not a pious hope but the record of an observed fact and the justification of essentially traditional societies.

Within communities the pattern of behaviour to which the individual is liable to find himself involuntarily conforming is, therefore, not a simple one. We are at the same time called upon to uphold the *status quo* and to destroy it, to conform and to rebel, and in neither case are our actions entirely independent of communal values, nor yet entirely dependent on them.

A fascinating series of experiments, which shows how values are the product of situation, was carried out with hens some years ago in America. A hungry hen with a heap of grain in front of her will eat a certain quantity and then stop, presumably because the hunger that drove her to eat is satisfied. But apparently if the food that is left is removed and immediately replaced the hen will, although previously satisfied, be stimulated to eat again. The removal, replacement, and recommencement of eating was repeated eight times. This is the result of a simple circular reaction such as that which makes a baby repeat 'Ma': hunger is associated with food and the action of eating it; food is necessarily, therefore, associated with eating and the sensation of hunger. The reappearance of the food in front of the satisfied fowl is a new event and wakes an echo of dissatisfaction. She eats and soon quietens the echo. After the eighth course even the echo has been stilled. The satisfaction of these pseudo-drives has a physical limit or the hen will burst. A further experiment showed that when a hen was offered a heap of 100 grains of wheat she habitually ate fifty; but that if a substantially larger heap were offered to her she might eat up to fifty more.

In both these experiments the element of incentive seems at first sight to have exceeded the element of drive, but what may have happened is that the incentive alerts and activates a residual unsatisfied drive which normally would be tolerated by the hens. Perhaps, after all, the satisfied hen was not really as satisfied as she believed? When we sit down to a particularly impressive meal we generally eat more than we do on normal occasions; the sight of excellent food in quantities stirs the appetite and makes a healthy organism feel the drive of a hunger which it had previously, perhaps, not suspected. The marginal area of safety which lies between satisfaction and discomfort and which contains the stage of repletion is brought into use by the presence of exceptional quantities of food.

The sort of behaviour described here depends merely on the individual and the presence of food, but it can also follow from a social stimulus. When, having finished a meal and not yet left the table, a friend comes in late and starts eating, we feel the re-stimulated pangs of hunger although we were previously satisfied, and we begin to eat again. Hens behave in the same way. If a satisfied hen is gazing lethargically at her heap of corn and a hungry hen is introduced, the well-fed hen will recommence eating at once. If two hungry hens are introduced she will eat even more, and if three, she will eat more still. But this result does not follow unless the hungry hens are superior to her in the pecking order. If she is the dominant character she will attempt to keep them from eating and chase them away. However, should our hungry hen be introduced to the company of three replete hens she will eat, but they will not. The social influence of majority behaviour or of superior social example are well known to commercial advertisers and we should not ignore the extent to which they may operate in the most sophisticated of us. Collectors know that in the Sale-room the presence of competitors will often increase the desire for possession well beyond that which they would have experienced had they had the field to themselves. We are like the sailor who, finding his bride a virgin, abjured her, saying, 'If nobody else wants you I'm sure I don't.' Sale-room prices, we all know, are rarely related to the excellence of the objects purchased, but if these hidden social patterns of behaviour can betray us into false judgements there, it is reasonable to suppose that the same patterns will be at work helping to formulate our likes and dislikes, our appetite for corn, even in our solitary moments. It is possible, but not always easy, to admire what all the world scorns, or to scorn what all the world admires; if everyone else adds two to two and makes four it seems idiosyncratic, to say the least, if we persistently make five. But these patterns will be the less compulsive with us according to the degree to which we are accustomed to make conscious judgements rather than to accept the formulae of our society. It is as easy to cultivate habits of nonconformity as it is to cultivate habits of conformity; it is possible, but more difficult, to cultivate the habit of individual judgement in which accepted corporate reactions are one only amongst the factors involved.

The subordination of the individual personality to patterns can either be felt as a sublimation or a degradation according to the need of the personality. It is at this point that the will enters and we elect to throw into the scales our personal weight, which at heart we believe may tip the forces of evolution this way or that, establishing the pattern of futurity for ever. For whether we may reasonably hope to influence the outcome or not there is a deep-laid conviction that there is, not an expedient, but a right side, and that when the time comes, whether it prevails or not, we may be found to have been fighting, however ineffectually, to maintain it; or, at the least, if this notion is fanciful, that we shall derive from our efforts in this direction a personal satisfaction more enduring than most. But if we reject the 'corporate' ideal of whatever sort it does not mean that we deny the interaction

42 *The Hermaphrodite, Museo delle Terme*

A picture will lose its essential quality as a work of art if we look at it as the instigator of an activity that goes beyond the picture itself; but the opposite view, that we should be cold to the subject in order to appreciate a picture, is nonsense and would turn us into aloof Epicurean eunuchs.

43 VELASQUEZ: *The Rokeby Venus*

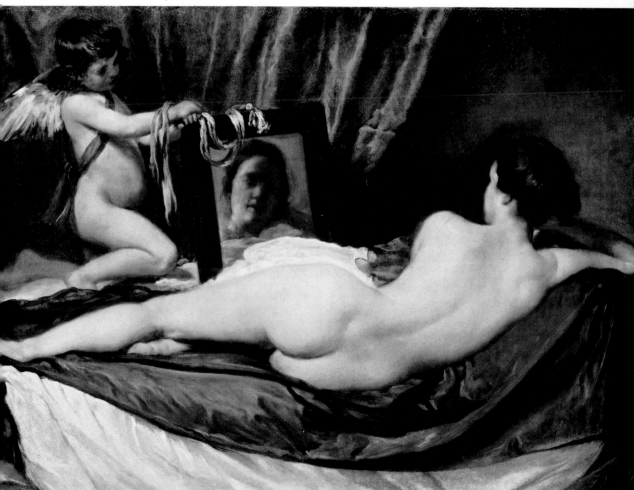

44 VINCENT VAN GOGH: *The Chair*

45 JUAN GRIS: *A Chair*

'I spent several minutes . . . being my Not-self in the Not-self which was the Chair.' Aldous Huxley

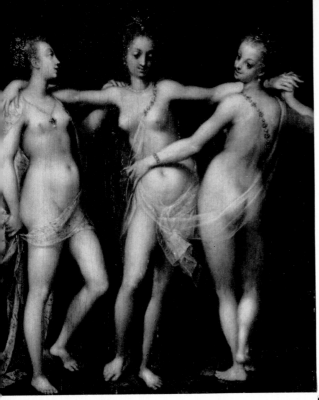

46 JOSEPH HEINZ THE ELDER: *The Three Graces*
'. . . the Spaniards imagine and prefer a type of beauty
quite different from that which we prize in France, and
just as they desire their sweethearts to have a different
figure, and features other than those we desire to see in
ours, to such a degree . . . there are some men who
will form an idea of their beauty from the same
features that we should consider homely . . .' Ogier

47 P. P. RUBENS: *Mars and Venus*
'That most outrageous demon, Rubens.'
Samuel Palmer

of individuals or the effect upon individuals of the corporate attitudes of groups. The question now rather is how do group attitudes arise and how is our happiness served by them; to what extent are they responsible for our liking for certain forms and for that flow of favour and disfavour which we call fashion; and does the recognition of corporate attitudes have any bearing on the ultimate question 'What is good?'

Every perceived form is a unique experience, but the human mind groups and classifies these experiences for ease of understanding them. The understanding of anything unknown is no more than the making of relationships between that thing and other things which have assumed the character of fixed points because of the observed constancy of their behaviour. Thus all observed life is like a great network, a spider's web which we have spun from salient point to salient point, and upon which our consciousness scurries about its business. This perilous tight-rope world exists in many dimensions and each fresh relationship increases its complexity and increases at the same time, if the new relationship confirms the pattern of the web, both its stability and its completeness. If follows that everything is capable of belonging at the same time to several groups and, according to the delimiting effect of the overlapping of these groups, the object acquires a more acute identity. For example the object out-there which is represented in Plate 8 is essentially unique and unknowable, and if we stop our reaction to the object at that point (the point at which Croce and Carritt wished us to stop it) we shall be able, in theory, to enjoy the experience of unencumbered sensations, but the process of perception initiates the process of classification, and our mind passes instantly from the bare sensation to the stage of classifying the sensation: it is a picture, an easel picture, an ornament, a two-dimensional image of a three-dimensional idea, an oil painting, and so on until amongst the classifications which our interest in such objects enables us to make is the fact that it is an English painting of the mid-nineteenth century.

If we are able to make a mental grouping or classification of this last sort it implies that the object has certain characteristics which are in their total effect peculiar to England and the nineteenth century. In practice we know very well that the more we have trained our sensibility by using it, and the more we have sharpened our intelligence by informing it, the more easy it is to say of objects we have never seen before that this is Japanese, this is Tibetan, this French, this Dutch, this German, this of the Ibo tribe, this Spanish, and so on. A few bars of music never heard before announce themselves to be Italian, German, Polish, even to an inadequately trained musical ear. In other words we are able to detect, though we may not be able to say from what feature it depends, a consistency of national character which pervades the form and which, despite an enormous degree of variation, is still discoverable in the most diverse activities of a social group and which can persist, not only throughout a considerable territory, but over great periods of time.

Groups of human beings, families, clans, tribes, nations, ethnic groups, have as their theoretical beginning a mating couple. The couple is a group composed of two individuals whose capacities and potentialities are diverse. From these spring the family which individualizes the variations in diversity which are inherent in the parents' joint potential, but which collectively are limited by that potential. Couples with black faces produce black children, couples with dirty pink faces produce children with dirty pink faces, couples with almond eyes have offspring with almond eyes, parents with long legs will produce children with long legs, dwarfs will give birth to dwarfs, a couple with small brains will produce children with small brains—were it not so we might as well sit down and wait for a couple of donkeys to produce a prize race-horse instead of carefully selecting our breeding strains to that end.

The common origin of the racial strain is one possible source of a family likeness of preferred forms in any social group. Heinrich Wölfflin, for example, was clear that there was an essential Italian quality of life and art which was due to an inherited bias based upon psychological premises. He seized upon certain qualities underlying Italian art and contrasted the attitude of mind these qualities evinced with other attitudes which he found to be characteristic of the German national temperament. The basis for the Italian concept of form was, he held, in the national feeling of the race for the body and for movement: 'With all its vivacity the Italian gesture is realized easily and effortlessly. The way a man leans against the door-jamb of a house, the way a woman lifts a jug from a well—these things look different in the South than in the North.' The basis of Italian pictorial art, as well as of architecture, is a highly developed appreciation of the body in terms of its proportions and possibilities of equilibrium, and Wölfflin believed that it was futile to work for the effect of Italian proportions in art as long as one did not have an Italian body. In effect he believed that Italian art arose from a racially different bodily organization, in which the entire body becomes gesture.

But only in societies which have been isolated for a considerable time is there a really consistent conformity to type in the species. In long-closed communities one may expect an inherent bias towards a certain type of person. When bodily conformations are similar it is reasonable to suppose that mental potential and psychic form will also have common characteristics. Where imbalances are in the same general direction, needs will be of the same general kind and tastes will not materially differ. Botanically the isolated communities of a genus steadily grow more and more like each other and less and less like other communities elsewhere in the world. For example, *Pelargonium cotyledonis*, which has evolved through countless ages in the isolated island of St Helena, is in many respects quite unlike any other member of that far-flung genus. (Plates 40, 41.) Amongst men the bushmen of Australia and of the Kalahari have become in their isolated habitats so stable that they have preserved virtually unchanged a neolithic culture for, perhaps, 20,000 years. Amongst such tribes not only does a flint arrow-head from year to year, from century to century, from aeon to aeon, remain a flint arrow-head constant in form, unchanged by fashion (for the forms of practical things such as weapons we expect to be dictated directly by needs), but such ornament as exists among them has remained equally constant; inherited propensity, reinforced by every form of communal pressure, has produced a homogeneous and unvarying culture.

High among the circumstances which create similarity within a community are the climate and the terrain in which the community lives, for these are essential ingredients of the 'situation' which controls the values of the individual. John Opie, in a lecture to the Royal Academy, chided 'a set of good-natured continental philosophers, who, confining taste to certain parallels, discover the genius of nations by a map and a pair of compasses, and wisely determine that no country, situated in a higher latitude than fifty degrees north, can succeed in the cultivation of the arts'. The theory of climatic control of culture has, like most theories, at times been carried too far, but its influence on the forms the culture takes, if not on the quality of that culture, is certainly great. The difficulty of maintaining life at all in certain areas—in the Amazon forest, in Antarctica, in the Asian tundra—is sufficient to employ all a man's energy and time to meet the challenge with an adequate response without allowing any excess from which the arts can be fashioned. Those tribes that live on the very fringe of habitable land develop necessary skills but few arts. As soon, however, as the conditions permit man to relax in his battle for survival he begins to employ his liberated energy on ornamentation and on the realization of ideas. The Esquimaux carves his whalebone and constructs his strangely assembled masks; the bushman paints the wall of his cave. In the one case the art springs directly from the aquatic economy which originated and still sustains the Esquimaux society; in the other it was an inherited fossil from the much earlier art of Stone Age hunting communities. Originally the direction of development was indicated by the way of life of the societies concerned, by the materials available to them and, ultimately, because both economy and materials arise from this, by the climate in the lands where the way of life originated.

At the beginning of his Italian journey Goethe wrote of the strange elation he experienced there: 'The soul expands; man feels himself to be somehow transfigured and has a sense of a freer life, a loftier existence, of ease and grace.' What was, or rather what is, for few people of European culture on entering Italy have failed to feel it, the source of this euphoria? Does it lie within oneself in the way that obviously it did with Goethe, in the fulfilment of a personal longing which had become identified in him not only with the spiritual ambience but the physical presence of Italy? Even Wölfflin, trying to prove his thesis of the importance of racial types, had to confess that plastic style implied a specific view of the world, a view which would inevitably to some extent be dependent upon and arise from the sort of world that was seen. The mood of a land, the quality of its air, the rhythm of its

seasons, the structure of its geology, unite to form a personality which is inevitably im-
printed on the people who dwell in it.

In all relatively homogeneous societies there is a circular flow of influences. A family, a
group of individuals of disparate innate capacities, by the community of their living evolve
a common manner of play; this in turn emphasizes the distinctive feature of the group
and binds them closer together by reason of their unlikeness to similar but disassociated
groups. Art at this stage, by a process of inbreeding, stabilizes its forms and, by limiting
them, stabilizes also the personalities of the members of the group.

This state of affairs, so beneficial to the individual in that it provides him with ready-
made points of reference for the construction and maintenance of his personality, is further
emphasized by the natural hieratic organization of the basic form of society. The child
learns the language of forms which his parents teach him; he accepts it on the authority of
those on whom he is dependent. His parents learned it in turn from theirs; and the child
on all sides finds himself surrounded by others of his kind whom he can understand, and
with whom he feels the security of limitations held in common. As the community widens
from the original family unit to the tribe or clan, so the mystique of parenthood becomes
extended to the elders of the tribe and in particular to the dominant personality in it. The
limitations which the chief imposes and maintains are his contribution to the well-being of
the society, and at his disposal for this purpose he finds as tools the traditional forms of the
society over which he rules and which he, as leader, has in his safe keeping. An innovating
leader destroys the psychological defences of his people. He may intend to reconstruct
them in a new form, but by his action he imperils their personalities and he does so at his
own peril.

The principal means by which societies ensure uniformity of conduct is by establishing
and maintaining what we may call Grand Universal Principles of Value. These are the
axiomatic, but often theoretic, moral foundations of the community, more honoured perhaps in the breach than in the observance, but providing a standard from which other
courses may be seen to deviate. To a considerable extent these standards are the common
property of most communities but, because we believe them to be absolute and of the
essence of human life, we are not always quick to recognize when they have no existence in
certain alien groups, or when the words which we translate as truth or honour or loyalty
or courtesy do not have in the original tongue the force, or even the general application, that
we have become accustomed to give them. These words, as representing ideal standards of
behaviour—but which we very well know, if we stop to consider them which we rarely do, are
only ideals because we conceive of them out of situation, but which in the normal commerce
of life have not by any means the universal application which we pretend to accord to them
—are like coloured lights in a room which lend their hue to all objects within reach, flattering
some and belittling others. These Grand Standards of Value, because they are so deeply

involved in our most serious theoretic judgements, and also because we so little understand them, their meaning, their application, or their origin, we rush to and use as a yardstick whenever more mundane or material criteria fail us or seem to be inadequate to the emotion we are experiencing. Truth, of which in the main we are very ill-equipped judges, is, for example, a common form of praise. We say that a line is true, that tonal values are true, that a picture is true to nature or, if this seems too defined and circumscribed in its application to express the inexpressible something which we are searching to say, we refer meaningly to the *honesty* of the vision, the *integrity* of the conception.

It is by their attitude to these basic values, by the relative importance which they give them, and by the extent to which it is their custom actually to employ them as values in everyday life, that societies acquire their peculiar bias towards certain excellencies and their apparent disregard for others. There is no compassion in Mexican pre-conquest art, for pity was not a virtue to the cruel Aztec gods. Chastity is not a characteristic of Hindu sculpture, for the lascivious line of a beguiling woman is to the Hindu symbolic of the physical and religious ecstasy that lies at the heart of life. Coarse and common materials were not admired at Byzantium, for poverty was ill-reputed in that particular form of urban Christianity, whereas among the Buddhists of Japan not only were vulgar materials greatly esteemed but the very work that went into their most precious tea-bowls was self-consciously calculated to express poverty, incompetence and humility. It is the moral attitude, the ideals of a nation, which provide those qualities which are evident in the most important work of that nation. It is the standards which are derived from their ideals which colour in one way or another all their activities.

Stable communities which have been evolved fairly simply out of the demands made by local environment upon inherited characteristics are, though still common, becoming daily less so, and are nowhere dominant in the world today. The societies in which we live and of which we are the product are, and have been, throughout all that period which we loosely call historic time, to a great extent heterogeneous, unstable and genetically unresolved. That, in fact, is what history is . . . the account of a genus in disequilibrium working towards a solution.

Our simplified description of the working of culture in society is broadly true of simple societies which circumstances have allowed to stabilize into near homogeneity, but most societies are far more complex than this and contain within themselves the rudiments of alien cultures which have been only partially absorbed. They are like children of disparate parents: some take largely after one, some after the other, whilst yet others, combining in a new way some of the capacities of both, are a hybrid form of totally different potential. In such societies the structure is dynamically stressed. There exist stratifications which are hieratic in character, as when a conquering people are perpetuated in the form of an inheriting aristocracy; and there are also vertical stratifications, as when several peoples of differing cultures have combined in the equivalent of a federal community.

Communal attitudes are identifiable though they are rarely purely national and never, perhaps, purely racial. It is easy to find, if we look at the scene from a great enough distance, types which transcend national divisions. For example, the Gothic culture of medieval Christendom was evidence of a wider cultural than national unity; and we readily recognize that European, African and Asiatic arts possess common features peculiar to their continental groups.

In a similar way, by looking more closely at the evidences of so-called national characteristics, we can split national types into smaller and smaller units, units based not only on locality, as when we speak of Florentine, Neapolitan, Venetian painting, or Prussian, Saxon, or Bavarian carving, but on religious beliefs, economic strata, traditional schools, and families, so that in place of the simple picture of Italian culture, or German culture, or Chinese culture, we are well aware that the unitary effects of the wholes are a simplification (though with its own truth) across which there is a network of alternative relationships not only within the national units but beyond them, and that it is within this all-embracing framework that the individual human spirit can seek its cultural associations.

Diversity of parents, and diversity of cultural associations, makes for a considerably increased diversity amongst their offspring. This potentiality to diversity in the second generation conflicts with social pressures towards conformity, and according to the relative strength of the two forces the direction of the development is determined. It may very well be that the individuals who compose the limited neolithic societies of the twentieth century have a potential very much less limited than it appears, but the important fact is that while they remain units of their closely knit communities they have every reason to develop that potential only in the direction and only to the extent which every other member of that community does. In the heterogeneous society on the other hand, there is not only a far greater variation of potential, owing to the absence of inherited limitations in common, but there is also a great measure of disagreement about the direction in which the potential should be exploited.

In fact, nobody can be said to have developed all his potentialities to the full, indeed it is not possible. The most highly trained individual with long legs may leap as high as it is physically and psychologically possible for him to leap, but most possessors of long legs, even if dedicated athletes, do not ever succeed in reaching their potential limits; with other training, other food, other mental attitudes, other climatic conditions, the man who can jump six feet might perhaps jump seven. Nor is it probable if such a man should devote himself to reaching his limit in one direction that he would also reach his limit in others. If he exploits the potential of his legs in leaping he will certainly not be able to exploit them as efficient instruments for swimming, and it is more than probable that his brain will be far from as fully developed as it had the capacity to be. We are therefore, all of us, in some respects—probably in many, perhaps in all—living far within our powers. Heredity may give us the capacity to leap seven feet, environmental factors and congenital predisposition will determine whether we in fact develop that capacity or do not leap at all. But no amount of adjustment of our environment (short of a move to the moon) will enable us to leap seventy feet. You cannot make a silk purse out of a sow's ear. By and large, the human species has a fairly constant potential if we view it through the wrong end of a telescope; it has a very variable potential if we look at it through a microscope. Both are perfectly legitimate ways of viewing the species; each is utterly misleading if it is employed as the only way.

It is not the potential alone, for that is never fulfilled, but the direction in which it is developed which is significant in giving a common character to groups of people. The way in which potential is developed depends on many factors, but not least on the considered choices of gifted individuals within the groups.

9. *The Ecstasy of Uninvolvement*

What is it that attracts the eyes of those who behold a beautiful object, and calls them, lures them towards it, and fills them with joy at the sight? . . .

PLOTINUS, *Enneads*, 1, 6, 1
(ed. Henry and Schwezzer, 1951)

OUR bodies contain a mechanism of chemical control in the form of glands which release hormones into the blood-stream. These hormones, according to their chemical composition, have the effect of making the nervous and muscular tissue more or less sensitive. It is easy to see that a stimulus which results in the secretion of a sensitizing hormone will lead to greater awareness of life, whereas if it results in secretion of hormones of an opposite type it will have a devitalizing effect.

The main function of the thyroid gland is to aid in the changing of the tissues of the body, the continual destruction and ultimate elimination of some and the reconstruction of others. If the gland is insufficiently active the waste products, the partially decomposed proteins, are retained in the tissues and the whole process of metabolism is slowed down. Those who suffer from an inactive thyroid become lethargic; they tire easily and are easily depressed, their blood pressure falls. But here, too, there is a healthy level of activity which, while it must be attained if we are to have a sense of well-being, must not be exceeded. If the thyroid is overactive the change of body tissue is hurried; the result is nervous tension and restlessness and excitability.

The thyroid gland is balanced by the parathyroid which functions in a reverse sense and acts rather like a retro-rocket, ensuring equilibrium. The mechanism by which the parathyroid gains its end is the control of the calcium balance in the body. If we have too little calcium in the blood-stream our nerves and muscles become too sensitive and we are overexcitable. If the parathyroid is overactive and provides an excess of calcium we become temperamentally quiet and slow.

If awareness of life is one of our great ends it would not seem unreasonable to encourage a little overactivity of the thyroid and a little underactivity of the parathyroid. The trouble is that oversensitizing the tissues, though it creates its own particular pleasure of excitement, has also unpleasing consequences. The response mechanism becomes disproportionately active and a need for response is simulated which is not related to what the situation calls

VI John Ferneley: *Portrait of Mr Stanley Standish*

for: we feel the urge to leap six feet when one would be enough. Those of us who by nature suffer from over-reacting know not only that life can be vivid but that it can also be nervously exhausting, and we also know the extent to which our vivacity can unbalance our judgement.

In 1954 Aldous Huxley published *The Doors of Perception*. It is an account of how under supervision he took four-tenths of a gramme of the drug mescalin, of his experiences while under the influence of the drug, and the conclusions he drew from them. Mescalin is the active principle of pyotl, the root of a cactus which has long been consumed by the Indians of Mexico and the South-western United States on account of the satisfactory mental states which it induces. Huxley summarized the peculiarities of the states of the majority of those who had taken mescalin under supervision, as follows:

(1) The ability to remember and to 'think straight' is little if at all reduced . . .

(2) Visual impressions are greatly intensified and the eye recovers some of the perceptual innocence of childhood, when the sensum was not immediately and automatically subordinated to the concept. Interest in space is diminished and interest in time falls almost to zero.

(3) Though the intellect remains unimpaired and though perception is enormously improved, the will suffers a profound change for the worse. The mescalin-taker sees no reason for doing anything in particular and finds most of the causes for which, at ordinary times, he was prepared to act and suffer, profoundly uninteresting. He can't be bothered with them, for the good reason that he has better things to think about.

(4) These better things may be experienced . . . 'out-there', or 'in-here', or in both worlds, the inner and the outer, simultaneously or successively. That they *are* better seems to be self-evident to all mescalin-takers who come to the drug with a sound liver and an untroubled mind.

Huxley's own experience tallied with this, although it is by no means certain that everyone would react to the drug as he did.

The immediate cause of such experiences appears to be an interruption to that normal chain of reaction whereby waves of energy striking the eye become visual sensations which are then interpreted as objective phenomena, are recognized, and appropriately reacted to. The brain, in which the most critical of these activities takes place, requires a constant supply of glucose which is provided by the work of certain enzymes; mescalin inhibits the production of these enzymes, and lowers the amount of glucose available to the brain cells.

If we remember that vision is a purposeful process involving certain identifiable stages, that the sensation of hue attracts our attention, that we then distinguish, chiefly by differentiating brightness, the form which the sensation takes, and that finally we relate the form to our previous experience and initiate the appropriate action, it becomes clear that anything less than the full circuit leaves the act of vision partial. A natural conclusion to draw would be that if some stage of vision were left out there would be a tension unresolved followed by a sense of incompleteness or of frustration. Instead it seems that sometimes we can very well do without certain stages and suffer no nervous discomfort from their absence. Hue, for example, is so little a loss that some people never see it at all and most people see it in a very superficial and rudimentary fashion, and we are all doing without it on this page. We are much more rarely called upon to see without distinction of brightness, but when we are, as for example in the work of some modern artists, we are soon able to accommodate ourselves to the shallowness of vision that results and some people quite clearly do not feel it as an inadequacy at all.

These are matters of common experience, but what particularly concerns us with Huxley's mescalin experiment is the actual stage of our chain reaction to observed phenomena which drops out when sugar becomes short. The visual sensation is there, apparently greatly increased in intensity; the power to recognize is there—no one suggested that they were no longer able to say what objects were; the ability to remember is unimpaired, as indeed it would have to be if objects were still recognizable, for recognition is only memory; the power to think, or to arrange ideas in order and to deduce other ideas from them, was not diminished. All of this is the same, but all appear in unusual proportions because of the removal of the sense of responsibility, the absence of the feeling that some reaction is demanded from us. With this conspicuous absentee, the slave-master who stands by our side at each moment of the day saying *Do this*, *Do that*, is also gone any serious interest in time and space; the mescalin-taker perceives them indeed, but they are now percepts only, forms taken by hue and brightness, their urgency has gone; time has become a eunuch and space an irrelevance.

Before we consider the wider applications of this we must notice the effect on all that remains. The object is still 'out-there', unknowable to us, nothing can alter that; but that which is knowable to us, the sensations that we derive from the physical being of that object, have thrown off the old-man-of-the-sea that sat upon their shoulders, giving them purpose and taking from them almost everything but purpose, and has left them, as representations of the object 'out-there', an extraordinary significance. The object is. What it was is nothing. What it is to become is nothing. Its 'is-ness' is everything. We remember it, we recognize it, but what we remember it to be, what we recognize that it is, does not appear to matter, so absorbed are we in our sensation of seeing it. But it is not truly the object's being that delights us, it is our being that delights us.

There were in a glass vase on Huxley's desk three flowers, a shell-pink rose, a magenta and cream-coloured carnation, and a pale purple iris. 'At breakfast that morning I had been struck by the lively dissonance of its colour. But that was no longer the point . . . I was seeing what Adam had seen on the morning of his creation—the miracle moment by moment of naked existence . . . "Is-ness". The Being of Platonic Philosophy—except that Plato seems to have made the enormous, the grotesque mistake of separating Being from becoming, and identifying it with the mathematical abstraction of the Idea. He could never, poor fellow, have seen a bunch of flowers shining with their own inner light and all but quivering under the pressure of the significance with which they were charged; and could never have perceived that what rose and iris and carnation so intensely signified was nothing more, and nothing less, than what they were—a transience that was yet eternal life, a perpetual persisting that was at the same time pure Being, a bundle of minute, unique particulars in which, by some unspeakable and yet self-evident paradox, was to be seen the divine source of all existence.

'I continued to look at the flowers, and in their living light I seemed to detect the qualitative equivalent of breathing—but of a breathing without returns to a starting-point, with no recurrent ebbs but only a repeated flow from beauty to heightened beauty, from deeper to ever deeper meaning. Words like Grace and Transfiguration came to my mind, and this of course was what, among other things, they stood for.'

This is very impressive, but before conclusions are drawn too confidently there are questions that need to be answered which do not seem to have been asked. To what extent was this intensified perception due to the novelty of a rearrangement of the mental process? If one became used to seeing three flowers in a vase whilst under the influence of mescalin, for how long would they maintain their singular significance? Was not the experience of the flowers so portentous chiefly because it was in such sharp contrast to normal experience? Did it depend at all on the fact that Huxley was nearly blind and did not normally see as we see? Might not the vision of the flowers as Grace and Transfiguration eventually, like the flowers themselves, fade if one became familiar with it, or could it be made to continue by maintaining the drugged state? One would also like to know if there were any regret at leaving these glorious perceptions, if it were hard to drag oneself away. And how about affection and gratitude? Do these warm human aberrations survive the change in the mind's behaviour, or do they too, go with space, time, and responsibility, out into cold storage while the religious ecstasy of perception reigns?

Again, one has, it appears, no responsibility towards these objects; they are felt as sensations only, but—and this is what is so curious—they do not appear to be only sensations, but recognizable sensations; they may have seemed to Huxley as sensum no longer overwhelmed by concept, but concept was still there.

Was everything perceived of equal significance? We know that a chair, a shelf of books, and these flowers, acquired an intensity of being that was like a spiritual experience, but was there anything that was not transfigured, or of which the vision seemed to signify less? The answer apparently was 'Yes'. 'Place and distance cease to be of much interest. The mind does its perceiving in terms of intensity of existence, profundity of significance, relationship within a pattern. I saw the books, but was not at all concerned with their positions in space. What I noticed, what impressed itself upon my mind was the fact that all of them glowed with living light and that in some the glory was more manifest than in others . . . A small typing-table stood in the centre of the room; beyond it, from my point of view, was a wicker chair and beyond that a desk. The three pieces formed an intricate pattern of horizontals, uprights and diagonals—a pattern all the more interesting for not being interpreted in terms of spatial relationships. Table, chair, and desk came together in a composition that was something by Braque or Juan Gris, a still life recognizably related to the objective world, but rendered without depth, without any attempt at photographic realism. I was looking at my furniture, not as the utilitarian who has to sit on chairs, to write at desks and tables and not as the camera-man or scientific recorder, but as the pure aesthete whose concern is only with forms and their relationships within the field of vision or the picture space. But, as I looked, this purely aesthetic Cubist's-eye view gave place to what I can only describe as the sacramental vision of reality. I was back where I had been looking at the flowers—back in a world where everything shone with the Inner Light, and was infinite in its significance. The legs, for example of the chair—how marvellous their tubularity, how supernatural their polished smoothness! I spent several minutes—or was it several centuries?—not merely gazing at those bamboo legs, but actually *being* them— or rather being myself in them; or, to be still more accurate (for 'I' was not involved in the case, nor in a certain sense were 'they') being my Not-self in the Not-self which was the Chair.' (Plates 44, 45.)

So in the mescalin-taker's world there are still values, for 'in some the glory was more manifest than in others'. Here, obviously, we are concerned with values which, superficially at least, appear to have no practical significance. If, always remembering that recognition had given these objects form, the experience was nevertheless one of pure perception, then it is there we must find the source of these values. Nor is this very difficult. To quote Huxley again: 'Mescalin raises all colours to a high power and makes the percipient aware of in- numerable fine shades of difference, to which, at ordinary times, he is completely blind.' The surfaces that give rise to these newly distinguishable shades of difference are pre- sumably those in which the glory is most manifest. Not only is the experience in this respect a fresh one and therefore bound to receive maximum attention, but, because our attention is now not related at all to the need for action, the mind has particular delight in exploring the novel sensation, in exercising its visual powers with such unparalleled fullness. Of the two drives of the mind, the drive to experience and the drive to reduce to order, the second has been inhibited, the first given full rein.

This fascinating account of experiences under the influence of mescalin would be important in showing something of the character of our mental processes in analysis, but it is much more significant than this, because these drug-induced states are not far removed from experiences which many of us have had, and do not infrequently have, in our ordinary lives. Mescalin is chemically very similar to adrenalin, a hormone secreted by certain duct-less glands which is necessary to our normal smooth functioning but which, in emergency, is produced in greater quantities and serves to heighten our powers of reaction. The essential difference between what adrenalin does for us and what mescalin can do is that adrenalin heightens our awareness in order to increase our chances of biological survival, whereas mescalin does it for no purpose at all save the pleasure it gives.

It would be easy to conclude from this that pure perception, the means divorced from the end, has no biological value. But in fact it may have value in the sense that it is vital play. The experiencing of pure percepts, in so far as that is possible, is like flexing the muscles or playing scales on the piano; it is a guarantee of the capacity to adjust to whatever challenge may arise; it is an exercise of the vital principle and contains the idea of power and is therefore pleasant to us. Some sensations and relationships of sensations are better exercises than others because they afford a wider preparation and reveal greater power. But in effect sensation is of potential biological value according to its capacity to give information, and of direct value when it does so.

What Huxley experienced in that strange group of flowers, in that cane chair, in the pattern of his desk, was not Grace or Transfiguration or the Buddha, but what we more simply know as the quality of wonder, which indeed may also be what those other ideas intrinsically are.

Wonder is consciousness exercised without the interference of pain or the inhibition of purpose; it may also be called worship, and is a principal one among the joys of life.

At no stage in the act of vision can we cut out entirely the participation of the mind, but it does seem that we can stop our visual experience short of the full sequence of mental processes and that this is precisely what happens when we experience things aesthetically. But what stages can we ignore and in what way do we gain from these various limitations?

The needs fundamental to the operation of the mind are activity and repose. In order to be mind it must fulfil its function, for its potential arises from its activity and is created by it. The form of the mind's activity is to inquire, to explore, to extend experience. The end of that activity is to determine, to recognize, to establish, and to know, which is to be at rest. The drive of the mind is from exploration to organization. The healthy mind, like the healthy eye, seeks its own satisfaction, but is unable to rest in it. It is not states but activities which result in awareness of life. As Stendhal wrote: 'The traveller who has just climbed a mountain sits down on the summit and finds a perfect pleasure in resting there, but would he be happy if he was obliged to rest all the time?'

Any visual percept of which we are aware involves both the eye and the mind. The eye's mechanism has built into it the principle that any stimulus must cause disequilibrium, but as the mind has a similar mechanism it follows that, unless one is subordinate to the other, there are in any act of vision at least two drives requiring satisfaction at the same time.

As when we eat it is not the sensation of hunger that is the source of pleasure, so in the case of the mind's activity it is not the state of curiosity which pleases, nor yet is it the terminal situation of knowing; it is the process of inquiring which takes place as the mind moves from curiosity to knowledge. Curiosity can itself acquire an aura of pleasure because we expect that successful search will succeed to it, and in the same way knowledge can please by its reflection of the pleasure we got in gaining it. A process from lack to fulfilment contains elements of both end situations in varying degrees throughout its course.

It is said by psychologists that mental activity is pleasant in so far as it is successful. As colour by itself cannot normally complete the act of vision, it should be the cause of dissatisfaction if the curiosity it has aroused is not then satisfied by further evidence supplied by perceived form. But this is not always so, for once the mind, having sent its scouts ahead— those antennae whose quivering is to alert the main battalions—has satisfied itself that no action is imminent, it is at liberty to forget about the matter, to cease to notice it, to consign it to the vast limbo to which most of our sensations instantly go. But if for some reason the mind is unwilling to let the experience pass from it, then it is able to concentrate those energies which would have been required to meet an active situation upon the passive savouring of its experience. Contemplation is no more than this: that a drive which is directed towards a terminal situation, being deprived of its end, is saved from the frustrations which normally result from such deprivation, by turning back on itself and becoming an unending circular experience. Now, this can only take place if the effort of the experience is neither too much nor too little for the mind concerned; for if it is too much the mind is discouraged, if too little the mind is bored, and in either event the sensation instead of being pursued is abandoned. Visual perception of any sort is a momentary identification of our own being with the being of an object out-there; we are, according to the degree of our absorption in the way it is modifying the waves of energy, the object itself; or rather, we are identified not with the totality of the object, for that is a mystery, but with the idea of the object as it has been created by our immediate apprehension of its visual aspect. This is normally felt by us in a very slight degree. The average visual sensation shadowily declares itself and is shrugged off, or it forces itself on our attention and we are driven onward to action; but if neither of these things happens, if we can only stay poised at the moment of experience, of held attention, we become pleasurably aware of our identity with the thing which we are seeing, and we are at the same time both intensely *it* and intensely *us*. This is the true aesthetic experience.

The extent to which we need to be personally uninvolved in a work of art has often been debated. It is perfectly true that in so far as visual experience passes the stage of attention and is converted into the need for action our experience ceases to be aesthetic. Time and responsibility come in at the door and contemplation and divine awareness go out through the window. But we have referred already to the antennae of the mind, and they indeed are perfectly well able to make contact with the world of involvement and, while declining any call to action, can re-convey to the attentive faculty a quality derived from the world of immediate objects. The often proclaimed view that in a picture of a nude it is neither here nor there whether, if it were living flesh, it would be sexually appealing or the reverse has been very properly corrected by Sir Kenneth Clark. No man or woman who had not an earnest, if unrecognized, admiration for the unclothed body itself could contemplate painted and sculpted nudes with anything approaching full awareness. If we are instantly alerted to sexual need by Botticelli's *Venus*, by the Farnese *Hercules*, or the *Hermaphrodite* of the Museo delle Terme, then these works cease to be works of art. (Plates 42, 43.) But if we have not had conveyed to us by the report of our advanced intelligence service that these bodies are essentially desirable, and therefore good, a great deal of the pleasure to be derived from the images of them will be withheld from us. The writer on aesthetic subjects who, to prove his point of the unimportance of subject-matter, illustrated together *The Slaughtered Ox* by Rembrandt and the body of Christ from the Isenheim altar-piece succeeded only in proving the incompleteness of his aesthetic experience and in demonstrating the reverse of his case. (Plates 48, 49.)

When we see a picture the mind says in effect to itself: 'This is all right. It is a painted lion. How fierce its eye! How gleaming white the ivory of its teeth! How exquisitely curled its mane!' We are open to experience all aspects of the beast that do not involve us in practical participation in its world. We see our terror, but we do not feel it. We may indeed enclose our lion behind bars, or view it through a cine-camera, or from the security of a motor car in a game reserve, and the efficiency and splendour of the animal may delight us, but all these are devices to enable us to concentrate upon those aspects of him which do not call for action. Our delight derives in part, perhaps, from the sense of a danger braved, but chiefly from our sense of relief that responsibility and time have been successfully evaded and that we are able to contemplate a fellow occupant of space in all his singularity without becoming directly involved with him in conflict for that space.

It is reasonable to ask whether it is possible to deflect energy from one field of the mind's activity to another. Because we do not have to run from our lion or to fight him does that necessarily mean that the force of the drive that would have carried us to that end is now available for absorbing his appearances? At first sight it might seem to be so, but actually our flight or our struggle are not themselves part of the visual sequence. Once our perception of the beast passes into action a fresh sequence begins, involving other drives and other terminal situations. The moment of transition from the act of vision to the act of flight is the moment at which decision is made and the will is involved. Choice is the link between the two events; and it is the residual faculty of making a choice that we are left with when we are not practically involved in a situation.

So, whether we look at a live lion or a plaster-cast of a decayed turbot is biologically immaterial once we know that we are not called upon in any way to act towards them; but, the faculty of choice having been released from its primary task of deciding what to do, being now free, floating, detached, is anxious for some opportunity of exercising itself, and it is, therefore, liable to be exercised, if we so direct it, upon the visual aspects before us. We feel urged to choose between them. Some people, it is true, not having cultivated the faculty of choice, are not conscious that there is a tension unresolved and do not, when faced with an aspect which does not require action, feel impelled to evaluate it. The connoisseur, on the other hand, is he who has cultivated a capacity for the distinction of fine differences and has a, possibly unconscious, scale of values to apply to them.

How are we to arrive at an appropriate scale of values? For as the question 'Which is to be preferred?' is biologically an unnecessary question, and as the values which we apply when making our choice cannot be directly biological ones, we must find others.

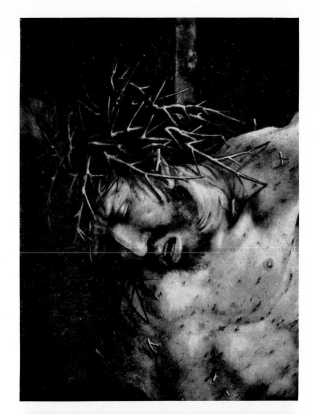

48 MATHIAS GRUNEWALD: *Christ on the Cross* (detail from the Isenheim Altarpiece)

49 REMBRANDT: *The Slaughtered Ox*

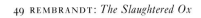

The belief that subject-matter is aesthetically irrelevant is a hang-over from art for art's sake.

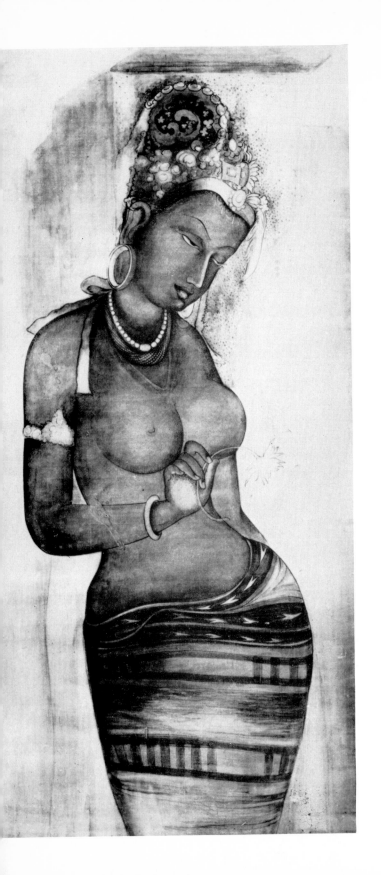

50 WALL PAINTING FROM
AJANTA

51 COSIMO TURA: *Virgin and Child*

52 RENOIR: *Jeune Fille Assise*

53 VITTORIO CORCOS: *Sogni*

54 VINCENT VAN GOGH: *Landscape with Cypress Trees*

55 CLAUDE: *Port Scene*

10. Taste

. . . men's formal, imaginative demands which vary so unaccountably from age to age. At certain times the average man can only look with pleasure at things of a certain shape and character. Why? Where do these shapes come from? How have they been modified? What ideals, what dream worlds do they express? To answer these questions the quality is irrelevant, for though the taste of a time is sometimes concentrated in a great work of art, more often men are satisfied with forms which seem to us devoid of grace, and a whole epoch may express itself very sincerely, but very unsatisfactorily. Beauty is a historical document; but a historical document is not necessarily beautiful.

SIR KENNETH CLARK

AS we walk about the streets of our cities and see the buildings of which they are composed, as we look in the shop windows and see the goods for sale there, as we enter the homes of our friends and see the circumstances with which they surround their most intimate hours, we are astonished by the appearances which our fellow creatures not only accept uncomplainingly but seem positively to seek out and to approve. It is well to remember that some, at least, of them are equally shocked by us.

Among the many divisions which may be made of the human race is that into those who are perceptually aware and those who are not. For many people the sensations of sight and sound and touch and smell and taste are means to ends; to a few they are ends in themselves. Neither type exists in purity. There is probably no one who is not at some time or another strongly affected by the aspects of things and there are none of us who can totally disregard their practical consequences. Though we call our two types the aware and the unaware, we are not really in danger of forgetting that the most aware are very imperfect instruments and that the most unaware are not without an aesthetic sense.

The distinction between the two types is one of mental set or degree of attention. It is not surprising if the man who only attends to what he sees in order to pass on to succeeding situations should, when he finds himself in a position to make a visual choice for other than practical grounds, in other words to remain *in* a certain perceptual sensation rather than to pass beyond it, choose very differently from those who have trained their palates and learned to perceive and find significance in relationships to which their companions are blind. The unaware, un-alert person, when called upon to choose between appearances, has no appropriate criterion. He is accustomed to make judgements for quantitative reasons and to choose the bigger, the more numerous, the more expensive, the stronger, the heavier, and so on. Seeking for a positive standard of this sort, he seizes upon a visual aspect which he can assess in the same way. He chooses fully saturated colours in strong contrast, or brightnesses of maximum impact, or smoothness of finish, or any extreme condition which he can readily recognize. But even here, as his eye is untrained, he is often unable to distinguish a saturated hue from one that is less so, or one quality of brightness from another that is near to it. His range of perception is small and his choice will not be exacting. One thing will do as well as another provided that they are more or less alike.

That such a person's visual preferences should differ from those of the aware man is to be expected, but we are apt to be genuinely surprised when someone, ostensibly as aware as ourselves, is unable to see with delight what we see, and takes what seems to be a perverse pleasure in the appearance of objects which we find inferior. The more alike our attitudes are in other respects the more shocked we are when our tastes do not coincide.

Unexpected differences amongst equally sensitive observers spring also from differences of attitude or set of mind. If two people of roughly equal experience and sensibility look at an object from the same aspect and estimate it for the same qualities according to the same scale of values, they will arrive at a similar opinion of its merit. But if a cricketer and a footballer look at a rugby football with an appraising eye the one will find it too large and too soft and the other will find it a ridiculous shape. Though equally experienced and discerning, they are looking for different qualities. We bring our standards of value with us.

It is clear that some standards are appropriate and some are not. Valuing the paintings of Veronese by the square yard or Maillol's nudes by the ton is an obvious mis-application, but other less ludicrously misplaced criteria of value are, on the face of it, equally inapplicable, yet we frequently make use of them. It is here rather than in marginal physiological differences that we should look for the cause of variations in taste.

When the work we are considering can be quite simply regarded *in situation* the problem of what standard to adopt is often a fairly simple one. For example, the choice for this book of typeface, of paper, of spacing on the page, and so on, has as its principal object legibility. It is not too difficult, once this is accepted, to regard everything that makes for that end as a virtue even if the virtue has to be moderated by such secondary considerations as expense. If a picture has a purpose to achieve other than that of simply being a picture, we can soon establish a reasonable scale of values by which to assess it. The fundamental criterion is *What will help it to achieve its end in the circumstances in which it is to be seen?* It must be visible, it must be noticeable, it must hold the attention for long enough to achieve its purpose. If it is a social protest such as Goya's *Execution Scene* we must be shocked into anger; if it is an illustration we must be led to the object or the event which it represents;

if it is an advertisement we must be persuaded by it. The attainment of such ends involves certain means, perhaps various and differing means. Our final verdict must be our reaction to what we are shown. If we are angry, if we understand, if we buy, the picture has fulfilled its purpose and is successful; if other circumstances intervene and prevent those ends, then the picture has failed. If we want to assess whether such a picture is likely to succeed or to explain why it has failed, we may consider in detail what means have been used and whether they are proper to that end. It is simply a question of the aptness of craftsmanship, of tools, materials, and method.

A common source of confusion is that when a picture is not clearly designed for some function beyond its immediate experiencing we are rarely in agreement as to what its purpose is. Often we give no thought to what it is intended to do, but immediately on receiving the message 'This is a picture' we proceed to evaluate it although our notion of the purpose of a picture *which is simply a picture* is of the haziest. So we evaluate it by what standards? Usually by several standards at the same time without our knowing it, but commonly by some at least of those which we have been accustomed to recognize as important in another context. For example, a machine-tool age will be predisposed to approve work that is as flashily decisive as a machine; and an age which is in the process of abandoning all standards but economic efficiency will favour work that is pared to its essentials, and its guarantee of aesthetic virtue will be a Certificate of Cost.

But do we know what are the essentials of a work of art?

It is as difficult for the aware as for the unaware to be consistent in their application of standards; perhaps more so.

There are two groups of criteria. Into the first fall all those values which depend upon our associating the picture, or statue, or building, or whatever it may be, with former contacts with the world out-there which have been pleasurable to us in another sense. The second includes those values which are basic to all visual art because they belong to the mechanical process of vision.

Inasmuch as we are human beings whose lives are one experience all our sensations must have overtones which are echoes, reflections, or shadows, of others. An example of the association type of pleasure is our enjoyment of a picture of sunlight gleaming through trees upon a woodland stream. In it we recognize that our pleasure, in part at least, belongs to some previous real enjoyment of the relief of cool shade and the refreshment of running water on a day of brightness and heat. The man to whom such an experience is strange, or one to whom it has unrecognized displeasing associations (because, for example, a childhood picnic in such a spot was marred by a parental quarrel), will hardly be able to feel for it as we do. Other obviously associative types of observation are 'I like pictures of ships' or 'I like pictures of windmills'. Less obvious, but still associative, are those criticisms which are based on character: 'Renoir is vulgar', 'Gainsborough is frivolous', 'Mantegna is too scholarly', 'Tura too dry'.

A practical consideration will often provide a powerful, if hidden, bias towards employing one set of standards rather than another. I know of at least one 'aware' person with a discerning eye for nuances of form and hue whose immediate reaction before any picture is of the order 'I should not like to live with that', or 'I would hate to have that in my dining-room'—a basis for judgement which is bizarre in its effect when the Isenheim altarpiece or the wall-paintings of Ajanta are in question. Such criticism, depending not upon our immediate relationship with the objects themselves but upon their power to contribute indirectly to the completeness of our lives, to play a part in a limited and prearranged ensemble, though not usually so frankly expressed, is more common among connoisseurs than they are aware. It is a hazard that particularly awaits the specialist collector.

It is common for collectors to transfer the delight normally reserved for the work of the master to the achievement of some insignificant follower which, moderate in quality, has the piquant charm of rarity. By this means items that complete a series become exceptionally desirable. Often, it is true, a collector can dissociate this form of pleasure from the so-called purely aesthetic one. He knows that the inferior object that he has manoeuvred himself into the position of prizing so much *is* inferior; but even here a tricky ambivalence can fog the matter, for there is a sense in which the work of art with which the collector is concerned is the collection as a unit and not the isolated part that helps to compose it. If this is so, if our attention is directed to a quite different whole, the blatant inferiority of one piece of it is of no significance so long as it contributes to the total. The value which it will have for us will be a reflection of the merit of the composite unit towards which it has so essentially contributed.

The personal possibilites of variation are so great that no regular pattern of behaviour can be depended upon. Observers who are consistent in their judgements are, one suspects, often using simple criteria which lie in the more superficial area of the mind. The basis for their taste is usually recognition. It is betrayed when it is seen that what they admire is not, say, all Constable or even the best period of Constable, but that type of Constable which is the popular image of the artist. The liking may be genuine, but the source of the liking is not usually in the direct relationship of man to picture but in the knowledge that one possesses, or esteems, so widely envied an object. The immediate cause of the pleasure is certainty. If the picture is not recognized for what it is, or if a doubt is cast on its authenticity, the pleasure is gone. This is perhaps too gross an instance of aesthetic judgement operating at a shallow level, but it is common, especially amongst wealthier collectors. What really command high prices in the market are pictures of which even the least cultivated can say with envy and awe: 'I see you have a Renoir', or 'What a splendid Van Gogh!' Appreciation of this sort puts a premium on readily recognizable idiosyncrasy and is ultimately dependent on other people's opinions and not upon one's own. The final form of this type of judgement is the satisfaction which flows from the knowledge that a picture 'ought to be like that'. It fulfils the standard demanded of pictures and is, therefore, *right*. In societies such as our own which lack self-confidence, this type of connoisseur is the most common of all and inevitably forms the group most exploited by commercial interests.

As what we enjoy is the conscious experience of the functioning of the mechanism of the senses, we derive some at least of our sense of well-being from fresh relationships, from those which extend our capacity for living and which open up a new channel of experience —providing, of course, that pain or some other taboo does not forbid it. But the novelty of an experience is a fast-diminishing asset. When Mr Gall advocated the character of *unexpectedness* in the laying out of grounds Mr Milestone asked, not unreasonably, by what name he distinguished this character when a person walked round the grounds for a second time. But unexpectedness, surprise, discovery, extension of our ideas in a new direction, is so much in accord with what our senses are all about, that novelty frequently overwhelms our judgement, and we experience from a new manifestation of moderate quality so great an excitement that we elevate it far above the status which it will take in our minds when 'we have walked about the grounds a second time'. It is because of this propensity to temporary euphoria, which is almost if not quite indistinguishable from the more enduring aesthetic experiences, that some people use as their criterion of excellence that an object should withstand the test of time. Rediscoveries can sometimes be as misleading as discoveries, and when we unearth some forgotten minor master his quality is often that which attends on the view from a window long bricked up, rather than the divine revelation we are inclined to suppose it. When we think of the astounding mis-judgements which throughout recorded history have been made on contemporaries by people of discernment, we can be consoled for our own shameful record of enthusiasms outgrown. And yet we must not make the mistake of supposing that a quality which long endures is in every way better than one which is evanescent. Novelty when it is fresh is as absolute in its charm as the flower of the Morning Glory which is as beautiful as an oak or as the Himalayas, *but* will not be there in the morning as the Himalayas will. When, forty years ago, I regarded Van Gogh's *Landscape with Cypress Trees* as the most wonderful landscape painting in the world, so it was . . . with me . . . then. (Plate 54.)

The relative strength of simple stimuli, the relationships that can exist between them, and our delight in what is fresh, are basic values of the organism which we are; but whether we prefer a greater stimulus to a lesser, or an easy transition to a difficult one, is not basic at all, but takes us far out into the world of the developed personality.

A further stage in the appreciation of the mechanical process of sight is the identification of ourselves with the object seen, in this case a picture, and our further identification with the act of making it and, eventually, our identification with its creator. It is not merely our admiration of the artist's skill that is the point here, though this certainly comes into it, but our delight in the firm stroke of the brush that *we* have made, our pride in exquisite colour that *we* have given to the piled-up forms, and so on. In the moments of our communion with a work of art there is to be seen in our eyes the intensity which meticulous care demands, or the flashing confident look which goes with the bravura stroke, or the Olympain calm which disposes masses here or there. There is also often to be seen in us a tensing of the muscles of the arm, or a vestigial movement of the wrist and hand, as though we were in fact conducting a great visual orchestra.

At a stage beyond this appreciation of manipulative skill we find that simple sensations begin to acquire values which are inherently functional—such values as clarity, noticeability, and so on. Although these qualities depend upon us and upon our perceptual capacity, they are values which do not belong to sensations themselves but rather to the use we put them to. And that use is to facilitate recognition.

In all vision recognition is the most critical phase and not unnaturally it is the phase which both the aware and the unaware most frequently rest upon.

An insidious trick of the palate is to accept as a positive standard some quality about which there can be no mistake merely because there *can* be no mistake about it; in other words because our need for recognition has been met. All that concerns most of us is that we shall have a standard of judgement around which, like the axis of the poles, we can revolve whether our standard be hang the Kaiser, burn the Pope, or I like Ike. Without such standards we become amorphous.

Nor are the sophisticated and the aware more free from this need than the unaware. It is the desire for a positive criterion which is at the root of praise of particular features such as 'drawing'. It is not difficult to train the eye to become aware of something that is 'out of drawing' and it has the advantage of being an objective criterion with the added charm of allowing us to demonstrate how discerning and how right we are. We are reluctant to say that such and such a picture does not weigh enough, although that is perhaps the sort of criterion we should prefer because that is even more easily proved.

Any incidental quality, even if much less susceptible to objective measurement than correctness of drawing, can be regarded as the touchstone that turns all else to gold. Meticulous attention to detail is still accepted by many people as such a touchstone and the mere presence of painstaking work will ensure their happiness. Others, who would scorn so jejeune a standard, pin their faith instead, for example, on spontaneity of handling, and apply it with the same oppressive universality. It is now less fashionable than it was to regard the attainment of true tonal relationships as the essential merit of a picture, but this was for long the voguish attitude and the quality above all others sought by the cognoscenti. It was in protest against this sort of thing that Roger Fry said of Sickert: 'Things for him have only their visual values; they contain no key to unlock the secret of the heart and spirit.' More subjective qualities, those involving the Grand Criteria of Moral Value, are much more difficult to assess and are never certain anyway.

The recognition of some positive quality, of subject, of drawing, of tone, of hue, and so on, can also be practised, as it were, in reverse. As black is experienced as a positive sensation, although it is no more than the absence of sensation, so we are able to cultivate not merely whatever value we choose but whatever anti-value we choose. There is very little difference. With a little practice we may learn to recognize anti-values as readily as values, and the pleasures of doing so are, in part at least, the same. As Picasso said: 'Pictures were formerly the sum of additions, mine are the sum of destructions.' Mathematicians can add together minus symbols as easily as they do plus ones. By this route we arrive at a pleasure which depends not merely upon the joy of destruction, or upon our increased knowledge of the norm which arises from it, but upon a sort of ritualistic retracing of steps which is only available to the knowledgeable. Only the most erudite can recognize the Mass being said backwards. We can do without imitation, we can do without recognition, we can do without order, we can do without line, we can do without bulk, we can do without tone, because, in fact, we are not doing without them, they are present in their absence. But it is a dangerous course because, though it may be all right when you are in process of doing without them, when the process is complete you *are* without them, the ground is bare where once the city stood. When Van Gogh wrote: 'Colour can replace tonal values, perspective, chiaroscuro—even, to a large extent, relief', he was merely advocating that the orchestra should be replaced by one instrument of it. We, driven by the demon of adventure, have gone on from there: we can do without colour too, for a loud shout can replace colour, and a sickening pain can seem like a noise, and at the end there is only sensation with nothing to cause it, at the best auto-aestheticism, and at the worst a shot in the arm with a hypodermic.

The function of all these value-indicators, drawing, tone, colour, association, subject, and the antithesis of these, is twofold. Firstly, by their unusual character or degree of application they attract the attention, alert the system, and create a general attitude of awareness into which, if the awareness is sustained, more enduring values can be introduced. Such values are felt by us more deeply because we are in a state of excitement. But by degrees these qualities which served to alert us pass over into signs which we recognize. 'What astonishing brushwork!' becomes 'Good gracious, this is a Frans Hals!' and finally, 'Yes, another Hals. Very good!' Recognition can in itself be exhilarating and a cause of euphoria, as when we see an old friend in an unexpected milieu or pick up a Crome landscape in a street market, but these too may, if repeated, slide into the merely gratifying rut which secures us in our mediocrity but excites us not at all. One thing alone guarantees us from this gradual loss of life: a quality which is the touchstone of our relationship with the friend and with the picture, a quality for which there is no other name but love.

The crux of the matter is that while every perceived object is a subjective experience, an aesthetically perceived object is peculiar inasmuch as it is a calculated and chosen subjective experience on which we elect to dwell. If we choose to have such experiences it is because we feel a need for them. If we feel a need for them it implies that we are experiencing a drive towards a terminal situation of which they contain the key. What we like depends upon what we lack and our longings are the clue to the direction assumed by our taste.

Many needs are superficial and transitory. Others are recurrent and reflect a basic need of the personality. We are drawn to the contemplation of certain objects because they promise us fulfilment. Some may satisfy us once and never again; they are those which complete the drives of curiosity, or those which depend for their efficiency upon their power to surprise and shock. More permanent delight is reserved for objects which fulfil recurrent needs, for those things to which we can regularly return for solace and not be disappointed.

Our needs are on many levels. The physical needs of our perceptual processes are one thing, the needs of the personality that lie beyond them are another. What we like to eat may seem to be governed by what pleases our palate, but if we take the matter further we see that it is the need of the stomach which lies behind the palate's preferences, and if we go further still we find that the stomach is no more than an intermediary at the service of the whole body. So it is with perceptual taste; what it ultimately serves is the personality, not the eye or the need of the mind for sensation.

There are, of course, infinite ways in which the multitudinous needs of the personality may be combined, but when all the so-called impure needs out of which our taste is largely composed have been winnowed away there remain two fundamental attitudes, upon one or other of which all aesthetic preference is built. Those needs are discipline and freedom.

Personality is the product of order. The first need of the personality is for form, for the boundaries and limitations that create. The deepest need, the greatest pleasure, is to feel form, to enjoy the *being* its restrictions give us. It is in this sense that Wölfflin wrote: 'We gather from the Italians' clear-cut adherence to rule that they found rule to be not a limitation of their freedom but, on the contrary, a manifestation of a wholly free and natural life.' But form is only felt in this way if we fill it, if we press against its boundaries from within and feel the tension which restrains us. If we do not press against it and fill it the form is inert. Thus the vital person feels the discipline of form as a creative limitation, but he also contains within himself an excess vitality which seeks release in bursting the boundaries of form. This is the second need of the personality—for growth and development and change, and for the feeling of freedom and escape which temporarily results from the sensation of breaking the bonds. On either side of form, when it is felt as a restriction, and when its dissolution is felt as an escape into a new world, the personality is most actively aware.

VII Guido Reni: *The Rape of Europa*

These contrasting attitudes, expressed in many different ways, are at the root of human life; tension and explosion, discipline and liberty, clarity and mystery, classicism and romanticism, the plain and the forest; an excess of the one leading to inertia, its tension lost; an excess of the other leading to diffusion and chaos, its energy dissipated.

The need of the vital individual, as of the vital community, is to maintain poise, to check too hardly felt a discipline with a corresponding freedom, and to balance too diffuse and destructive a liberty with the certainty of clearly defined form. The need to compensate, the oscillation between restraint and freedom, is felt only by those vigorous organisms in which energy increases to the point at which the bonds of form are oppressive and in which the creative spirit is strong enough to force the exploding energy into another discipline. The workings of this compensating mechanism are not always evident because we can compensate in one field for imbalances in another and so screen from our view the very need we are fulfilling.

For example, the growing spirit of enquiry in religious matters which led away from order and authority in fifteenth-century Italy was matched by an artistic development which emphasized order and authority in architecture. As soon as the process was reversed with the Counter-Reformation and authority was restored in Church and State, the baroque replaced clarity with mystery, and substituted for the articulated order of human proportions, easily comprehended, a new type of form in which man was no longer the measure and in which the calm intellectual harmonies were abandoned in favour of a direct appeal to the passions. So far from art being the expression of the dominant characteristic of an age there is a sense in which it is always the reverse of the dominant characteristic, that the form it takes is dictated by the organism's needs, not by its surplus.

Often the compensating movement is not simultaneous with the condition it balances, with the result that either state becomes extreme and the oscillations between them are so violent that the organism is sometimes destroyed by it. The régime of Louis XIV produced a condition of this sort. Individuals could find some petty compensation for the over-powering authority of the king in the dangerous world of court intrigue; but for society as a whole there was no safety valve and the pendulum was subsequently forced to the extremity of the Revolution.

History abounds with instances in which rigidity of manner is succeeded by licence, in which establishment is ousted by anti-establishment until it in turn is forced to assume the mantle of authority and it imposes its own forms. Heresy when it succeeds becomes orthodoxy. How many sons whose only guiding principle in life was to be unlike their fathers have found, in pained astonishment, that their sons look on them in the same way!

Less obvious are those instances in which an imbalance receives a contemporary check in some apparently unrelated field. At least one reason for the passion for living in psychological danger—of which the present condition of art in Western societies is a symptom—

lies in the material security that those societies provide. It does not matter if Western civilization is, in fact, insecure; the point is that it is felt by individuals in their daily lives to be oversecure. Food, housing, health, education, come easily and as by right; the basic uncertainty of being able to provide them has largely gone from our lives. To the price we have paid for this, a world of bureaucratic discipline, of concrete roads upon which we may not even turn round, of tickets for this and passes for that, we respond like an over-restrained child, with a screaming fit. We stamp and roar and rage over acres of canvas and hardboard, finding our release from order in the anti-order of our demonstration. More simply we grow great beards and adopt the farouche demeanour of social pariahs, sitting upon pavements and hurling abuse at anyone who will not listen to us. We cultivate moral depravity until we find on the one hand that we have destroyed ourselves or, on the other, that all our efforts at nonconformity have resulted in a new brand of conformity of which we are the arch-type. It has all happened before. Suddenly the new generation becomes the old generation. Of England in 1900 W. B. Yeats wrote: 'Everybody got down off his stilts . . . nobody drank absinthe with his black coffee; nobody went mad; nobody committed suicide; nobody joined the Catholic Church.'

The comparatively mild Romantic Revival at the end of the eighteenth century was a display of anti-order designed to compensate for the rigid forms imposed by the so-called Age of Reason. That in Britain the swing of the pendulum did not produce either political revolution or total rejection of traditional art forms was because the formality of British art and British society in the eighteenth century was by no means without simultaneous compensating factors. Tory was balanced by Whig. Palladio found a counterpoise in Strawberry Hill and Fonthill Abbey, and some escape from order was at least provided by public executions and by the exhilarating depredations of footpads. Consequently anti-order when it took over was not extreme and was soon struggling to find for itself the semblance of a new order. That the new order should also contain a good deal of the rejected old was one cause of Victorian eclecticism.

These same variations of the compensating principle occur in our lives as individuals. If the routine of commuter-trains and office-work keeps us in a state of low energy, no pressure is felt against the unrelenting form and we contentedly allow other patterns of customary behaviour to take over control of the remainder of our days: golf, walking the dog, digging the garden, looking at the telly, and so on. If, however, the foreseeable order of our lives is felt as a restriction by the spirit, we find our release in the dreams of Walter Mitty, in novels of violence and depravity or, if we have a leaning to the mock-esoteric, in dadaist, tachist, and pop art. Our taste or, in other terms, our consciousness of a drive to satisfy a need, does not necessarily imply that we are aware of our need: the palate that signals for beef does not trouble to explain that the body needs protein; nor does it imply that because the exquisite order of the Parthenon is called in to balance the horror of the unplumbed, salt, estranging sea that it may not be equally efficacious in imposing calm after a day of petty frustrations, burnt fingers, and degrading personal absurdities. It may even acquire its efficacy from a previous overindulgence in Swinburne or James Bond. The power of its order is sovereign in all such cases.

Order and anti-order are fundamental. But we commonly base our personal preferences on considerations that are less so or which, while still essentially of one or other type, are not apparently so. For example, a picture, romantic in subject and concept, may be very highly finished; the man who is unaware of finish will applaud it because it satisfies his need for doubt, for the excitement of uncertainty, for mystery, for freedom, for anti-order; on the other hand, his companion, whose attention is almost solely concentrated on the technical certitude of the work, its accuracy of line and smoothness of finish, will find in it relief from the undisciplined irregularity of his own customary affairs, and like it for the opposite reason. What is solace for the one can also be solace for the other, according to which aspect is turned to the view.

We can also be predisposed to certain types of form upon what at first sight appears to be quite a different principle. We can recognize characteristics as being an echo of our own most valued qualities and feel flattered by the mirror image. In this case our real need is for self-esteem. There is, for example, often a marked divergence of taste between those who value qualities of line in a work of art and those who concentrate their attention on the relationship of the bulks which the lines circumscribe. Experimental evidence is not available, but it would be surprising if it were not found that the majority of those who prefer Botticelli to Titian and Rembrandt were in their youth slim, agile, and swift runners. The pleasure of their prowess and the praise it attracted combine to cast an aura over the sensation of easy movement which flowing line essentially is.

But we are all, at some time or another, in one way or another, subscribers to all these codes of value and our preferences depend upon the way in which the infinite variety of possible standards are integrated into one personal attitude. The history of the fluctuations or evolution of our preferences is the story, not merely of a more cultivated distinction of differences, a progressively educated eye, or a more ordered sense of harmony, but of the changing emphasis which the circumstances of our lives and the needs of our personalities give to our underlying attitudes. It may be that a certain change, for example, in my own character, perhaps a more relaxed social sense resulting in a loss of arrogance and a consequent gain in charity, might make it possible for me to appreciate, say, Turner, whose innate competitive vulgarity seems to me so deplorable that his virtues are to be discerned only with an effort. Whereas others, to whom competition is no affair of sweaty night-caps and spiritual degradation, are not even aware that every picture he made smells of his effort to win a prize and to demonstrate his superiority over all rivals, a pettiness which is so apparent to me that it destroys the rest. Here a super-sensitivity to a certain aspect of character ruins what can evidently be a real pleasure, and the loss is, perhaps, mine. But in cases where others stand before a picture which is redolent of the assurance, the humility, the greatness of character of its maker and which has itself that character, and can only see there a fault in drawing or a tonal discrepancy, I, who have also seen these things but can discount them, am a manifest gainer. It may even be that the absence of a flaw of this sort could make the work unsympathetic to me as displaying an improper degree of perfection offensive in a fellow human, or perhaps as lacking the deviation into error which establishes the whereabouts of the truth. In any event it is not so much capacity to distinguish differences that divides us, but the attitude that emphasizes one aspect rather than another, and which tomorrow we may both, for the time being, have changed.

Clearly it might be all gain for us if we were able to derive from every work every pleasure of which it was properly capable. To some extent we do this and adjust the set of our minds according to the opening signs which the object gives us. We know, for example, when we see a drawing by Andrea del Sarto that the quality of sublimity is not in question and we use an appropriate measuring-stick. In this respect we are in advance of the woman who did not fancy the Isenheim altar-piece for her dining-room. But the set of mind which some works require of us is so strange that we cannot readily accommodate ourselves to it. It is this fact that is at the base of the historical approach to art appreciation.

According to the historical school of thought, quite contrary to that of Croce but near to that of Plato (who wrote that to estimate correctly the achievement of an artist it was first necessary to know what he had set out to achieve), comment on a picture 'may be open to the damaging criticism of inappropriateness' if all the factors contemporary with its production are not taken into account. We have, in other words, to reconstruct imaginatively and as a result of profound scholarship the cultural world of Bongo-bongo if we are to derive the delight we should from its coconut-fibre masks. To put the matter like this is, of course, to weight the scales. It cannot be doubted by those of us who have some historical knowledge that we gain immeasurably from it. But how much of it is due to the deep satisfaction the psyche derives from having established more and more firm points of reference? The soul, sick for certainties, gets so many dusty answers that it is often well pleased if it succeeds in making even a little progress towards firm ground.

But a good deal of the knowledge we may obtain in this way, while it may make the object more interesting, does not make it aesthetically more commendable. Titian's curious picture of three heads in one is an example. It has little appeal and at first glance is meaningless. (Plate 56.) When we learn that it is an *Allegory of Prudence*, that the three faces, in addition to typifying the three stages of human life, Youth, Maturity, and Old Age, also symbolize the three aspects of time, Past, Present and Future; that these in turn represent Memory which learns from the Past, Intelligence which acts in the present, and Foresight which provides for the future; that furthermore the three faces are portraits respectively of

Titian himself, of his son Orazio Vecelli, and of his adopted grandson Marco Vecelli—we are fascinated. But when to all this is added the discovery that the tricephalous monster which the portraits surmount is the distinctive feature of one of the greatest gods of Hellenistic Egypt, Serapis, and that as early as A.D. 400 it was described by Macrobius as denoting Past, Present, and Future; that Petrarch rediscovered the interpretation in 1338; and that thereafter in one form or another it was frequently republished until it appeared in what was probably the immediate iconographic source of the picture, Piero Valeriano's *Hieroglyphica* in 1556; and that it is highly probable that Titian painted it in 1569 when Orazio was confirmed by the Venetian authorities as his successor to a lucrative broker's patent, or, in other words, on the occasion of Orazio becoming Present to Titian's Past—then we are astonished and delighted, for the portals of the past have been opened to us. But the picture is no less a thoroughly uncomfortable picture for all that. As Professor Panofsky, who elucidated all this and much else besides, wrote: 'It is doubtful whether this human document would have fully revealed to us the beauty and appropriateness of its diction had we not had the patience to decode its obscure vocabulary.' But if an object speaks to us in the language of a common humanity we do not need an interpreter. We will cope with a dialect whether it be of Abyssinia or Rome or Japan, of High Gothic or of baroque, provided that it is a variant of our human tongue; but if the language it speaks is peculiar to the time in which it is made and to the people who made it, then a glossary is necessary and the work as we experience it is then perhaps more word than thing. It may be a poem or a tale or a history or a philosophical treatise, but it will only be in a moderate and superficial degree a work of visual art, for the mind does not receive words at the same level at which it receives pictures. A painting which is an intellectual puzzle is of the same order as one of the literary paintings of the mid-nineteenth century—it cannot rest upon the ingenuity of the puzzle any more than the other can rest upon the intrinsic interest of its tale. Paintings that do so are visual tales and puzzles; they are a valid art form, but they must do more than this if they are to be significant visual experiences: they must be that which they contain.

Like all other attitudes to art the historical attitude has dangers as well as advantages. Some art historians have become so absorbed in discovering when and where and for whom a picture was painted that they seem never to have understood why it was painted at all or why we should care that it was. It is this type of art historian, the mathematician *manqué*, the sociologist who can only comprehend works of art as links in a chain of evidence, who gave rise to Geoffery Grigson's *cri de cœur*: 'What strikes me as among the balmiest heresies of all cultural time is *de rigeur*—that everything from the poems of Tu Fu to the novels of Joseph Conrad, must be read, not in the context of one's own needs and satisfactions, but in the context of its time.'

With this complaint against the aridity of a certain self-sufficient scholasticism one must sympathize, but the true justification of the historical attitude lies not only in the fact that it can ensure that we adopt an appropriate stance before a work of art and seek in it for the virtues which are truly there, but also in the merit which the historical attitude itself possesses. The present contains the past and grows in dimension by its relation with the past. Those of us whose lives have touched upon the lives of Aeschylus, of Hadrian, of Akbar, who have fought at Troy and been at the sack of Rome, live longer than others, which is an advantage. The present is infinite; the historical attitude is one way of making ourselves a little more aware of its infinity. Though the stone images of the gods of Mexico or the little bronze native offerings of Luristan may mean little in the context of our own needs and satisfactions, our acquaintance with them may well widen those needs and satisfactions and then they will mean much. The personality itself, like brightness and hue and shape, can exist only in situation, and the more situations and the more varied the situations which can be imaginatively experienced the greater will be the mind's scope for life.

11. Fashion

Some praise at morning what they blame at night;
But always think the last opinion right.
ALEXANDER POPE, *Essay on Criticism*

THE gibe that though a Thing of Beauty may be a Joy for Ever it is not a joy always, expresses a fundamental truth. Sensations are not absolute conditions, but are activities which have a past and a future but no autonomous present; we know the moment only in terms of other moments. The colour changes as we look at it, the form alters, the implications are modified, all is fluid, not because of the changing nature of the energies which they are, though these do change, but because of the changing nature of ourselves who perceive them, and because without that change our organs of perception would no longer function. The neurons whose content of energy is discharged to the brain would become decreasingly sensitive and suffer damage if the nature of the stimulus never altered.

This dependence of continued perception upon contrasting experience—white needing black, red needing green, sound needing silence—has an analogous need within the mind itself where any total sensation or idea if presented in unvarying form loses its keenness of edge, its emotional significance. We do not step in the same river twice.

The saying of the Abbé Dubois that 'a swift shifting of our emotional life comes from the first need of man', which is the need to escape boredom, is based on the recognition that persisting sensations progressively lose their savour. Metabolism is the process by which our physical cells change, the process by which external physical matter, food, is turned into us; that which cannot be changed lies dull and heavy on the stomach until it is rejected. There is a similar metabolism which converts sensations into ideas and ideas into the personality. As the needs of the body will not be satisfied if we serve up to it, say, tinned peaches for every course of every meal, but will demand their rejection by turning our palate against their flavour, so the needs of the personality are not satisfied by the continual flow of an identical sensation. Too long-held a sensation becomes first flavourless and eventually poisonous; a varied diet is needed if the personality is to grow into its full organic complexity. Mere repetition of an experience can result either in the mind becoming dull and inactive so that Keats's *Ode to a Grecian Urn* becomes a tedium, and the *Venus de Milo* as banal as a picture on a pencil box, or until it excites the mind to a violent rejection so that Beethoven's *Fifth Symphony* played once more becomes an excruciating torment.

Repetition and tedium apart, when that particular poise and completeness which is a work of art has been changed by this spiritual metabolic process into us, so that our need for it is finally satisfied, it has nothing left to give us. When we *are* the *Ode to the Urn*, when we *are* the *Fifth Symphony*, when we *are* the *Venus*, then we have no more need of them. As to whether we are ever able to absorb so utterly such major works, or if so, whether we should be able to retain their harmony without occasional recourse to them, is altogether another matter.

If this analogy is valid the ideally healthy individual will intuitively seek a varied diet to accord with the needs of the growing personality and, as at the various stages of our physical growth we require more of one vitamin than another according to our need to produce bone and so on, so at corresponding stages of our spiritual development we will require this food rather than that. Fortunately the essential nutrients for the personality are to be found in many experiences, just as vitamin C is not only to be found in carrots, or protein only in Gruyére cheese, but in other foods which are available in lands where Gruyére and carrots are unknown. It is possible for many quite different diets to produce healthy personalities provided that the essential vitamins are concealed within the multiplicity of forms. Neither the arts of Europe nor of Asia, of Ancient Greece or Renaissance Italy, provide uniquely a spiritual regime on which the personality can thrive; each may do so, each has done so.

But what is true of individuals is true also of communities. Adolescent communities have certain clearly defined needs in the satisying of which the communal pattern or character develops; and once the community has evolved beyond a certain point, its psychological needs, or its appetite for personality-building experience, alters also.

The pattern now becomes complicated because the developing individual personality exists also as part of a developing social personality. The individual is rather like the earth which, while revolving about its own axis, is at the same time involved in another broader movement of which it is not the centre at all, but from which it cannot break free but is held on a dynamic path by the contrary tensions of centripetal and centrifugal force. The further movement of the solar system hurtling into space is like the evolution of life itself.

Were all individuals healthy, and if all societies were so, it would perhaps be possible to prescribe an ideal diet-sheet. Not only are they not so but we do not yet even know with certainty what health in this context is, with the consequence that our appetites, our changes of diet, our inclinations towards certain flavours, are not necessarily governed by essential needs, but may well be at the mercy of very superficial ones, as when a child eats a brightly coloured pill though its consequence is death, and as a man consumes alcohol for the satisfaction of an immediate need though the end result will be *delirium tremens*, sclerosis of the liver, and general debility of the personality.

On top, then, of the healthy rhythm of change set up by the interlocked needs of a smoothly developing individual in a smoothly developing society which would compose an

56 TITIAN: *An Allegory of Prudence*

57 WIGS

Art, like nature, is constantly experimenting to find the limits of the possible.

58 *Venus de Milo*

59 A PARTERRE AT VERSAILLES

60 THE GARDEN OF THE RYOANJI TEMPLE, KYOTO

ideal pattern, there is an infinity of cross-currents which confuse the surface and give the impression that the whole thing is a matter of wayward, irrational and wanton caprice. Yet even in this confusion it would be possible to plot certain regular currents of change provided that we kept clear the different levels of our observations.

Unfortunately we do not keep them clear. Every experience, every sensation, has a potential existence on many different levels and on each one of these levels its value to us (that is our need of it) may be entirely different. We may reject it on one level and welcome it on another. The brandy we drink for society's sake, conforming with an after-dinner custom, may taste vile, may create a temporary euphoria, an ultimate hangover, and an improved digestive process. Faced with these five functions of a glass of brandy we will welcome or reject it according to the level at which we are conducting our affairs, whether social conditioning or physical well-being are uppermost, whether immediate gratification or ultimate satisfaction is our instinctive criterion. We conduct our lives not according to any simple scale of values but by a very complex variety of scales, and we do not normally take sufficient care to keep separate one scale from another.

Our capacity for change arises from our need to be poised, ready to adjust ourselves to changing circumstances. Our desire for change arises from the need to escape boredom. Change operates by compensation, by providing what we lack . . . or attempting to do so. Compensation may take place in one field for what we lack in quite another; indeed, it usually does so. As the body is not much concerned whether it gets its protein from egg or cheese or beef-steak, so the personality, provided it is fed what is essential to its well-being, does not greatly care if it comes in the disguise of a song in Tamil or a portrait bust of an American President in Coade Stone. If we have no children to love we may expend our affection on cats or eat too much chocolate and in either way make our personal sum come outright.

Because of this confusion of scales it is necessary if we are to explain fluctuations of taste to look not merely at that group of activities in which taste and fashion are generally thought to operate but at all others which compose the lives of man. It will be possible to find the missing factor now here now there, now in political liberty, now in economic servitude, now in a puritan morality, now in a quietist philosophy. Nor is the balance a simple one or else it would have been more widely understood and commented upon. Everyone has his own fulcrum of indifference. What is a negative force to one may be a positive force to another; that which overbalances me may restore you to equilibrium. All men may lack liberty, but all do not feel it as a lack; to some it is a desert of horrors. All men may exist within the boundaries of form, but not all actively delight in the tension of discipline. All may be involved in the destructive dissolution of formlessness, the fraying at the edges of our consciousness, but not all feel equally the need to grasp chaos and concentrate it into being, because not all men are creators.

Again it is a matter of stance, of where we choose to stand, and which way we choose to look, and whether we maintain balance by keeping our eyes on things far off or by grabbing at things which are near.

In practice—and we are discussing what *is* and not what might and may one day possibly be in some, allegedly ideal, egalitarian society—this question of stance, and depending from it the operation of taste and fluctuations of fashion, are very largely socially conditioned and, in many people, have no other basis whatsoever.

The stance of a society is a consequence of its history. A national culture grows into being in the ways we have discussed, but within its limits the chief determinant for the great majority of the individuals who compose it is the spirit of emulation. The greater number of all peoples of the earth are consumed by the necessity to think well of themselves. Of all driving forces this is the greatest, and even the most modest, self-abasing, and humble of persons gratifies himself with the undeclared knowledge that modesty and humility are characteristics of which he thinks well. To establish values by which he can, satisfactorily, measure himself, is every man's unrecognized purpose. If he is a man of religious beliefs his ethical and social, although, alas, not commonly his aesthetic, standards are prescribed for him. In this lies the enormous strength in times of stress of the convinced religious. If, however, he is a man of intellectual courage (intrepidity, perhaps, is a more appropriate word) he may seek to establish his values by the decision of his own mind. But for the most part men, at least in modern western societies, are without religious creeds and without the courage and intelligence to attempt a complete code of values, so that they turn automatically to the only standards available, to the most superficial of social standards. One measure that can be clearly understood by almost anybody is the extent of social approval and disapproval which is earned.

There are two ways of achieving social acceptance. The first is the way of the animal who practises protective behaviour by making himself conform to the appearance of the mass. Those who do this lose themselves against the background of their fellow creatures by accepting as their standards of right and wrong the customary behaviour of those they believe to be in their own category. They in turn are accepted by the group and made to feel secure. Such people are also able to think well of themselves, because amongst their acquaintances there will always be some who in some respects less adequately fulfil the canon than they do themselves. The second course is that of the hen who eats because her superior in the pecking order does so. Where there is awareness and acceptance of social gradations in a vital society there will usually be a steady movement whereby individuals from the lower grades pass into those above, or whereby the whole standard of a lower grade becomes modified in the direction of the standards of a higher one. Higher strata of such societies do not necessarily imply higher ethical or aesthetic standards, but may well do so, and when they do all society gains from it. Where social status and power become separated in the community the confusion of those whose nature it is to emulate, or to reach after higher values, is greatly increased for they are no longer sure where the higher values are to be found.

The same forces which make for the establishment of codes in matters of moral behaviour operate also in matters of taste or aesthetic behaviour. The greater number of people admire that which they have been accustomed to hear admired by those whom they want to be like. As Archdeacon Fisher wrote to Constable: 'Men do not admire pictures because they admire them but because others covet them.' If they seek to identify themselves with the sort of people who live in their street they will conform to the aesthetic standards of the street; if, on the other hand, they wish to differentiate themselves from their neighbours they may do so by acquiring the judgements of a group other than that in which they find themselves. Within the most highly developed (or degenerated, according to one's point of view) communities there exists an infinity of variants of these two main attitudes, whereas in the simpler and more homogeneous societies the simpler are the attitudes of individuals in them, for their tastes are more straightforwardly adjusted to the prevailing canon.

As each community contains within itself micro-communities, so the individual may identify himself with one of these rather than with the greater unit, or he may in some part of his activity identify himself with one minor group whilst in another part of his living he will see himself as belonging to another. He may consort with dukes at Ascot, with millionaires at Miami, with pseudo-intellectuals in Chelsea and with yeoman farmers at his local market, transferring easily, and perhaps without any essential falsity, from one milieu to another and, like a chameleon, taking colour from the group in which he for the moment finds himself to be.

The movement of the tides of taste depends, then, upon the unaware multitude hardly at all except in so far as they determine which leaders to follow. An entire community may manifest a liking for art of a certain type which cannot be said to be appropriate to its need, for its need is not to be experienced in this way, but which has been evolved to satisfy a genuine need of a small section of that community—a section upon which has devolved the leadership of fashion if of nothing else, but whose social, moral, intellectual and aesthetic positions may really have very little in common with those who follow them. The need of the followers is to think well of themselves, and the standards of those whom they seek to emulate are the only criteria they have. The need of the leaders may equally be to think well of themselves, but they have other criteria. It is confusing to the superficial observer that the same objects may meet with the same applause, may seem to be equally satisfying to the multitude who follow and to the élite who lead, although in fact the sources of these identical satisfactions are different because the drives which have been completed by them are different. We are at a variant of the simple problem *Which is more full when it is full, a pint pot or a gallon jar?* The new version reads *Is a pint pot more full when it contains whisky than when it contains water?*

To understand the fluctuations of taste, the movements of fashion in any society, it is necessary to relate the changes to those sections, or to those individuals, in the society which initiated them. Why the multitude follow any particular lead is worth inquiry, but why they applaud this painter rather than that, approve this style rather than the other, drink their tea from a cup or from a saucer, is not a fruitful question. The answer to such questions is nearly always the same as to the question: Why does that sheep go through the gap in the hedge? Because the rest of the flock have done so.

Change is necessary to preserve the life of the organism in a changing world. It operates by attempting to fulfil needs. Can we discover any tendency for it to operate always in the same general direction?

Life is subject to the grand cycle of growth and decay. The most long-lived form of it known to man, the Sequoias of California, at 3,000 years or at 4,000 or at 5,000 will one day cease to take up sap and will become old. 'Generations pass while some trees stand, and all families last not three oaks.' Mayflies and galaxies are born, expand to maturity, decay and dissolve. Not only is this the law for individuals of a species but the species itself follows the same course. Life is an energy that grows to a head, achieves its perfect form and, losing creative tension, relaxes its form and runs down.

The nineteenth-century evolutionists, looking closely at these cycles, rediscovered what had already been observed by the Greeks, that living forms on their upward path show a tendency to diversify and specialize their functions. This is by no means a general law—all things do not observe it; some creatures specialize but do not diversify, others have reached a position of genetic stability and evolve no more. Because some evolutionists appear to forget that evolution is not an end in itself but a method forced upon the germ of life if it is to survive amidst changing circumstances, they naturally tend to fix their gaze upon things which do evolve and to be unaware of things that do not. But an evolving species is merely one that has not yet succeeded in stabilizing itself in a form that allows it to adapt to a fluctuating environment. It is like an acrobat whose violent oscillations to achieve balance we watch entranced while his companion remains poised, enduring and ignored, his dangerous purpose already achieved.

If we regard, as we should, evolution as a process designed to correct an unbalanced relationship between an organism and its environment, the simile of a man on a tight-rope is a fair one. If he is falling to the left he must transfer his weight to the right. Should he carry his weight so far to one side or the other that he cannot return he will be carried by it away from his balancing-point until he reaches some new position at which it is possible for his balance to be restored. If a living organism is genetically unbalanced it will sometimes develop in the direction of its unbalance and continue to develop in that direction until a new poise is achieved, or until the organism is no longer competent to survive.

Cases of excessive development in one direction are common enough. The herbivorous dinosaurs became unbalanced in the direction of bodily growth. They enlarged to such a size that the swampy earth could not bear them up and the field of their limited wanderings had not herbage enough to feed them. It is as though the Life Force said: 'Let us see what happens if we blow these creatures up beyond all other creatures. Let us discover the practical limit of size for a mammal.' And when at last the great masses of flesh could no longer be moved from place to denuded place the experiment was given up and these vast animals yielded position to others with more modest appetites and greater mobility. But in the sea the experiment was successful. The whale, the biggest mammal of all, managed very well, he achieved not only genetic balance within himself and became a stable genus, but he also achieved a satisfactory balance with his environment . . . or had done so until man discovered a profitable use for his carcass. Of all those creatures which achieved vastness the whale alone found a situation in which stability was possible.

Exploration of differing lines of development is going on all the time and we are not to be sure, until a path is finally closed by the extinction of a species, by which route the germ of life will be able to endure. It may well be that in the human species the mind, with its built-in lack of stability, is about to proliferate to such a degree that the organism of which it is a part will become totally unfitted for survival. It is not too fanciful to imagine that the great dinosaurs, well satisfied with their bulky superiority to all other forms of life, pressed on, in the name of progress, to become bigger and bigger just as we are pressing on to become more and more intellectualized. Or it may be that the specialization of function is also on the verge of going so far that the composite organism which alone can carry such specialization is quite unable to form a synthesis of its elements, so that societies of what we at present call a civilized type will simply fall apart and give way to better-proportioned entities.

Increasing specialization and diversity, which is an observed condition of the evolutionary process, is one way in which an organism may develop in its effort to adjust itself to a position of imbalance. A change of posture and emphasis is a property of life, which means, after all, that it is a property of living things; it can hardly be a property of things that do not live. The rock which, worn by weathering, tilts from its high place, caught by the tug of gravity, will fall until it is again lodged. But the rock merely obeys the law and any change it undergoes does not spring from within itself. So that when it is said that Art evolves according to the principle of increasing specialization and diversity it cannot mean that Art itself illustrates this principle. Art in the collective sense of all pictures, all sculpture, all buildings, and so on, is inert, it does not evolve, it does not do anything. It is we, mankind, who *do*. It is we who shape it, we who make it, we who respond to it. If our successive products in this way are increasingly diversified and specialized, then the increasing diversification springs from us and our need; it is not inherent in paint or marble or bronze.

The direction of change may, however, be inherent in an existing condition. If we, for some psychological or commercial reason, feel impelled to design a tea-cup or a motor car or a picture that is unlike any that has been made before we can do so in one of two ways: we can co-ordinate the ingredients more closely, welding them into a better-integrated whole, or, if the form is already fully integrated, we can only exaggerate some feature of it. Let us suppose that a lunatic desire for change at all costs were to afflict the designers of tea-cups so that they enlarged and over-ornamented the handles. To improve on this their successors would naturally be inclined to follow the route already entered upon and would enlarge and ornament the handles still more until they outgrew their function and had to be made separately from the cups and to be reassembled before we could use them. The first woman who washed her hair and arranged it becomingly was not aware that the desire for change, for novelty, would ultimately involve shaving the head and replacing the natural hair with a powdered confection two or three feet high which had to be put on and off like a hat. Nor did the maker of a simple leather sheath for a cutting-edge of steel foresee the extravagent flowering of his invention in the sword furniture of the Japanese metal-smiths. Yet these developments were inherent in their innovations.

A similar urge to exploit a difference is responsible for much of what is generally called 'development' in the fine arts. We may exaggerate the linear aspect of things seen and reduce pictures to the sparest of lines, the record on paper of a single gesture; or we may exaggerate the feature of hue and try to make our pictures out of colour alone; or we may push to an illogical conclusion the intellectual significance of vision and by emphasizing this reduce our pictures to a short story, to an esoteric conundrum, or to an algebraic demonstration.

The end to this sort of proliferation is imposed by natural physical limits. The mountainous wig, like the brontosaurus, became impossibly big: the head would not bear it, doorways would not admit it, husbands could not afford it, the State intervened and taxed it . . . and the wig became, virtually, extinct. (Plate 57.) Upon the upward, the differentiating specializing process the evolutionist keeps his eye, but in a broader sense the downward movement, the so-called devolutionary phase, is as much a part of evolution. Our destination is balance and the road to it will sometimes be uphill and sometimes downhill; the higher the ascent the steeper must the descent be, and the longer and more arduous will be our journey.

The tides and movements which we loosely call fashion arise from the complex network of individual need which forms the structure of human society. The new science, the Ecology of Taste, will have to concern itself, not with what we call the aesthetic sense only, but with the whole of human experience.

12. Excellence

*The thirst for every kind of experience, encouraged by a philosophy
which taught that nothing was intrinsically great or small, good or evil,
had ever been at strife in him with a hieratic refinement, in which the
boy-priest survived, prompting always the selection of what was perfect
of it kind, with subsequent loyal adherence of his soul thereto. This had
carried him along in a continuous communion with ideals. . . .*

WALTER PATER, *Marius the Epicurean*

I AM an awareness at the heart of a complex arrangement of sensation. The awareness
is like a pair of mirrors placed not only so as to seize images of the world outside but
also the reflections from each other. Somewhere in one of these mirrors is that germ which
is 'I'. This 'I' is shaped by the images in the mirrors, but the mirrors did not call it into
being, they are not its ultimate creator. Nor is this 'I' totally passive. Within limits I can
adjust the mirrors and I can concentrate my awareness on some reflections and not on others;
I can look only at the images of objects out-there and live out my life in what I think I know
of their company; or I can look directly at the mirror and see myself looking at objects out
there, and I can spend the brief period of my awareness puzzling over this strange relationship of inwardness and outwardness in which the existence of each seems to be dependent
upon the other; or I can look into the heart of the mirror and see the image of myself looking
at the image of myself in the hope that somewhere at the end of this diminishing tunnel
I will be able to discern the ultimate reflection, the 'I' which is 'I'.

To explain the human personality in this fashion is not to explain it away. I am an awareness shaped by my power to react differentially to energy. I may also be an immortal soul,
a fragment of the Godhead, the flickering of a light on an old wall. In any of these events,
while the spirit of life is in me, I am a subject of wonder, capable of delight.

An animal, a bird, a butterfly, they are also such an awareness, but they differ, or so I
believe, from the awareness that is me, because they do not see themselves as I can see
myself, they cannot separate appearances from things and they cannot separate themselves
from the situation in which they are. But they are more graceful than I, more harmonious
in their movements and in their lives than I, they are more beautiful than I. And all this is
because they are more completely integrated than I am. I look with longing and admiration at
them. I can rarely look with such admiration at you . . . or you . . . or you . . . or at myself.

There are two ways of answering the problem. The first is to re-enter the Garden of

Eden by eliminating the knowledge of the distinction of good and evil, by allowing all our actions to be reduced again to the level of automatic response. And the second is to attempt to achieve integration self-consciously, in other words to be the architects of our own beauty.

When Socrates asked Hippias for a definition of beauty and Hippias, hedging, suggested that it was a quality to be found in a beautiful maiden, Socrates pressed on with the suggestion that as a beautiful horse and a beautiful lyre and a beautiful pot are all called beautiful it should be possible to say wherein their common quality consists. Hippias, still unable to extract the common denominator, tried to produce something that was always beautiful and suggested that gold was such a thing. Socrates pointed out situations in which gold would not be considered to be beautiful, so that Hippias was made to see that what was required was some quality that was present when gold was beautiful and absent when it was not. This quality Hippias discovered to be suitability or fitness for purpose. The eyes of Phidias's statue of Athena were not of gold, because gold was not an appropriate material for representing eyes (we are not told why), and a ladle with a handle made of wood, being suitable to the work it has to do, is more beautiful than one made of gold.

What, then, constitutes beauty? How do we arrive at it? How do we conceive it? The beauty of the maiden, the horse, the lyre, which Hippias had distinguished, have one quality in common and this quality is beauty itself. Beauty that endures is better than beauty that perishes: in any case when the maiden perishes her materiality dissolves, but Beauty itself remains, for is it not in the horse and the lyre? Therefore Beauty in its advanced positions is not a quality of form at all but a quality of ideas, a quality of learning, and of knowledge, of customs, of laws, of mathematics. Man is a creature compounded of body and soul; the beauty of materiality is variable, mortal, it is a shadow of the real beauty; the beauty of the mind involves the finer half of man's being, and this is what the wise man seeks, for in this way he will free the immortal and immaterial from the transient and the gross. But beyond the beauty of ideas, of science and reason, lies The Absolute, The Beauty, of which all else is a reflection, a Beauty that is beyond being and beyond knowledge.

This is roughly the idealists' position. But a modern Hippias would have stood his ground against Socrates with more vigour. There is no question of beauty or ugliness . . . everything is itself alone. This we call beautiful and that we call beautiful; we do not mean that they are alike. We are putting them together into a file or docket according to what seems to us to be a similarity in the emotion which they arouse. But the objects are different. The reasons why they please us are different. Is the pleasure, then, the same? A song is beautiful, a woman is beautiful, a flower is beautiful. And nowadays we have so extended our ideas that everything is beautiful. Men speak of the exquisite rose-like beauty of a shrapnel wound, and of the strangely beautiful forms of the human wreckage of Belsen. This can mean either that the word beauty has become meaningless, as a file becomes useless when everything goes into it; or that we have learned to see beauty in everything and are adopting

VIII Naum Gabo: Linear Construction no. 4

a new attitude to the phenomena which surround us . . . an attitude of delighted acceptance, rather than one of critical selection.

If our nature is the sole arbiter of good, and if our appetite is the manifestation of that nature's need, and you, owing to your need to exercise your senses pleasurably, should drink a bottle of gin at a sitting or hang a Jackson Pollock in your boudoir, can I query this even though you will lose the lining of your stomach and will diminish your capacity for making visual distinctions? After all the pleasure was *your* pleasure and derived from the needs of your organism, and if your organism is self-destroying it must still, if the pleasure principle is sound and the only criterion of aesthetic judgement, be right that you should destroy it. Perhaps it is. Perhaps life is no more than a potential in process of becoming actual and perhaps this alone is what is right and in accord with the cosmic purpose, and we should follow our destiny like the lemmings.

The machine of life appears to be self-adjusting, and its purpose can be distinguished, if at all, by its processes, just as the end of a road may be discovered with reasonable accuracy from a study of its general course. If this is true, then what we term a purpose is really a consequence and each event has within it an unfolding, a potential striving to become actual, which arises from what the event is and not from what it is to be. So far we have an infinite number of events each seeking its own unfolding, but often in conflict with one another; the expansion of this form of life meets with the development of that, so that the one or the other must yield and fail to resolve itself into its ultimate form, into the state which contains no further potentiality whatever.

There is a picture, then, of a universe containing innumerable events, each pursuing its own course, fulfilling the potential that is within it, competing with its neighbours until its energy has run down. The sun hurtles on its appointed way; the earth, spinning, revolves about the sun; the moon desribes its orbit; the cyclone rises, rages, and blows itself out; the flower blooms and fades—all for a certain time and no longer, until their respective energies have dissipated or fused into a new identity.

Which survive? Those that can. And clearly if a million events set out upon their journey and one endures longer than the rest, then it has done so for a reason, the reason that its aptitudes were best fitted to ride out the challenge to its continued existence; but it may not survive the very next challenge, and if it does not, another event will have joined the Dodo and the brontosaurus and the comet that burned itself out a hundred million years ago, and another path has been closed to evolution for ever. So, if survival is the criterion of rightness, the standard which makes Methuselah most admirable of men, how are we to know which cause is right? Who is to know which road is longest? Only the man who reaches the end of it. But if it ever ends, then there is failure after all in the long run, for only the endless, the circular road, can solve our problem.

That everything *is* and that what we are really concerned with is to be increasingly aware of is-ness and thereby to raise ourselves to higher levels of being is not a doctrine of Stoic and of Quietist philosophers alone. By a different course St Augustine at one time found himself at a not dissimilar conclusion. He accepted the Pythagorean notion of harmony as underlying the cosmos, but held that the harmony in objects which makes them bearers of delight is not an attribute of things as independent entities but a reflection in them of their divine origin. Their origin is the One, the Absolute, the Indivisible, but they, His works, the created ones, are multiple and divisible. It follows, then, that for the multiple and divided to emulate and to echo the One-ness of their Creator they must reach out for his unity in their diversity. And that is what harmony is. Nothing can exist without concord and He, the Creator of all things, is the key of that concord. The Supreme Good is One-ness, evil is . . . Two-ness or conflict and division. This distracting Two-ness which is our torment we must seek to recompose into One-ness. We may achieve our goal by grasping at the formal essence of sensual things and so approach to spiritual Form itself. This is the use of the shadow of reality to approach the reality of the shadow.

Augustine's attempt to work back from the Essential to the created has much in its favour. God is order. All things are created from Him in harmony; it could not be otherwise. Whence, then, comes the ugliness? Ugliness, says Augustine, unlike beauty, is not absolute, only relative. 'There is nothing either good or bad but thinking makes it so,' said Renan. Augustine, too, found himself in these regions of the subjective, for according to him the mutual harmony of things cannot be perceived by souls which are not attuned to it. Souls which are in tune will look at all things in their contexts, they will discern the nice adjust- ments of parts in wholes which at first sight seem repulsive, and they will appreciate how contrast and gradation are the inevitable ingredients of harmony. Beauty depends, in fact, upon assuming a correct posture, looking at things from the right point of view. Nothing will bear the test of an isolating examination, for things were made in combination. As an example Augustine points out that sin when punished becomes a part of the beauty of justice. Ugli- ness is merely a feature of the great contrasting pattern and bears its part in the ultimate harmony; it exists solely in the untrained eye of the beholder and not at all in the nature of things. 'Everything is for the best in the best of all possible worlds,' said Dr Pangloss. And how else is it to be resolved if the Omnipotent is also the Beneficent?

> 'All nature is but art unknown to thee,
> All chance, direction which thou cans't not see;
> All discord, harmony not understood;
> All partial evil, universal good;
> And, spite of pride, in erring reason's spite,
> One truth is clear, whatever is, is right.'

But, unfortunately, we cannot get far enough from the pattern to see it entire; we are part of the pattern and cannot get out of it.

A similar but more satisfying explanation of the matter was given by Plotinus. In his view we, individual souls, are making a sort of progress. We originate in the Fountain of all Being, the Perfectly Good, the One. It is the character of this Creative One to act and multiply. From it proceeds the Intellectual Principle, then the World Soul, and finally the individual being which we are. But in this progress matter, formless Non-Being, becomes involved and the brilliant path of the Original Energy becomes dimmer as it proceeds further from its source. The soul is conscious of its separation from its true home in the One and with a restless longing seeks to retrace its steps to where the energy is stronger, the unity clearer, and the elements more pure. Beauty is something perceived at the first glance; the soul recognizes it as a radiance from the Source, welcomes it, and enters into unison with it.

The effect of this view of our affairs is to place emphasis on the creative faculty, for the One is inevitably a creator and its energy is our being. It is the presence of this creative energy, dimmed though it be by its distance from the Source, which we call the beautiful in a work of art. A current of creative energy flows into the maker from the underlying idea and from him it is transmitted to the thing made and remains inherent in the thing, statue, poem, building, what you will, for us to recognize and reach out for and to identify ourselves with, because only in this way can we find our way home towards the One. For Plotinus it is not proportion, or harmony, or this colour, or that shape, which is beautiful, it is life which is beautiful. The enemy of beauty, the source of all ugliness, is Not-Being, the unstirred, unresponsive mass, the inept, the expressionless, that which has been unbreathed upon by the Primal Energy.

The nature of this primal energy is explained by those who think along the lines of Heraclitus and of Aristotle in this way; all things are in flux and what we experience as harmony is essentially a balanced adjustment of opposed tendencies. The material world in Heraclitus's view was very close to our modern conception of matter as energy. All that exists does so at the point of conflict; without strife there would be nothing, because one principle alone unless held in check by its opposite disintegrates into nothing. In this way good and evil are seen as essentially one, for we cannot conceive of good without evil: black and white are one, for we cannot know black without experience of white; life and death are one; chaos and order are one; the pendulum swings from side to side, the present position of the weight IS, all else is not, but without the tension of opposite tendencies IS cannot be, without the opposition of forces there would be no pendulum and no being; all is in a constant state of readjustment; we cannot step twice into the same river, for not only is the water flowing by not the water that passed yesterday, but we who came to it are no longer what we were. All things are coming-to-be or passing-away; happiness is not a state of mind but an activity; the soul is not a spiritual essence but a principle of life; nature is energy working towards a goal. It follows that nature contains her goal within herself and that nature's creation is truly an evolution, a growth of potential, a fulfilment. The beginning and end of nature's act lies within itself; the acorn and the oak are in themselves the cause and purpose of their flowering.

Much of all this strikes us as being true as far as it goes. In so far as we are concerned with rising to ever-greater heights of being, so we must identify ourselves increasingly with the is-ness of things whether that is a reflection of the unity of God or the consequence of conflicting energies or both at the same time. In this case all that will concern us about them is their absolute presence and nothing else about them should matter at all. If we take this point of view we shall live like the Epicurean gods, remote observers of the distant scene, or like the Omniscient and Omnipotent of Augustine and of Dr Pangloss, in whose eyes 'whatever is is right'.

But Augustine did not, in fact, find everything to be equally beautiful; he did not pretend that he was himself aloof from the mêlée and could see the pattern as a whole. He was thoroughly involved in it and said: 'As we must often swallow wholesome bitters so we must always avoid unwholesome sweets. But what is better than wholesome sweetness or sweet wholesomeness?' In other words, he might have repeated Addison's thought that 'there is not perhaps any real beauty or deformity more in one piece of matter than another, because we might have been so made, that whatever now seems loathsome to us, might have shown itself agreeable'. And Augustine might have added to it the gloss that though all is good in the sight of the Creator—for He is without limitation—all is not good to us simply because of our finite character, and we, after all, are Us not Him.

All things are different indeed; a thing is what it is and not another thing. But is not the atıttude which accepts them all equally liable to become, rather than one of delighted acceptance, one of dreary endurance? And is one thing never better than another? For if one thing is, if once we admit inequality in one thing, we admit it in everything, and choice re-enters the world. Is there, then, not one thing better than another? Better for its purpose? Of course. Then betterness and choice do exist. But is our life not extended beyond purpose? Is it not a 'thing' in its own right, and not merely a biological happening, which leads to other happenings which lead to other happenings? We can see the oak as such a thing because we are outside it and outside any purpose it may have. And we can see ourselves if we stand outside ourselves and outside any purpose we can conceive that there may be for us.

Our affairs, then, can be conducted at two levels. We are travellers being passed from one event to the next, treating each one as a stepping-stone in some monstrous progression towards a destination we do not understand, making ourselves more and more the slaves of time, dragged forward by what is not and hustled on by what has been, resting less and less in the dazzling brilliance of what is. In so far as we live on this plane, and some of us live on no other and none of us can avoid living on it to a considerable degree, values are a compound thing. The criteria for our judgement may be derived from brightness, and hue, and form, and movement, and sound, and echo, and complexity of relationship, and simplicity, and harmony, and success, and failure, and vitality, and grace, and truth, and love, and a thousand others, and when we have compounded them into one criterion, that criterion becomes the measure of the good life, the standard to which all should be referred. We heap together a great agglomeration of slightly unstable values, and the result is a mound which in its general form is more or less stable. This Grand Value, derived from the good life, casts a reflection on all things made. If we look at a picture with the eye of a craftsman we will see in it a craftsman's virtues. If we look at it with the eye of a preacher we shall see in it a preacher's virtues. If we look at it with the eye of a salesman we shall see in it commercial values. But if we look at it from the standpoint of a man we shall see in it the virtues of the good life, in which all other virtues are comprehended in their appropriate proportion.

Between these two levels of living, the purposive-progressive-temporal, and the contemplative-eternal, art is a bridge. 'The beginning and the end of Nature's act lies within itself, the acorn and the oak are in themselves the cause and purpose of their flowering.' But man the artist is outside the thing he makes. The beginning and the end, the purpose and the plan, are not from the first within the picture or the statue; they are put there by man, the beginning and the end are transmitted from him to them. Nature's dynamic is from within. Art's dynamic is from without. It is in this sense that to be complete, as Nature's act is—that is, to be a union of dynamic and form—man's creation, Art, must also be made to contain its dynamic. The only way in which it can do this is by the observer becoming also the creator by identifying himself with the creation. By this metamorphosis the competition for space is suddenly made to cease and we become what we all seek to become, an awareness without responsibility.

A work of art, having been created by man on the pattern of nature's creation, not a copy of what nature has created but a copy of nature's way of doing it (that is harmoniously, with a beginning and a middle and an end, an organic whole, as with nature's potential becoming actual), when freed from its maker can become in certain conditions a source of pleasure for others. The principal way in which this pleasure operates is through the identification of the spectator with the action seen. The appreciation of art is the transfer of things into act. When we see a picture we are acting it. The most early, and in some senses the most complete, work of man-the-artist was the stage drama in which the idea of the identification of the spectator with the dramatic action was relatively easy. The next step, by which the spectator was able to identify himself with the patterns of music and eventually with quite simple sounds and forms and colours, would be made to follow naturally. From this process of becoming what one sees, and experiencing what the character before us experiences, arises the power of art to correct imbalances. Essentially what takes place is the creation of form in the soul, or the re-imposition of discipline without which there is no being. Man in an over-emotional state, charged with an excess potential of pity and fear, is in a disturbed condition, the form of his being is unbalanced and to that extent he is on the verge of not being. This formless proliferation of energy is given form by the channel which art forces it into. In the theatre, for example, a poisonous fog of pity becomes Pity for Oedipus, or Pity for Lear, passing through all the processes which the rational mind must experience before pity takes its proper healthy form. Equally, when fatigue has loosened the tensions which keep the soul in form it is the application of perceived order, the metre of the poem, the repetitive movement of the dance, the harmony of music, which draws together and re-creates the being.

Over the bridge made by art between the purposive and the contemplative worlds passes the shadow of our sense of values. Not entire, for if it were to do so the contemplative world would become subordinated to purposive standards and itself become only purposive; or the purposive world would in turn lose that criterion which is chiefly responsible for hastening us from one event to another, the value of fitness for purpose. But inasmuch as Contemplator and Doer are one person the habit of mind adduced on one plane of existence will not be quite discarded on the other, but we will try to bring both worlds into harmony, to create a unity out of their disparity. Some echo of the agglomeration of values of the good life, the Grand Values, will haunt our contemplative experience and we will feel to be most beautiful and worthy of contemplation those forms which seem, however remotely, indeed the more remotely the better, to fulfil the standards of the world of time and events. But the reverse is also true and we carry back with us from the golden world of contemplation the reflection of its disinterested values and bring to our purposive scramble a precious sense of the absolute. In this way we are no longer purely detached acceptors of the sensations of life, nor only the deeply implicated chasers after we know not what. Each plane of existence is modified by the other.

To ourselves we seem to be creatures of free will. Perhaps we cannot steer against the current, but we can steer a little across it. The self which we seek to attain to is perhaps Augustine's emulation of the One-ness of the Creator; or Plotinus's unity with the Creative Source; or perhaps what we are really seeking on our most precarious journey amongst the crags and precipices of choice is to evolve once more into a creature that acts beautifully and nobly by instinct, or, if this hope is forlorn, at least to create such a life by intellect, by reason, and by will. For ultimately, as Paul Klee said, the art of living is the most important art of all; and man is himself his own greatest artifact.

Index

ACKNOWLEDGEMENTS OF ILLUSTRATIONS

Plates: 1, 2 3: The Vatican; 4: Alte Pinakothek, Munich; 5, 43, 55, 56: The National Gallery, London; 7, 8, 10, 44, 45, 54: The Tate Gallery; 9: The Courtauld Gallery; 12, 52, 58: The Louvre; 13, 29, 39: The Zoological Society of London; 14: Associated Press Photos of India; 16: Radio Times Hulton Picture Library; 17: The British Museum; 19, 37: The Wallace Collection; 21, 26: Press Information Bureau, New Delhi; 22: Camera Press Ltd; 24, 53: Galleria Nazionale d'Arte Moderna, Rome; 25: Museo Preistorico, Rome; 35: Private Collection, Chicago; 42: Museo delle Terme, Rome; 46: The Baltimore Museum of Art; 47: Dulwich College Picture Gallery; 48: Colmar Museum; 49: Glasgow Museum and Art Gallery; 50: Govt. of India Tourist Office; 51: Accademia, Venice; 57: The Mansell Collection; 59: French Govt. Tourist Office; 60: The Japanese Information Centre.

Colour Plates: I, British Museum; II, Courtesy Mouradian & Volloton; IV, Philadelphia Museum of Art (George W. Elkins Collection); VIII, Courtesy *Studio International*.